AF229471

Dedication

To the doctors practicing medicine who remain their patients' advocate and oppose the radicalization of this noble profession.

ACKNOWLEDGMENT

I had no problem writing this book, but I could not have gotten it ready for publication without the help of my son, Mark.

Prognosis *Guarded*

Marvin Ginsburg, MD

ISBN: 979-8-35092-525-8 paperback
ISBN: 979-8-35092-526-5 ebook

❦ 1 ❧

A Reason to Leave

The anxiety he experienced as he drove along desolate Highway 14 was making it difficult to breathe. It was only made worse by his inability to cast from his mind last week's medical staff surgical committee meeting at Woodland Community Hospital. The sun drenched the opaque mountains splattered with patches of yellow and gold. Immediately, he found himself squinting in an attempt to hide from the sun's blinding rays. His meeting was scheduled to take place in one hour with the owners of Palmdale Hospital. Dr. Mark Gaines was desperate to move away from the den of iniquity he had blindly entered.

Leaving the University Hospital in June 1995, only a few short months ago, he decided to enter the practice of internal medicine with the subspecialty of pulmonary medicine in the west San Fernando Valley. Never in his wildest dreams had he expected to witness the shocking state of the practice of medicine he had come to know so well.

He had rapidly become disenchanted with the practice of medicine in the Valley. Too often his ideals and moral fibers were tested and caused him to develop defense mechanisms and symptoms of anxiety in order to cope with these problems. *What kind of people are these who hold themselves out to be healers and yet they march to the tune of Mammon, God of Money? They have no compassion and do not measure their self-worth by the satisfaction of their performance or the warm feeling that comes from helping the sick.*

He made his decision to escape from that pit of hell because he could not stand to see the cheating games played out daily. The indignation and "holier than thou" attitudes, as well as the grandiose declarations and pontification by those doctors of medicine, were more than he could endure. They proclaimed innocence of their incompetence to their colleagues, who were just as inept. If you had a large patient base, then you were king because you controlled their referrals, and no colleague wanted to alienate you for fear of losing that source of patients. It was so bad that there were many physicians who found that the indication for a procedure, surgery, or test was entirely predicated on the type of health insurance. He had had it! Last week he had decided he would leave, although, despite his conviction, he continued to agonize over his decision.

How could he have stood silently by and allowed that young girl to undergo a needless thoracotomy by that so-called surgeon? When Dr. Kovacs had asked him to evaluate her for elective surgery because she had asthma, he never imagined the web of entanglement that would follow.

She could have physically undergone the surgery, but that wasn't the point; her chest X-ray had revealed a six-centimeter cyst in the left lower lobe. The film, taken ten years previously, had shown the identical cyst. It had not changed in size; the girl was entirely asymptomatic, and her breathing tests were normal. After evaluating all the facts, he had concluded that this was a simple congenital lung cyst that required no surgical intervention. In his written consultation, he so stated this, which was interpreted by Dr. Harvey Kovacs as depriving him from a healthy four-thousand-dollar fee to carve open her chest, leaving a hideous scar.

After all, he told me he was the surgeon and the one who must accept the responsibility for this patient's care. "I have asked you to evaluate her for her ability to undergo the anesthesia and to tolerate the surgery, and I am not interested in hearing what you have to say about the lung lesion." Gaines was shocked that Dr. Kovacs was attempting to coerce him into removing his objection for this patient's surgery. There was no doubt in this doctor that this caused him some element of financial distress.

Mark was adamant about his position, which he knew was correct, and he was incensed over the fact that Dr. Kovacs was so motivated by money. Then Mark said, "What you are planning to do is malpractice, and I will take this to the surgery committee."

Dr. Cohen, the chief of surgery, was notified and was in accordance with Mark's position. He felt the quickest way to deal with the problem was to select an ad hoc committee to hear the issues and decide on their merit.

The next day, the ad hoc committee for the Department of Surgery was called to order, and Gaines was requested to present his case in detail. When he finished, the floor was turned over to Kovacs for his presentation and rebuttal. If he had only known that what he had started was a holy political war, Mark might have elected to walk away from the confrontation.

Those doctors who derived referral patients from Dr. Kovacs were lined up on his side of the long table. They were showing their support for their colleague. The others were seated with Gaines on his side of the table. Honesty was defined here as not being in the referral pattern of Dr. Kovacs and his friends. The others, of course, looked at the good doctor as a continual source of revenue enhancement.

Dr. Harvey Kovacs was a man about fifty-five years old, five feet ten inches tall, with shocking white hair much more extreme than a man his age deserved. He had a fair complexion and piercing light blue eyes. He was revered by many of his colleagues and loved every minute of it. Harvey spoke with deliberate purpose and a slight New York accent, sounding like a charming politician exemplifying the classic con man. Mark was convinced that Kovacs might have missed his calling. He explained away his rationale for wanting to operate on his patient with total disregard for anything even slightly resembling the truth. His opinions were bathed in untruths, omissions of facts, and innuendos, and like an artist, he produced a picture that only could have been created by his dishonest mind. It was his intention to sway and lead his supporters in his direction. "After all," he said, "this may be a malignancy; one can never be sure."

Dr. Mark Gaines interrupted, "But there are no risk factors, and her entire evaluation is normal." Harvey's eyes scanned each of his friendly colleagues seated at the conference table. He attempted to transmit the dollar signs that referral patients signify. "I have been doing chest surgery for twenty-five years," he said using his soft-spoken convincing voice. "I strongly object to you questioning my opinion." Mark asked, "Why haven't you done a lung scan, which would easily answer this question? This is a simple lung cyst requiring no surgical intervention, and, if you are wrong, you will only inflict upon your patient a large, hideous scar forever. I can't let you do this to her," Mark said. Harry Cohen, chief of surgery, called for order, and after he had asked a few choice questions of his own, he then allowed the discussion to continue. He then called for a vote on the issue. Mark's position was affirmed by the committee, and the good Dr. Kovacs was ordered to cancel the surgery for the lack of an appropriate indication.

Dr. Kovacs, upon hearing this decision, ejected himself from his seat by throwing his chair back against the wall and began a barrage of self-serving statements. He shouted, "I have never been so humiliated before my colleagues! I have been a surgeon for more than twenty-five years, and you have prevented me from performing a needed surgery on my patient."

Dr. Gaines got up and left the room. In seconds he was confronted by Dr. Kovacs. "You will never see another patient in this valley, I'll see to that," he snarled while positioning himself between the hospital entrance and Gaines. "You'll regret this, you son of a bitch!" he shouted, shaking his long, delicate surgical finger in Mark's face. "I'll get you one day, you bastard. You'll be black-balled in this town. I know everybody, and you will pay for this." Kovac told him much more than his verbiage.

For but a fleeting moment, Mark again felt the fear of losing a practice that he had only just begun to build. "You money-grubbing incompetent. Go screw yourself." Dr. Gaines stormed out of the hospital.

The freeway sign read "Avenue S Exit." Mark entered the right lane without signaling, feeling that it was unimportant since he had only seen three other cars on the freeway the entire time. As he approached the stop sign, he saw strange plants along the adjacent hillside. They were five to seven feet tall, were very straight, and their leaves were long and stiffly pointed. He dimly recalled that a small town in the desert was named after the plant: Yucca Valley, he thought. The sign pointed to the right for the hospital. He turned right and traveled the road about a mile to the stop sign. Carefully looking both ways, he scooted across the intersection and drove another mile, where he noted an American flag waving from a flagpole. The flagpole was situated in front of a low-profiled building that was sprawling on two sides. As he turned right to approach the building, he drove through a barren desert for a quarter of a mile. This hospital seemed out of place, situated right in the middle of the desert surrounded by junipers, yuccas, and jackrabbits. To the right of the hospital was another single-story rambling building that extended along the street to the main road he had just turned from. He walked into the small entrance and approached the telephone switchboard operator who was sitting behind an enclosure.

"May I help you?" she asked.

"Why, yes. I am Dr. Gaines, and I have an appointment with Dr. Small."

"Very well. If you'll have a seat, I will let him know you are here," she announced in a loud voice.

"Thank you," replied Gaines, slightly annoyed at the operator. Her loud voice was brash to him, and it made him feel ill at ease.

He looked around at the tiny area that was obviously reserved for patients' families. The wall lacked color coordination, and the hanging pictures were desert scenes, some of which were ghastly and certainly didn't belong in a hospital. This was especially true of the one picture depicting a circling vulture about to descend upon a dying cow. He thought the other pictures were just as harsh. The yellow-green walls were not pleasing to the eye, and the carpet was a hideous blue with green designs that resembled a Rorschach inkblot test. Dr. Gaines studied the design and was sure he could see a dragon's head.

"Hi, glad you could come and visit with us. My name is Dr. Rick Small," he said in a manner that indicated perhaps he wasn't sure of his own name.

What a weirdo, Mark thought. They walked down the hill and entered the rear door of the other building that he had passed on the way to the front of the hospital. After a few feet, Mark was led through a door that opened on the left side of the hallway. They were in a large dining hall furnished with many oak tables. On the left side was a serving line where white-hatted servers spooned food onto large plates. The line ended at a cashier strategically positioned to collect money from the diners. He was motioned by Dr. Small to enter the line, upon which he did so with gusto since it was already one o'clock and he hadn't eaten anything since 6:00 a.m. As he passed through this line, he became aware of a silence that blanketed the room; the initial voices and conservations were now gone. He barely noticed the questioning glance that the cashier directed at Dr. Small. Dr. Small grunted something unintelligible and led the way to a far corner of the room where a large, round table was situated. It seemed to be purposely placed so as not to be too close to any other table. In the center of the table was a black telephone. They sat at the table, and Dr. Small introduced him to Dr. Bob Lund.

"So, Dr. Gaines, are you interested in practicing here with us?" Lund began. Somewhat stunned at the direct salvo, Dr. Gaines gazed about the table. He was aware that all the diners in the cafeteria were now staring at him as though he were a Martian. Perhaps he had food on his mustache. His wife was forever alerting him whenever he had tried to feed his mustache. His hand slipped quickly to his lap, and with a single motion, he drew the napkin to his lips, sneaking a brush over the mustache. Feeling certain that nothing was there, he lowered the napkin and looked directly at Dr. Lund. Dr. Small was a man of fifty years of age, medium build with sparse white hair and a large bald area in the center. He had a ruddy complexion and was clean-shaven. His eyes were dark brown so that the pupils were not easily visible, and he wore a white doctor's jacket that was badly stained. It looked as if it hadn't seen starch in many a year. Mark was suddenly acutely aware that he hadn't answered the question.

"Oh, ah yes, I am."

"Mark, I'd like you to meet our hospital administrator, Bill Hendrickson," said Dr. Lund.

Mark stood up and leaned forward slightly while extending his hand across the table. Bill was at least six foot two, trim, with curly sandy hair. His eyes darted between Drs. Lund and Small and had that wily and insecure appearance. It was obvious that Hendrickson was a pawn. Mark concluded that his function was to validate everything said by the doctors. This became immediately apparent as Hendrickson bobbed his large head in agreement with Lund, who had just made an insignificant remark. Mark's antennae were immediately tuned in.

Mark told them Dr. Reed, the radiologist at Santa Clarita Hospital, informed him that a well-trained internist was badly needed in Palmdale. He told them he was interested in relocating to another area and in exploring the opportunities that their group had to offer.

"Well," began Dr. Lund, "we have only one internist here, and that's me. I am a general practitioner though. Our hospital must transfer many patients down below for their acute hospital care because I can't handle the high workload in the hospital as well as the office. Also, Palmdale has an overwhelming number of seniors who are seriously ill and really require someone in Internal Medicine."

"Where's this down below you mentioned?" Mark interrupted.

"That's the San Fernando Valley," he replied.

"How often does that happen?" Mark inquired.

"What would you guess?" Dr. Small asked abruptly, directing his statement to Dr. Lund.

"Oh, five to six times a week," said Lund shaking his head up and down.

"What are the usual medical problems involved?" asked Mark.

"Half trauma and half acute medical problems," said Bob Lund.

"Where are the closest internists?" asked Mark.

"In Lancaster, about fifteen miles away," replied Bob Lund.

"Won't those docs come here?" Mark asked, wrinkling his brow with disbelief.

"Nope. They are at war with us," interjected Bill Hendrickson.

"Why is that?" asked Mark.

"Well, it's a long story, but in a nutshell, they have their own hospital and want to hurt us."

"I still don't get it," answered Mark looking confused.

"It's like the Hatfields and the McCoys," piped up Dr. Small for the first time.

"Who owns this hospital?" he asked. All three of his lunch companions started to answer at once.

Dr. Lund replied, "Dr. Small and I are the owners."

"I see. It's a battle of economics then, and, if they won't help, they think you will eventually fold."

"That's right," Lund said in despair.

"Do you think that I can build a practice quickly?" asked Mark eagerly.

"No problem there," Hendrickson volunteered. "We will refer to you all the medical patients seen in the emergency room as well as the patients from the managed care plans, not to mention the patients we would refer to you for consultation."

"What about your pulmonary services, and who reads your EKGs?" Mark asked.

"Well, said Dr. Lund, "we could contract those services to you." Small and Hendrickson both eagerly nodded their heads in confirmation. Mark liked what he heard. He then felt very excited, for this was an opportunity just waiting to be seized.

He mulled the possibilities over in his mind as he left the hospital after saying his goodbyes and told Dr. Lund that he would call him in a day or so. All the way back to the San Fernando Valley, he replayed the recent conversation with Dr. Lund over in his mind. Mark wondered if these doctors could really be trusted to fulfill their part of the bargain. More specifically, he was concerned whether there was really an opportunity as good as the picture just presented to him. He knew this area of LA County had recently seen a population explosion in both the working-age groups, as well as the Medicare ages. In his specialty he was certain that he would see more patients in the Medicare age group. The doubt he had was related to the fact that the people who were over the age of sixty-five were, for the most part, signed up with managed care groups who administered the medical care for the large health maintenance organizations (HMOs). It was funny, he thought, that no mention of any HMO patients or group practice who had an HMO contract was ever mentioned at the meeting. He'd give them a call tomorrow to explore those issues. If most of the patients were already signed into a medical group for their care, how would he get referrals from private Medicare patients? He already knew he had to be a member of the referral doctor's group or of the independent practice association in order to provide medical care to a patient. Gone now were the days when a patient chose his own doctor and was not controlled by a gatekeeper who directed all his medical care. Today, patients were referred to doctors who had agreed to accept a marked reduction in their fees in order to gain patient referrals. Some doctors had even been capitated for their specialty services and would thus receive a fixed dollar amount per patient assigned to them per month. In one way, this was a good thing. If the patients were not ill, the doctor would not have to see the patient, thus allowing the doctor more time for other paying patients. The only problem with the scenario was that there were not many "other" patients. All the patients were assigned to group medical practices, and those groups were trying to stay alive by accepting large numbers of patients into their group in order to increase their capitation and enhance their profitability.

He had an unrestful sleep that night, and upon awakening the next morning, he placed a call to Dr. Bob Lund.

"Hi, Dr. Lund, this is Mark Gaines," he said cheerfully.

"Good morning, Mark. Have you thought over our proposal?"

"Uh, yes, I have," he said, somewhat unsure of himself. "Tell me, who has the major share of the HMO patients in the Antelope Valley?"

"Why, we do, right here in our group. Didn't I tell you that yesterday?" questioned Lund.

"As a matter of fact, you didn't," answered Mark.

"Mark, we have fifteen thousand capitated lives assigned to us by US Care. You know who they are, don't you?" asked Bob in a positive way, as if to ensure an affirmative answer.

"Oh, sure I do," replied Mark with authority. He really didn't have a clue who US Care was. "Tell me, how many are Medicare enrollees?"

"I'd guess about ten thousand or so," Bob replied.

Mark performed a mental calculation based on what he had read about group capitation and estimated that each patient was capitated to the group at $120 per month. He then quickly computed that the group received one million two hundred thousand dollars a month, or about fourteen million dollars a year. And that was not counting the five thousand non-Medicare or commercial insurance patients.

"If that's so, then I would guess that I would be paid on a discounted fee for service?" asked Mark.

"We would rather pay you a yearly salary and have you work directly for our group," replied Bob.

Over the next fifteen minutes, Mark haggled out a yearly salary of one hundred fifty thousand dollars, four weeks' vacation, one week sick pay, one week paid medical education seminars, and a one hundred thousand dollar a year disability policy. He agreed to start the following week.

~2~

MAKING NEW FRIENDS AND HEARING GOSSIP

Upon arriving at the clinic, Mark rapidly acquired information through the grapevine common to all medical groups. He made friends with some of the nurses and clerical help. At lunch one of the secretaries told him the group was losing a lot of money because they had to refer so many of the very sick patients to hospitals in the San Fernando Valley for hospital care. This turned out to be costly since the group had no contracted rates with any of the larger hospitals. These hospitals knew that groups located away from the Los Angeles basin were at their mercy. Medicine was now a cut-throat business, and for hospitals to survive, they charged what the market would bear. They had to pay all the doctors who provided care as well, and since they had no contracts with these doctors, they were being raped. Since they never knew what doctor would be assigned to their patient, it would be impossible to contract with all doctors. This was coupled with the fact that this area of the desert had seen a massive influx of retired elderly patients who had migrated because real estate in Palmdale was cheap. Many had sold their expensive properties at the apex of California's real estate boom seven years earlier and had relocated to preserve their wealth. There were now living in the Antelope Valley this large group of seniors who had moved there with their illnesses. They had not always resided in the area, so the statistics for predicting disease in this given population were skewed. They had all moved from urban areas elsewhere in the state with their illness in tow. Now they were part of a large, senior managed care plan sold

~11~

extensively in the Antelope Valley. The Palmdale Medical Group had flourished at the beginning when the senior enrollment had been three thousand, and it was said they had profited extensively. The Medical Group had spun off a profit of one and one half million dollars during the second and third year of existence. The first year was a wash for the group because they were in the growth stage. Until the group's enrollment exceeded fifteen hundred enrollees, the profit was minimal, if any. When the enrollees' numbers were low, there were high costs, and it seemed that everyone was sick. There were no healthy patients who did not require care. The over age sixty-five gang also utilized at least five times the group's resources. This meant that they used more office visits than their working counterparts. As a matter of fact, they were in the office ten times as often and required many more referrals to specialists and diagnostic procedures. Of course, they were sicker because of age alone, but no one had taken into consideration the fact this unique group of elderly patients had been gathered from all over and relocated in one small area with all their ills. This resulted in multitudes of cancer patients who required expensive radiation and chemotherapy. The assortment of skin, orthopedic, gastrointestinal, pulmonary, cardiac, and metabolic diseases was phenomenal. The internal gossip was that the medical group was deeply in debt and struggling to stay afloat.

Mark enjoyed the day-to-day practice of internal medicine and very quickly developed a close friendship with some of his peers. He especially liked Dr. Gerry Walker. Gerry had a great sense of humor and had no difficulties in addressing issues head-on. He was a specialist in the field of gastroenterology who shared several patients with Mark. "Rumor had it," said Gerry, "the medical group might have to downsize the total number of primary care physicians." Mark also found out that in addition to owning the hospital, Drs. Lund and Small were also partners in the medical group. Gerry said there was also a third silent or investor partner, who no one had ever met. The rumor mill also had it that the third partner practiced elsewhere in California and was very wealthy in his own right. Recent scuttlebutt was the hospital was now seeking to contract with the state for Medi-Cal patients. (California had seen fit to rename the federal Medicaid program "Medi-Cal.") The state had nearly bankrupted the federal Medicaid funds because of the liberal granting of these health benefits. The hot medical care programs were now managed care medical groups. California wanted to shift the medical costs into medical groups through a capitated program. This would limit the amount of money the state would have to cough up for medical care of the indigent. The Medical Group had taken on twenty-five hundred Medi-Cal managed care enrollees, and more were assigned each month by the Department of Health Services. The state was determined that all Medi-Cal recipients would be assigned to medical groups on a capitation basis. Because of the distant geographical area, the state had negotiated a full-risk contract with the hospital. It made perfect sense to contract all the medical services to the group and the hospital. In this manner the state paid the hospital and medical group two hundred dollars per member per month for the total medical care. This amounted to a capitation of five hundred thousand dollars per month for the complete medical care of these twenty-five-hundred patients who were on the Medi-Cal program.

Mark thought about what he had just learned and then asked, "What do you think the overhead costs will be for these Medi-Cal patients?"

"Can't be as much as all the others," said Gerry. He shook his head negatively.

"Why is that?" asked Mark, now becoming curious.

"They're younger and not as sick," replied Gerry.

"That makes sense," answered Mark, somewhat disappointed that he didn't figure it out himself.

"Rick, we have to talk immediately; come on over now!" said Bob Lund. He slammed the receiver down so hard that it bounced off the cradle. In a moment there was a knock on the door. "Come in," said Lund. He was red-faced and obviously angry.

"What's the matter, Bob? I have an office full of patients to see."

"We must do something to stop our losses!" shouted Bob.

"Like what?" said Rick. *What the hell can I do,* he thought. *I'm no business guru and I'm working as hard as I can now!* He was irritated at the suggestion that he had to do something more than he already had to ensure the success of the hospital. There were, however, pangs of guilt that nagged at his thought process of rationalization. He knew he was just as responsible for the economic success as his partner, and his attitude was a cop-out.

"I have just heard from our illustrious partner, who has an idea that he wants to tell us about," replied Bob with scorn in his voice.

"When will he be here?" asked Rick. *I sure hope he isn't coming today,* he thought. *I am just not in the mood to listen to that egotistical jerk dictate his orders to me.* He was remembering the previous occasions when Kovacs met with them to form action plans. Kovacs loved to bark orders at them as though he were an army colonel directing his subordinates on how to perform a task. The three partners met a minimum of four times a year, and he had never missed a meeting over the years. After adjournment of each meeting, he always swore he would never attend another, but he always did. He felt driven to be at every meeting because he had paranoid feelings about Bob and Kovacs meeting alone. He was sure that Kovacs would try and elicit Bob's support, and the two of them might try to put a fast one over on him. It would drive him berserk if a meeting were held and he was absent, because he would be totally unaware of what they had discussed. Small knew very well he wasn't blessed with business acumen but felt content that his partners were unaware of his deficiency. Just because he never had any suggestions to offer, it didn't mean that he was stupid . . . or did it? He was now starting to feel very uneasy about himself and his relationship with his partners, especially Kovacs. In the past, he had always followed the lead of Bob Lund in any type of decision-making process. Thinking back about the time they met for a lunch meeting, he became incensed. He was eating his usual lunch meal, which consisted of a large bowl of salad and a bowl of soup. He had added a large portion of tabasco to it and then, rather than eating his soup first, he elected to empty his bowl of potato soup into the bowl with the salad. This was met by Kovacs with a look of disgust. Not only did he look at Lund and roll his eyes upwards, but he even put forth a sarcastic comment. Kovacs said something about how it reminded him of a horse's feed bag that was used long ago so they might pull a wagon and eat at the same time. When the horses were finished, all one had to do was dump more grain into the bag. The more he thought about it, the more furious he became. He was still daydreaming when Bob's voice interrupted his thought.

"Tomorrow night at seven o'clock," replied Bob.

"Okay by me. Just order some food so I won't starve," said Rick. He hated those night meetings because they interrupted his television time.

"Will do, Rick. See you in my office tomorrow night at seven. Okay?

"I'll be there Bob," replied Rick, placing his left hand on the doorknob.

"Fine, but be on time for a change," ordered Bob, who remembered all the times that his colleague arrived late for meetings.

"Righto," said Rick, as he saluted Bob in mockery.

~3~
MARITAL BLISS NOT

Erin Kovacs had just come home from the hospital. She was employed as an x-ray technician at Palmdale Hospital and was married to a doctor's son. Her marriage to Alex Kovacs was one of convenience and had been that way for three years. He was physically attracted to her from the start. Erin was just a shade over five feet and one-half inches tall with long, dark hair that hung to her waist. She tipped the scales at one hundred twelve soaking wet. Her small waist was accentuated by her well-endowed breasts, and her legs were long and muscular, no doubt a result of her years of roller-skating. Her hands were graceful and ended in long fingers and nails to match. Erin's face divulged noble features of high cheekbones and full lips. When she laughed, a dimple on her right cheek came into sight. Her skin was olive, with a smooth, velvety texture, and her teeth were straight and brilliant white.

Alex Kovacs was a dark-complected, dark-haired, medium-build man who weighed one hundred sixty pounds and stood five feet ten inches tall. His eyes were dark, and he was good-looking. He was employed in Hollywood California by LMB Special Effects Corporation. He had received a lucky break when one of the artists became ill, and temporary help was needed. Alex was hired to help the company meet a deadline. One of Alex's friends got the job for him since he worked for the company. Because he was so talented in the art of special effects, he was asked to remain working permanently. He had shown Erin only once the way he made life-like masks for the film industry. She had picked it up immediately. Alex was so good that his name had become well-known in the field.

He drank heavily and used drugs. This combination was at least in part responsible for battering his wife. Erin had come to the realization that divorce was inevitable, but in the meantime, she had found solace in fantasizing about a life of leisure and riches. Each evening after work, she would pour a shot of Jack Daniels straight over ice and slowly nurse the drink for an hour while she experienced the world drifting from her. A wall of pleasant solitude with indifference eased her pain.

Alex turned on the TV, grabbed a can of Coors, and slumped onto the couch. He was worn out, tired, and agitated. The cocaine use had become unmanageable, not only from the cost perspective, but also because it caused him so much marital stress. His wife bitterly complained just yesterday that there wasn't enough money between both their jobs to sustain his habit.

Erin closed her eyes and pretended she was asleep while trying to block out her real thoughts but was unable to do so. She knew she could stop the alcohol because she only used it as an escape from Alex. Erin knew Alex was spending at least fifty dollars a day on cocaine, and she was certain he was also spending money on uppers. *How did it ever get this way?* she thought to herself and downed a shot of Jack Daniels. As the warm liquid warmed her throat, she felt a bit stronger. *I hate him big time. Just as soon as I have enough cash, I'm out of here.* She knew on her salary as an x-ray tech she could never afford to divorce Alex. She was desperate to walk out of the marriage, but she couldn't afford to now. That didn't prevent Erin from dreaming about a different lifestyle. Many times, she fantasized about having the wealth to live a life of leisure. She longed to become an artist and indeed was gifted in her abilities. In the past three years that she was married to Alex, she had demonstrated her talent to Alex. He had once shown her some of his own techniques of making facial life-like masks, and she had copied his style exactly.

Erin sat dreamily on a soft-backed chair and let her mind wander. She recalled the time that Alex was sick with an unexplained fever for three weeks. His stubbornness prevented him from seeking medical help, which would have been very easy to secure. His father Harvey Kovacs, the renowned surgeon of the San Fernando Valley, would have referred him to one of his colleagues. In this situation, of course, there would have been professional courtesy extended, and

Alex would not have been presented a bill. The only difficulty with this freebie was that Alex feared that any friend of his father would violate the sacred physician-patient confidentiality relationship and report the drug use to Dr. Kovacs. Alex hated his father and did not want him to know anything about himself. His father was a control freak, and if his father were made aware of anything at all concerning Alex, he wouldn't hesitate one bit to use it for his own gain as a tool to manipulate Alex.

Erin shuddered as she recalled the violent memory of the fight that had occurred on that winter night. It was a rainy night in the desert, the winds were picking up, and she remembered Alex bursting through the front door. Her thoughts were interrupted suddenly.

"I'm home," he slurred, his speech in that characteristic manner she had learned to recognize as a warning that he had been drinking. She hated it the way he said "home" in that sing-song, double-syllable, *ho-em* aggravating way that implied there was some type of a love bond between them. She sat in the chair and tried to ignore him.

"I don't feel well," he shouted when he drew no response from her.

"What's the matter?" replied Erin in a monotone.

"I'm burning up. I'm shivering," he shouted louder, hearing no response.

"I'm in the living room," Erin managed to mutter in a low groan. It was an effort for her to respond. She loathed him immensely.

"My teeth are chattering," said Alex. He entered the dimly lit room and sat on the couch.

"You look terrible," she said in an affected manner.

"Sounds like you really give a damn," he replied.

Erin smirked and instantly thought, *I really don't.* She got up and approached the couch, standing in front of him, staring with icy eyes. *I hope you croak.*

"What the hell are you gaping at?" asked Alex with malice in his tone.

She just couldn't control her response. "What a worthless piece of trash you've become," slipped from her mouth.

"What the hell do you mean by that?" inquired Alex.

"You come home loaded and tell me that you are sick, and I'm supposed to be concerned?" shouted Erin in anger.

"I don't care one way or the other," replied Alex. He was now fuming with hostility.

She stared directly at him and put her face right up to his. "Go to hell!" It was only then that she saw it. Alex's eyes were yellow-orange, and the white of his eye was no longer visible.

"Oh my God," she cried," you've got hepatitis!!"

"How the hell would you know?" he asked in disgust.

"Well, Mr. Big Shot Movie Man, I do happen to be an x-ray tech who works in a hospital, and I have seen many cases that look exactly like you. You're in deep trouble." She walked away smirking in satisfaction.

"BS. Erin, you're no doctor," he answered with agitation.

"I may not be a doctor, but I still know what jaundice means," she said. "Whether you want to hear it or not, my man, you've got hepatitis, and no doubt it's from some of those wonderful drugs you've been using. I told you this would happen, but no, don't listen to me, I'm only a dumb x-ray tech who doesn't know a damn thing. What are you going to do now, Alex?"

He stared at her dumbfounded, not really having a good answer readily available. "Maybe I should see a doctor," he finally answered.

"Why don't you break down and call your father?" she asked.

"So he can give me a load of crap and sing me the 'I told you this would happen' song? No thanks." Alex stared at the floor, trying to block out Erin's voice.

"We can't afford medical care. You know how expensive it is, with blood tests and all," Erin raised her voice authoritatively. "I told you not to let your policy lapse last year."

"I don't care," he shouted, "leave me alone. You know I didn't have the money for the insurance."

"You sure as hell would have, had you not stuck it up your nose," Erin screamed.

"Why don't you shut your big, fat trap?" Alex answered in a voice of disgust.

"I will not, you idiot," she screamed back. In a split second he leaped from the couch and struck her in the chest with his clenched fist. He then slapped her in the face with his opened hand. Erin fell backwards and tripped over the ottoman, which sent her sprawling onto the floor. She found it hard to breathe as she sat up on the floor.

"You bastard," she cried, gasping for a breath between the words. The pain, first dull, became sharp and seemed to travel from the front of her chest directly to the area between her shoulder blades. Blood trickled from the corner of her mouth, and her lip began to swell. "I hate your guts and hope you die," she screamed. The pain was excruciating and was magnified by each gasp. Her crying jags were punctuated by short sobs accompanied by involuntary deep inspirations. She got up and limped off to the bedroom, locking the door behind her. Erin threw herself on the bed and wept. Soon she was asleep.

The next morning was just like all the previous times they had fought. She felt sore over her chest where Alex had slugged her with his closed fist, and her left lower lip was swollen and bruised. Dragging herself out of bed, she went into the bathroom. Then she turned on the shower, adjusting the hot water to be hotter than she normally liked it, thinking that the heat would feel good against the bruise. She peered into the living room and saw that Alex was gone. Stepping boldly into the shower, she let the hot water immerse her face and chest, and after standing there for what seemed like an hour, she got up enough courage to open her eyes and look at her face and chest. She gaped at the large, bluish area that was on the upper inside area of her left breast. There was no flat area where it once used to be between her breasts. She began to cry as she felt the area and quickly pulled her hand away because of the extreme tenderness and pain. *I have to leave him, and fast, before he cripples me,* she thought. But how? It was getting late so she dressed hurriedly and left for work.

❧ 4 ❧

SICK FATHER AND SICKER SON

Alex had awakened early with shaking chills. He felt very weak and exhausted but couldn't return to dreamland because of fear. He knew that he needed some help, but he also knew he had better get financial help if he were to stay alive and healthy. He owed a lot of money to his drug supplier, Tony, and Tony had extended all the time he could to repay the debt. After all, he also had bills to pay, but more likely, since he was only the pusher and was controlled by the big boys, he also had a healthy fear. If the money wasn't received every two weeks by the syndicate boss, a new pusher spontaneously appeared on the street and assumed the distribution route of his predecessor. There were never any questions asked, for to do so might be detrimental to one's health. As rapidly as a dealer disappeared, a new one arrived on the scene. Alex knew that his days were numbered if he couldn't raise the five thousand dollars he owed by the first of the month, which was only five days from now. As if that were not bad enough, he now was very sick and couldn't work. He rolled this over in his mind and rapidly concluded that he must see his father and ask him for help.

He hadn't seen his father, the good Dr. Kovacs, in almost two years because of his drug abuse. His father suspected that he was using drugs when he had been told by Alex's previous employer that Alex was always late and had unexplained absences. He told him that the word was out about his son's habit. Of course, Alex never knew how his employer had ever come to relate this information to his father. As fate would have it, Alex later found out from his father that his employer had been a patient of Dr. Kovacs. Alex and his father had a bitter fight over this issue, which caused Alex to isolate himself from further contact with him. He had stolen his father's expensive stereo set from his home to pay for his drugs because he had fallen behind in his financial obligations to Tony. He was forced to do it. *After all*, thought Alex, *he's got plenty and can afford it*, so he made it look like robbery so his father could file an insurance claim. In this way, Alex rationalized that he really wasn't stealing since the insurance would pay for the goods and his father would again have the stereo. He enjoyed the fact that his father would be unconvinced, with the red tape of filing and the wait that was inherent on all insurance actions. Dr. Kovacs had suspected that his son had stolen the stereo, but he could never prove it. It was that very event that had led to the fight. Now he had to eat crow.

He continued his drive south along the Antelope Valley Freeway and approached the intersection of the Golden State Freeway. Tuned to his favorite early talk show program, he was reminded that it was only 6:00 a.m., and his father lived only twenty minutes away in Encino.

Dr. Kovacs usually left home before 8:00 a.m. on Wednesday to join his friends at the tennis club. This had been his tradition for years. He wasn't a bad tennis player considering he had only begun to play the game when he was forty, some twenty years ago. He sipped a cup of hot coffee that had just been brewed by his coffee maker. One of his favorite pleasures was to sip two steaming mugs of Irish cream-flavored coffee brewed from freshly ground beans each morning while watching CNN for his daily news briefing. He was a news buff, and as important as his morning fresh brew was, CNN news occupied equal status in his life. The weather segment was just about to be shown but held no interest in Dr. Kovacs since he lived in Encino, California, where the weather was monotonous anyway. He heard a car pull up in front of his house. In another moment the doorbell rang. He opened the door and stared in disbelief at his son. Dr. Kovacs felt a combination of fear and pleasure, for here in front of him stood his son appearing disheveled and somewhat humbled. "What happened to you?" he asked.

Alex bit his lips and looked down at his feet. "I am sick and need help," he said. He waited for a response.

"Come inside so we can talk," said Kovacs. Alex walked through the door into a palatial foyer that led into his father's study. The television was still on, but the green, muted sign appeared on the screen. "Please turn it off," he said, as he fell into the chair. There was a long period of silence before his father said a word. "Is that the way you greet me after two years?" he asked.

"Dad . . . I need your help." He raised his eyes, and for the first time, he looked directly at the piercing omniscient eyes of his father.

Dr. Kovacs couldn't believe what he saw. "You are jaundiced. Do you have pain anywhere?"

"Some pain in my right side, that's all," he replied.

"I knew it," blurted out Kovacs. He shook his head vigorously from side to side.

"You knew what," said Alex.

"I knew that those damn drugs would get you, Alex. You don't have a brain in your head."

Alex took a deep breath and forced himself to again look at his father. "I've come to you for help, not a sermon. Must we always start off like this? I've lost twenty-five pounds over the last month, and I can't eat. Can you give me something for it?"

Kovacs quickly evaluated his patient. His skin was deep yellow, and his eyes were the same color. His son's face reflected the weight loss, and he knew very well Alex's liver had been the victim of an attack of hepatitis.

"We must get you into the hospital and do some testing right away. You need medical treatment," said Kovacs.

"You know I don't have health insurance," Alex said.

"It doesn't matter. I will make all the necessary arrangements," said Kovacs with a voice of authority.

"What hospital?" asked Alex quickly.

I will call some friends in Palmdale and have them admit you to the hospital there," responded Kovacs.

"Okay, when?" asked Alex.

"Why don't you drive back to the hospital now, and I'll make the necessary arrangements. I think you should present yourself to the emergency room. They'll have a bed waiting for you." With that, he grabbed his tennis bag and was already standing at the door gesturing to Alex.

"I'll be late if we don't get a move on," said the surgeon in a disgusted voice.

Alex got up and walked out the door and to his car. He opened the door and slid behind the wheel, slipped the key into the ignition, and drove away. He headed north on the 405, passed the Sepulveda Dam, and felt his stomach twinge with pain while he thought about what had transpired between himself and his father over the last fifteen minutes. *That bastard could not have cared less about me. He couldn't wait to get me out of the house so he could play tennis. That selfish son of a bitch lives only to satisfy his own desires. Why did I even think that he would show concern like a real father? He never has and never will. That egotistical sperm donor.*

As soon as Alex drove away, Dr. Kovacs re-entered his house. He moved quickly to the desk in his den and dialed Dr. Small in Palmdale.

"Dr. Small's office," the receptionist answered, conveying an attitude of arrogance.

"This is Dr. Kovacs. May I speak with Dr. Small, please?" he said in his soft, flattering voice.

"Oh, certainly, Doctor, I'll get him on the phone right away." Kovacs was always amazed at the change in the receptionist's demeanor from that of a bitch, who was impressed with herself because she worked for a doctor, to becoming an agreeable, oversolicitous phony. To make it even worse, she didn't have the slightest clue that her boss was an incompetent moron who just happened to have a license to practice medicine.

"Hello, this is Dr. Small speaking," he said.

This also inflamed Kovacs. It was just that every time that idiot identified himself as "doctor," he became infuriated. He had always wanted desperately to respond to Small with something like, "I don't really think you are."

"Drop that 'doctor' shit, Small," he said emphasizing the word doctor.

"What can I do for you?" asked Rick, trying to be solicitous.

"Look, Rick, my son is jaundiced and appears pretty sick. I want you to admit him to the hospital, okay?"

"Gee Harvey, you know I don't feel I can give him good care," Rick said with a nervous laugh. "If you can't treat it with penicillin or diagnose it with a urine test, it's out of my league. If you don't mind, I'll have our new internist admit and treat him, okay?" asked Rick.

"That's fine with me, Rick, and I would appreciate it if you would call the emergency room and let them know that he is on the way," replied Kovacs.

"Sure will, and by the way, don't be late for the meeting tonight, okay?" He didn't want to miss his favorite television sitcoms.

"I'll be there at seven o'clock," said Kovacs, as he slammed the receiver. He walked away muttering something about the intelligence of his partner.

~5~

FINANCIAL FRENZY AND THE SALVATION PLAN

Promptly at five forty-five that evening, Dr. Kovacs drove away from his home and headed for the north on ramp of the 405 freeway. The drive had been uneventful, and soon he pulled his car into the doctor's parking lot at Palmdale Hospital and parked in a reserved space for doctors. The meeting was always held in the large conference room located in the subacute unit. Kovacs entered through the rear entrance and headed toward the conference room. Opening the door to the room, he was greeted by his two partners.

"Glad you're here," said Lund, standing to shake hands.

"Good to see you," echoed Rick Small, following Bob's lead and waiting to shake hands with Kovacs.

"Let's get on with the business at hand," said Kovacs, pulling up a chair.

"Since I haven't been here for a while, I would appreciate it if you would update me on our financial status."

"Sure," said Bob. "You know we are losing big bucks now, and we can't seem to plug the losses. Our expenses are exceeding our income, and we need to do something quick."

Small, with his usual stupid expression on his face, piped in, "I think we should sell everything."

"You mean the hospital, subacute center, and the group practice?" asked Lund.

"Yep, everything," answered Rick, nodding his head up and down like a yo-yo.

"Wait a minute, gentleman," said Kovacs. "We have been showing large losses for the last six months or so. It would be foolish to entertain a sale until we can show a profit. Businesses are valued partly on how well the bottom line appears."

"That makes sense," said Lund, and Small nodded in agreement.

"Look guys, I've got a plan I want to run by you," said Kovacs, then, sensing there was no objection, he continued.

"The way I see it, we receive five hundred thousand dollars monthly from our Medi-Cal contract with the state, but we are paying out about six hundred thousand dollars monthly in total operational costs. We are upside down a hundred thousand dollars a month. If we can reverse this, we will be in a better position to sell. Our biggest losses stem from the Medicare age group. If we unload the whole practice and retain the hospital and subacute care center, I think we can come out okay. We can make our money on the shared risk hospital pool like we have in the past years. If you recall, that is the pool money we split with the HMO at the end of the year when they calculate any savings that result from reduced hospital admissions."

"Well, tell us more, already" said Small.

Kovacs continued, "I have been talking with the Department of Health Services in Sacramento about leasing out some of our empty subacute care beds for long-term respirator patients who have tracheostomies and are respirator-dependent. There is a similar setup in a subacute center in Delano, and I've spoken with their administrator about the economics of the operation. The state pays between four hundred and four hundred fifty dollars a day for care, and the profit is about fifty percent. If we fill a dozen beds, that will bring us about five grand daily, or one hundred fifty thousand a month, which will buffer our current losses."

"How quickly can we get patients?" asked Lund. His interest was now piqued.

"I think we can safely assume that we would have our beds full in sixty days," responded Kovacs with a smile.

"What happens if we don't fill them?" asked Rick.

"Well, in that case, we will put Plan B into operation," replied Kovacs, annoyed that Rick had jumped the gun on him.

"And what's that?" asked Lund, looking at Kovacs in doubt.

"All right, gentlemen, hear me out on this one. I have uncovered a way to keep our subacute beds full, and it's all right here in our own backyard," said Kovacs.

"What?" asked Small, wrinkling his brow with doubt.

"Whenever we have a patient on a respirator, we get paid, right?" asked Kovacs. Both Small and Lund nodded affirmatively.

"Now then, we stop getting paid when the patient dies, so I have a plan to keep them alive permanently, and we continue to bill the state, and we continue to get paid. Brilliant?" asked Kovacs gesturing with his hands outstretched.

"Uh, I don't get it," said Small.

Figures, thought Kovacs. He went on. "Let's say we have a chronic lunger, say an emphysema patient that is respirator-dependent, and he dies. Let's call him Mr. Lunger. We then substitute patient Jones for Mr. Lunger if Jones is one of those indigent patients we must take in as mandated by our state contract. As you know, in order for us to have become licensed as a subacute center, the state mandated that we must always keep ten beds available in our chronic care nursing home. Therefore, we will always have a supply of indigent patients that are already in our care. The catch is that these patients must be screened for family members. As you already know, the big problem we have always had with these patients is that we could never get them discharged home because most of them don't have families. This, of course, is exactly what we want—patients with no families."

Kovacs was now caught up in a frenzy as he continued to explain his scheme. "All right, so now we have a patient without a family, and this patient can be substituted for the real respirator-dependent one when he dies. Of course, this will mean that we will continue to bill the state for daily care, even though the patient is dead. We sign the death certificate with the name of the substituted patient who has no family, and as far as anyone knows, it appears that 'Mr. No Family Jones' died. He now exists in his new identity as 'Mr. Lunger' and is placed on the respirator. If he doesn't need respirator care, all we need to do is drip IV-paralyzing drugs into him to make the respirator necessary for him to breathe and stay alive. When 'Mr. No Family Jones' dies, all we do is sign the death certificate with his predecessor 'Mr. Lunger's' name. He is then buried, and no one is the wiser." Kovacs looked at Lund and Small, waiting for them to digest what he had just told them. "Any questions so far?" asked Kovacs, all smiles.

Dr. Lund sat back in his seat and rocked back on the rear legs of his chair. "Harvey, here's where I lose you. Once Mr. No Family Jones takes the place of Mr. Lunger, on paper it looks good, but in reality, he doesn't look like Mr. Lunger, and the family will know."

"Eureka, you get the prize, my friend!" blurted Kovacs gleefully, rubbing his palms together. He knew that Lund would pick up on this major flaw in his plan, and he was also certain that Small was so stupid he would never see it. His prediction was again correct, and he smirked ever so slightly. "Now, my partners, hear me out. For me to reveal the solution, I must tell you a little bit about my past." He continued to talk.

"I grew up in the Bronx and was raised, if you want to call it that, by my father. When I was eight years old, my mother died in an auto accident on the Merritt Parkway, killed by a drunk driver. My father became an alcoholic and a heavy gambler. He was financially comfortable prior to my mother's death, but he lost almost everything he owned shortly thereafter. This gambling addiction was the cause of his death. My father was a mortician and owned his own mortuary as well as a crematory. After accumulating severe gambling debts, he found that he was beholden to the mob. You see, if you owe the organized crime syndicate money, your life becomes a bargaining tool—that is, if you have something of significant value to offer them. In this case my dad was fortunate because they thought he had something to barter.

"A mob boss by the name of Emilio, to whom dad had become financially indebted, called upon Dad for a favor. This mobster had come under scrutiny by one of the local 'families' for hiding the fact that his own sister had stolen cash receipts from a weekly collection of bookie money. He had convinced his sister to leave the country because he knew that once 'The Family' heard about this infraction, they would put a contract out on her life. He secretly was also worried about his own life. Since she had stolen the cash from him, he had no doubt that they would think he was responsible for the theft. Emilio had not been vigilant with their money; therefore, he could not be trusted anymore. The family was not known for their forgiveness in matters such as these. She was a heavy drug user and did whatever she had to in order to keep her body in drug satiety. Emilio bought her plane tickets and arranged for her to disappear in Mexico and thought up a scheme to get the mob heat off him and his sister.

"Emilio went to see my dad and told him he would forgive his gambling debt, which was already fifteen thousand dollars, if he would do him a favor. My dad told me years ago that when he heard this, he began to sweat and develop palpitations, no doubt experiencing an acute anxiety reaction at hearing the proposal. He knew it would have to be a hell of a favor to cancel a fifteen-thousand-dollar debt. At this point, I want you to understand that I had no knowledge of any of this on that day when I walked into my father's office. I was only thirteen years old at the time.

My dad wasn't in the office, so I walked through his rear door and entered the mortuary where I heard a radio. I approached the area and saw that a lady was preparing the face of a person for a funeral service. I saw that she was placing a long, blonde woman's wig on the head of this male body and then proceeded to spend the next two hours applying makeup to his face. I had watched her off and on during this time. When she had finished, she had transposed the face into that of a woman. It was unbelievable magic. I remember asking my father about that event, and he brushed it off, but I knew by his expression he was upset that I had seen it. It wasn't until many years later when I asked my father about that event that I discovered the truth. He told me about the debt he had agreed to repay to Emilio. What he had done was to convince the Family that Emilio's sister was dead. He accomplished this through the artistic abilities of a friend who was a cosmetologist and for whose services he paid dearly. The dimly lit casket had remained open throughout the ceremony, and it convinced all present that this was indeed Emilio's sister. The Family and their representatives were satisfactorily convinced the sister was dead. Since my father also had a crematorium, it was easy for him to fake the family request for cremation of the dead man and issue a death certificate properly signed by Dad. I was impressed with this deception and thought then that it was a great scheme and have never forgotten about it. My father, however, didn't realize that he could never escape the demands of the mob. In the future they did call upon him to perform other tasks, which finally led to his conviction and incarceration in the state penitentiary. He had been caught up with mobsters who sold their stories for their own immunity. Unfortunately, one of those stories related my father's involvement in a case where another body was switched to conceal a killing of a high family member who had been repudiated to have retired in Sicily. In reality he had been murdered by one of the mobs, and in order to keep all the mob factions at peace, it was arranged that his body be cremated without a death certificate.

My father was found guilty of aiding and abetting the mob and many other violations of his undertaker's license. I hated the bastard and never shed a tear for him, nor did he ever for me I might add. He was always too busy for me and would revel in calling me names and insulting me in front of my friends. He never really loved me. That bastard cared only for money and his own selfish desires."

Kovacs went on in a barrage of words that seemed to serve as a catharsis.

"You know," he said, "I was beaten so many times by that drunkard, that I wonder how I ever made it to my teens without being killed. When he died in jail, I felt relieved, and I never lost any sleep over it."

A thought crossed his mind at that moment. He now understood why his relationship with his son was what it was ... nothing. He saw that it was all because he had none with his own father. That, no doubt, was why he couldn't or wouldn't attempt to develop one with his own son. He finally was able to see it clearly. It had never dawned on him, before probably because it had been so painful. He could never bring himself to remember his childhood, and so, by repression, he never had to deal with his feelings. He had never revealed anything about his past to anyone and knew he had done just that but only because he had to make his partners understand that his plan would work. He had already witnessed its success once. Kovacs was determined to gain the approval of his partners for implementing his plan. He was now playing for big stakes. There was a fortune to be made if the sale of the medical group and hospital were consummated, but there also loomed the very real possibility that he could lose everything as well.

The reason for the void in his relationship with his son was now crystal clear to him. He did not love his son, and as a matter of fact, he felt no feelings for him whatsoever. Kovacs had not allowed himself to be put into a vulnerable position. When he was very young, like all children, he tried to become close to his father, but he was shunned. He came to understand that relationships cause pain, especially upon separation, and vowed he would never place himself in that position again, not even with his own son. In the past, Kovacs had learned how to engage defense mechanisms whenever he began to feel anxious about issues. One that worked very nicely for him was to concentrate his thoughts on money. This always exhilarated him and dissipated his anxiety.

"Now, let me return to the present situation," continued Kovacs.

"What we need now is the ability to make the face of Mr. No Family look like Mr. Lunger, right?" asked Lund. "Exactly," answered Kovacs. "All right, now get this," he continued. "I know someone with extraordinary talent who works for a special studio effects company and does most of the special effects for the big movies. The company makes lifelike masks of people, and duplicating a live face is a piece of cake for this guy."

"I remember seeing a TV special on how they do that," said Lund.

"I saw that too," piped in Small.

Kovacs continued, "They first make a plaster mask of the face then follow through with other techniques to produce the lifelike mask. It ends up as a perfect duplicate which can't be differentiated from the original."

"But the most important question is, can we trust this guy?" asked Lund.

"Now therein lies the crux," said Kovacs. "But trust me boys, I have always produced in the past, haven't I?"

"This is really scary stuff," said Small. "Are you sure you can get this done? How can we be sure that someone won't rat on us? I'm all for making a buck, but not at the risk of going to jail! What kind of guarantee do we have someone won't blow the whistle?"

Dr. Kovacs peered at his colleague with disdain. "I, as usual, shall take all the responsibility, Small. We will all go up in smoke big time if we don't turn this hospital around financially. There aren't enough patients I can operate on, even if you send me all yours and Lund's. Oh, by the way, I have the cash I owe you for those last six cases I operated on, and I believe that will put us even to date." He pulled out a roll of hundred dollar bills and began to peel them off. After he made two piles, he said, "I grossed eighteen thousand on those surgeries, and you get half, amounting to forty-five hundred apiece. Keep them coming, lads; I do appreciate the opportunity to serve you." Kovacs laughed. Lund and Small both joined in the laugh. Kovacs was laughing over the fact that he had just screwed his own partners out of three thousand dollars. He had neglected to tell them that he had collected twice as much on one patient because of his unscrupulous billing practices that were much too sophisticated for his partners to ever discover. He had billed a patient's insurance company in a piecemeal fashion known as unbundling, thereby receiving much more for the surgery. This required multiple billing codes and indicated to the payor that much more surgery had been done, which was a blatant lie. The billing codes had been agreed upon by his comrades, and they were all aware of the fees that these billing codes would generate. Lund and Small were duped into thinking that the fees Kovacs received were as a result of their agreed-upon codes. Every now and then Kovacs would unbundle and bill at the higher codes, never telling his partners. He would, however, calculate their percentage based on the single anticipated code. "Let's meet again next week. It will take me that long to arrange the rest of the details." Kovacs said goodnight and walked out to the parking lot.

~6~

ALEX SEEKS MEDICAL HELP

"Paging Dr. Gaines, Dr. Mark Gaines," blared the overhead speakers. He walked to the nearest phone at the nurses' desk and dialed the operator. "You are wanted in the ER," said the operator."

"Okay," he replied as he hung up the telephone, left the nursing station, and headed toward the emergency room.

"Hi," he said to the nurse as he opened the door and entered the ER. He was met by a scene of chaos. There were six gurneys, each separated by a three-foot space and a draw curtain. On the first gurney lay a middle-aged white male with a tube inserted through his nose into his stomach, which was draining coffee-ground appearing fluid. He had an IV of dextrose and saline running rapidly, and the nurse was taking his blood pressure while the overhead monitor recorded his electrocardiogram in green. The next two gurneys were occupied by a man and a woman who were being evaluated for multiple injuries they suffered in an automobile accident. The fourth gurney held a mother holding a screaming infant who had a croupy cough. The infant would not remain still despite the mother's attempts to confine her baby to her bosom. On the fifth gurney was a Black man being sutured by the emergency room doctor. He had been cut rather severely across his right cheek in a drunken brawl. A Los Angeles County Sheriff was standing at his head, recording information on a clipboard.

"Dr. Gaines, there is a patient in bed six who was referred to you by Dr. Small," said the nurse cheerfully as she hurried by, handing him the patient's chart. He walked over to the closed curtain and opened it. Then he walked inside the enclosure.

On the gurney lay a man who was severely jaundiced and appeared extremely ill. "Hello, I'm Dr. Gaines. Dr. Small has asked me to see you," said Mark.

"Okay."

"Well how long have you been sick?" inquired Gaines, who then spent the next thirty minutes taking the medical history from Alex Kovacs. He performed a thorough physical examination and told Alex, "Your liver is enlarged, your skin is yellow, and you are dehydrated. You need to be admitted to the hospital for treatment," explained Gaines.

"I should have known this time Erin would be right!" muttered Alex.

"You know, I knew a doctor in the San Fernando Valley whose name was Harvey Kovacs."

"That's my father," answered Alex.

Mark was surprised. Here he was seeing the son of that despicable excuse for a doctor that had caused him so much grief. "Does your father know you are ill?"

"Look, Doc, I am old enough to take care of myself, and he doesn't need to know anything about me, Okay?" answered Alex angrily.

"Whatever you say," said Mark. "Let's get you admitted and start treatment right away."

He left the ER and walked to the nurses' station on the east wing, requested a chart from the nurse, took out the doctor's orders, and began to write. The first order was for isolation, because he really felt that Alex was suffering from an acute hepatitis B infection secondary to drug abuse. Alex had admitted to him that in addition to his heavy cocaine habit he had also shot up with heroin at a party four months ago with a shared needle. Gaines now had to be concerned with treating the physical effects of cocaine withdrawal as well as the dehydration and the liver failure. He ordered Catapres orally three times a day to decrease the withdrawal symptoms and judicious amounts of Librium to both sedate and prevent the muscle spasms of withdrawal. After that, he wrote for the usual and customary laboratory tests to properly diagnose the liver disease among other tests.

Alex slept well that night and the following twenty-four hours. The Librium had worked very well. When he awakened, he saw someone standing next to his bed with a tray in her hand that looked like a plumber tool box that was full of tubes filled with blood and other things. "I'm here to draw blood from you Alex," she said. Erin was sitting in a chair next to his bed. She whispered to Alex, "I told you that you had hepatitis, didn't I." Erin raised both of her eyebrows, slightly cocked her head, and opened her mouth in a haughty attitude.

"Lay off, will ya," said Alex, closing his eyes and hoping desperately she would leave.

The technician placed her gloved hand on his arm and tightened a tourniquet. She drew blood into four tubes with different colored stoppers and applied pressure to the puncture sight. After a few minutes she left the room and was followed by Erin.

Dr. Gaines entered the room wearing a blue paper gown used for protection by hospital personnel. He was also wearing a mask and a paper cap covering his head. The cap was angled forward in such a way that it made him look like a French pastry chef.

"Feel better today, Alex?" inquired Mark, smiling.

"Yes, I do, said Alex, "and I'm starving."

"No wonder—you have been asleep off and on for four days now. I have good news for you, Alex. I think you can go home tomorrow, but you can't return to work for at least a month."

"Just great," moaned Alex. "I've got to get back to work, Doctor; I can't afford not to."

Alex groaned out loud as he thought about his drug pusher and the money he owed.

Mark Gaines returned to the nurses' station and removed Alex's chart from the chart rack. Opening it to the lab file, he reviewed all the reports. The blood tests revealed Alex was suffering from an acute hepatitis B infection. Since arrival to the hospital, Alex's bilirubin level had dropped from a level of seven to three and one half, and his liver enzymes had dropped from a level of 820 to 310 units. This was good, thought Mark; it indicated the liver was healing and the cells were no longer dying. He knew that another month of rest was required to promote the healing process of the liver to complete restoration. He also had some doubt whether his headstrong young patient would follow his directions. He had seen this behavior before, where a young patient began to show a recovery pattern from hepatitis, but because he ignored his doctor's instructions for rest, severe relapse occurred. In this disease it could very well be disastrous and result in complete liver failure which more times than not was fatal. He flipped through the pages of the laboratory results and read the next report. Hepatitis C antibody had been detected by the laboratory. This was unexpected, and Mark now knew that Alex's full recovery might never happen, since a large percentage of these patients went on to develop cirrhosis of the liver. As Mark glanced up, he saw his friend passing the nursing station on the way to the Intensive Care Unit. Dr. Walker had just finished performing a colonoscopy on an elderly patient with severe anemia. "Be right back, Mark, I've got to write a few orders first, then let's go to the doctor's lounge for a cup of coffee, Okay?"

"Sure Gerry, I'll wait here for you."

In less than two minutes, Dr. Walker exited the swinging doors of the Intensive Care Unit and signaled to Mark, who scooted back his chair and hurried to join his friend.

They walked to the doctor's lounge and poured a cup of coffee into sterile white Styrofoam cups. "Want to hear something funny?" asked Mark.

"Yup, I could use a laugh or two about now, it's been a bad day."

"A few days ago, I was asked by Rick Small to admit a patient with hepatitis, and it turned out this guy was the son of the surgeon I told you about. The one who caused me to leave the San Fernando Valley, remember? He was very sick, but he recovered and will probably go home tomorrow."

"So?"

"Well I got to know him, and we had a few conversations. He told me that his father was one of the owners of this medical group and that he was partners with Small and Lund in both the acute hospital and subacute care center, including the chronic skilled nursing facility."

"You've got to be kidding!"

"No, I'm not, Gerry. Furthermore, he told me his father keeps this under tight wraps and that he only found out about this recently by accident. This kid hates the old man, and I really can't say that I blame him. In my short exposure to the good Dr. Kovacs, I came to hate his guts rather quickly, so I feel sympathy for his son. This kid also got serious problems at home, too."

"Is he on the skids with his wife?"

"You bet he is. He told me she wants to leave him and that she doesn't love him. I really felt sorry for him."

"So where will he go when you discharge him tomorrow?"

"I guess home."

"What kind of hepatitis does he have?"

"Acute hepatitis B with a chronic C as well, poor guy."

"Did you check him for other hepatitis viruses Mark? You know B and C may not be the only hepatitis pathogens."

"Thanks for reminding me about that, Gerry; it slipped my mind. I'd better write more orders tomorrow."

The next morning after he was discharged from the hospital, Alex walked to the parking lot where he had left his car. He was just about to open the door when a dark vehicle pulled alongside and stopped. The shaded window rolled down to reveal a man that Alex had never seen before. Fear overcame him as he felt a shiver up his spine.

"Hey Alex, I want to talk to you," said the man.

Alex glanced over his right shoulder at the face framed in the car's window and froze. He couldn't remember ever having seen a face this frightening. There was an angry red scar running from his right lower eyelid straight to the jaw, which then made a right angle and rose to the crease next to the nose. As if that weren't enough, there was another scar running parallel on the other cheek, each one ending at the lips. *This man's face had been a great challenge for some surgeon,* he thought. He felt his heart racing as though it was trying to eject itself from his chest, and his mouth had instantly become dry, making it difficult to speak. Alex turned around to face the stranger head on and began to speak.

"I don't know you, do I?" Alex said in an unsteady voice.

"Na, you don't, but I got a message to give you from Tony," replied the stranger.

Alex's heart fluttered violently with the sound of the name Tony. His fears had just now been confirmed. He was already a week late with his payment to Tony.

"What's the message?" asked Alex cringing.

The man opened his car door and walked toward Alex. He wore a smirk on his face, which changed to a serious demeanor as he came closer. "Tony says you got till next Monday to pay him, or I'll be back to collect for him," he said, his eyebrows raised in a questioning manner that demanded an answer immediately.

"I . . . I'll have it for him. I've been sick and just got out of the hospital. Tell Tony, Okay?" pleaded Alex with the sound of obvious desperation.

The stranger closed his right eye partially as he lit a cigarette and blew the smoke directly at Alex. "I'll pass the message on to him, but let there be no doubt, if the bill ain't paid by Monday, you and I will be goin' for a ride, and you ain't got no return ticket."

"I'll take care of it; don't worry," stammered Alex rapidly. His mind was a blur and thoughts were in disarray.

As the messenger of doom drove off, Alex slumped against his car. He was frantic with fear. His mind raced as he tried to come up with a solution. His hand shook violently as he put the key into the ignition and started his car. He knew he didn't have the financial resources to pay the six-thousand-dollar debt, and his credit was nonexistent. Long ago his credit cards had been canceled because they were always overdrawn using them to finance his habit. Debts continued to snowball, and the huge balances that resulted had been more than he was able to handle, and the cards were voided by the companies before he had ever made one payment on them. It then took him three years to pay them off because his wife had no access to money, and he had no friends. As he drove up his driveway, Alex thought about asking his father to help him but rapidly dismissed the thought from his mind. He walked into the house and found Erin sitting on the couch watching television. She looked up at him and smiled as she shut off the television.

"Guess who just called you?"

"I have noooooooooo idea," said Alex.

"Your father, and he said to tell you he was on his way here to speak with you."

"Look, Erin, I've got some real problems, and I want to talk to you for a minute before he gets here, Okay?" *I've got to tell somebody about this,* he thought.

"Fine," replied Erin.

Alex then told her how he had fallen into debt to Tony for drugs.

"I have been off all drugs for ten days ever since I became ill, and I no longer have the craving," he said with conviction.

"I'm happy for you," Erin said in a low, soft voice.

"I wonder what my father wants. Maybe he wants me to loan him some money," he went on laughing. They had no further discussion between them.

An hour later a car drove up to his condominium. Dr. Kovacs walked to the door and pushed the buzzer. Alex opened the door and stared at his father. "Come in," he said in a flat affect. Dr. Kovacs walked into the living room and sat down on the sofa.

"Alex, I want to talk to you about a proposition I have for you. As I'm sure you know, I hold a financial interest in the Palmdale Hospital and the Subacute Unit," said Kovacs.

Alex couldn't believe his ears. His father was actually talking to him like he really cared that he knows these matters. He had never been told anything of substance before by his father.

"We have had financial problems that have caused us to pursue other solutions in order to reduce our losses. One of these approaches has to do with the Subacute Unit and its patients. My plan is quite complex but, suffice it to say, I need somebody with *your* talents to work for us," stated Kovacs.

"What do you mean by talents?" asked Alex inquisitively.

"I'm getting to that, Alex. You see, we need someone who knows how to make a facial mask like you do in your capacity as a special effects artist for the movies. It is crucial that whoever we hire be tight-lipped about the job, and in return for the silence and the work, we are prepared to pay extremely well," replied Kovacs with pride.

"Now, just how much would that pay be?" Alex's mind was racing now. He was excited, but didn't want to tip his hand. If ever there was a time he could use an income boost, it was now. By the way his father had spoken, he suspected there was something illegal about the whole thing, but he didn't want to alert his father he was suspicious.

Dr. Kovacs continued, "This job will require you to be available to do our work on an intermittent sort of on-call basis."

"Can I still work at my other job?" asked Alex.

"You may, Alex, as long as you can perform the task for us in a timely and efficient manner," replied Kovacs.

Alex was now in deep thought trying to guess exactly what he would be required to do, when his father spoke and broke his train of thought. "Alex, I'm going to level with you on this. I want you to make the facial masks of certain patients so that we can place them on others. The patients who will wear the masks of the others will be ones who are on respirators, and since they are long term, there will be visitors only rarely who might raise suspicion. I don't have a feel yet for just how frequently we will need your services, so I suggest that we pay you on a per-patient basis. We will set aside space for you to work at the hospital, but I think it would be most advisable for you to do most of your work at home. Our thrust here is to keep this entire operation secret. No one must ever find out about this, or we may all go to jail, but the benefits here do outweigh the risks. We are prepared to pay you twenty-five hundred dollars per mask." Kovacs awaited a response.

"Boy that's a lot to swallow at one sitting," said Alex, wiping his brow. He thought a long time and weighed the risk of all he was just offered against the risk of not being able to pay Tony. There was only one choice. "There is one pressing problem, however, that I must deal with now," said Alex.

"What is it, Alex?" asked Dr. Kovacs.

Alex knew that he had the upper hand. Now that his father had disclosed the scheme, he felt he had to strike while the iron was hot. "Since you have trusted me with your plan, I will tell you the truth about my problem. I am in debt to the tune of six thousand dollars that must be paid by Monday."

At this juncture, Dr. Kovacs felt uneasy, as he knew he had just opened a can of worms. In the past he had been able to remain isolated from his son by staying distant and never discussing personal issues of any type. This had allowed him to build a wall between the two of them and sheltered him from emotional trauma that he had left behind when his own father died. He wasn't sure, but he thought there was a trace of paternal reflex attempting to rise in his conscious mind, and this was frightening to him.

"I'm listening," he said and was acutely aware of his voice as he spoke those words.

Alex's face blushed slightly, and he felt the warmth on it. He realized that he was blushing because he felt embarrassed to ask his father for help. He couldn't remember the last time he had felt this way, and it made him very anxious.

"I owe a guy six thousand dollars for the purchase of cocaine and a few other drugs that I bought from him when I didn't have the cash, but from now on I'm off drugs forever … I've learned my lesson. My life has been threatened if I don't pay this guy by Monday …" Alex thought it better if he stopped here and awaited his father's response.

"All right, Alex, you want me to advance you the money?" asked Kovacs. He wasn't terribly surprised at what he had just heard.

"Yes, I would be indebted to you forever," replied Alex with enthusiasm.

His father was just waiting to hear those words. He now felt in control again, and a surge of strength ran through his body as adrenalin was released that caused his heart to beat rapidly.

"I'll agree to do it, if you agree to take this job as I have outlined," Kovacs said, staring at his son with icy-blue eyes. He knew he had hooked Alex as well as any drug might have, but he was disappointed that Alex hadn't even attempted to bargain for more money. He was sure that Alex did not inherit his genes. Alex was too placid and much too easy a mark for anyone wishing to take advantage. *He must have his mother's genetic complement,* thought Kovacs, *no wonder he is such a zero.* "I will let you know when we will need you to start on the project Alex. I'll call you soon."

Dr. Kovacs walked to the door and let himself outside. As he started his car, he thought about the great deal he had just made. Little did Alex realize that his father stood to make a tidy fortune in this endeavor but wouldn't easily be able to do it if he had refused to take the offer.

~7~

Making the Mask

Alex spent the next few days at home resting and trying to gain back his strength. He noticed that every afternoon at about 2:00 p.m., he became exhausted and had to lie down for an hour or two. On Wednesday morning at ten o'clock, a federal express delivery was made to his house. Alex tore open the seal of the large envelope, put his hand inside, and found another letter-size envelope, which was sealed with tape. He opened the envelope and was met with a stack of hundred dollar bills and a note. The note said, "Enclosed is six thousand dollars per our agreement," and was signed simply HK.

Alex was suddenly shocked into reality, since he had forgotten all about his debt to Tony. Because of all his sleeping, he had dismissed it from his mind. He felt exhilarated and confident now that he had the money in hand to settle the debt. He called Tony and planned to meet him and settle the debt. The next day, he kept his appointment with Dr. Gaines.

He entered his office and told the receptionist he was there for his appointment with Dr. Gaines.

"Please have a seat; the doctor will be right with you," she said.

To his surprise, he was ushered into an examining room within a few minutes, where Dr. Gaines was seated reading his chart. "Hi Alex, good to see you again."

"Ah, sure, Doc, good seeing you too."

"Why don't you have a seat on this table if you don't mind?"

Alex stepped up to the table and lifted himself up on to it. "I really feel a lot better than last time we talked."

"I'm glad that you do. Please lay back so I can examine your abdomen."

Dr. Gaines palpated his abdomen and specifically tried to feel the spleen as well as the liver. He knew that the liver was easily palpated a week ago to extend three finger breadths below the lowest rib, and he expected to feel it in about the same place today. His examination proved him to be wrong, as the liver was indeed much smaller. This bothered him, because he knew on occasion when a hepatitis liver diminished rapidly in size it indicated that it would collapse. This would result in overwhelming liver failure and coma. He felt the left-upper quadrant of the abdomen and was shocked to find that the spleen was now enlarged. He walked to the hand basin and washed his hands. "Alex, I must tell you that your liver is worse than it was the last time I saw you. I don't like the fact that it has become smaller, and your spleen has enlarged."

"What does all that mean, Doc?" asked Alex, as he sat up and tucked in his shirt while his legs dangled off the end of the table.

Gaines walked back to the table and sat in a chair while opening Alex's chart to the section containing the laboratory reports. After a few moments he spoke again. "Your lab tests show an elevation in the enzyme level, which indicates that your liver cells are being destroyed at an increased rate, and this might lead to liver failure and even coma. You notice that your eyes are still yellow, don't you? This means that the liver is still very sick and cannot excrete certain breakdown products, and as a result, these products remain in the blood. They cause the yellow color most easily noticed in the white sclera of the eye. The liver is a filter of sorts, and functions to remove toxins and byproducts from the blood that result from metabolism. When the liver is sick, it can't perform its function efficiently, and this is what we refer to as liver failure. It also manufactures many different proteins that are necessary for life, and when it fails to do so, it can cause a host of other illnesses." Gaines thought better of continuing the dreary picture of end-stage cirrhosis and hepatic failure. Being a compassionate person, he saw no advantage in certifying a depression and anxiety state in his patient. He knew that there was not much he could do about restoring the liver to normal. It was a well-known and accepted medical fact that the liver will heal after an insult caused by the hepatitis A, B, C, or D virus, but only the body could make it happen. He doubted whether Alex's liver would ever heal completely. His examination and the liver function tests, not so much the real numbers but the trend that they were starting to establish, were of ominous significance. He stood up and opened the door, asking Alex to wait for his blood to be drawn, then suddenly almost as an afterthought, he turned and reminded him to make a return appointment for two weeks.

Alex stood up. "Look, Doc, remember what I told you before about my father. I don't want him to know anything about my problem, Okay?"

Dr. Gaines unconsciously bit down mildly on his upper lip, looked down at the floor, and nodded.

It was about one week later when Dr. Kovacs received a telephone call from the hospital administrator, Bill Hendrickson, notifying him that they had just received the contract from the state. The State of California's Department of Health Services was requesting to contract with the Subacute Unit of Palmdale Hospital for the care of long-term respirator-dependent patients. Hendrickson said that the word was, they were to receive six patients over the next week from Los Angeles County Hospital as well as patients from Martin Luther King and Harbor General hospitals. "We're going to get paid at a rate of $460 a day for their care. I am in the process of arranging leasing for all the equipment we will need."

"That's great news, Bill, let me know when we have those machines cranking," demanded Kovacs.

Within ten days the respirator beds were all occupied as a result of a recent flu outbreak that struck the county. Many chronic lung patients were affected by the illness. Some succumbed to the ravages of the flu, while still others became chronic respiratory cripples. As their ability to breathe was further reduced from the flu, it rendered their lungs incapable of performing gas exchange. Respiratory failure was the outcome, thus requiring permanent respirator support.

Dr. Bob Lund never missed the opportunity to review the financial data generated by the hospital's computers on a monthly basis. At the end of the first month of operation, the twelve respirator patients yielded a bill to the state for $165,600, which would be paid within fifteen days. He was exhilarated at the thought that this venture would now spin off a profit of more than a million dollars a year if these beds remained one hundred percent occupied. It was his and Small's responsibility to care for these patients, which necessitated each of them visiting six patients every Monday to chart a progress note and order any medications needed for their care. In addition, whenever a patient experienced a problem, the nursing staff was instructed to call them, at which time they would arrange to visit the patient and render care. The Respiratory Care Unit had been created from space located at the end of the Subacute Care Unit, which already housed some twenty-five patients but had the capacity for another twenty. The type of patient population varied between long-term care patients, who required supportive care that prevented their placement in a board and care facility, and those who were recuperating from fractured hips and other types of surgery and were only destined to remain for a short period of time. Most of these were receiving some type of rehabilitation program and eagerly awaiting their discharges home.

Administration had instituted a computer-generated selection process that identified all of the MediCal patients who had no next of kin. Whenever a patient was assigned to the Palmdale Medical Group, they were interviewed by personnel to extract that specific information, and then those patients were only assigned to Drs. Lund and Small for their medical care.

One day, James Carson, a sixty-five-year-old White male, came to see Dr. Lund complaining of weakness of his right arm and leg. Dr. Lund examined him.

"I believe you are suffering from a small stroke and will require an aspirin each day to prevent further damage."

"Is that all I need, Doc?" asked Carson with a quizzical look.

"Yes, that will do it for you, but I want to see you in a few days for a recheck."

Lund then went to his supply of office drugs and gave his patient a bottle of Tylenol, which he labeled as aspirin. He knew that aspirin would be very effective in preventing further blood clots and brain damage, but he was more concerned that there were no chronic care patients in the Subacute Unit who could be available at a moment's notice. Patients were needed to substitute for one of the respirator patients should the need arise. He had just returned from making his weekly rounds on his six assigned patients and was certain that it wouldn't be too much longer until one of them would die, and he had no potential replacements. As he thought about the money he would split, he chuckled to himself and thought how perfectly legal it was to give his patient an innocuous drug like Tylenol . . . *after all, Mr. Carson would eventually stroke anyhow.*

Dr. Lund was advised on the following morning that his patient, Mr. Carson, was in the emergency room with a full-blown stroke, unable to speak and paralyzed on the right side of his body. He called the emergency room and had the patient admitted to the hospital for testing. At Mr. Carson's bedside that morning, he noted his physical findings and the results of the laboratory tests and made an entry into the chart. "This patient has no next of kin and will require long-term rehabilitation. Will transfer to the Subacute Unit tomorrow."

On the next morning, Mr. Carson was transferred to the Subacute Unit with a page of orders. This was the first patient to establish the beginning of the "No Family Club," whose entire existence was dependent on their doctor's care.

"Dr. Lund, this is Marple in the Respiratory Care Unit," said the voice in authority. "Homer Benson in bed five has taken a turn for the worse. Can you come over and see him now, please?"

"Sure thing. I'll be right over." Lund walked briskly from his office and out the rear door of the medical office building. He quickly crossed the small street that divided the medical building from the subacute center and entered the rear door, taking larger than normal strides to hasten his arrival at the Respiratory Care Unit. He was already feeling panic as he thought about the money that would be lost if Mr. Benson were to die now. How could he have neglected to notify Kovacs that he had a patient in whom death was imminent, especially after Kovacs had instructed him to do so? They needed to have enough time to prepare a substitute with the designated facial mask. Ms. Marple, the nurse, met him as he entered the Respiratory Care Unit with a chart in her hand. She accompanied him to the bedside of Mr. Benson and immediately took the patient's blood pressure.

"It's eighty-four over sixty, and the pulse rate is falling . . . it's now down to fifty-two," she said.

Lund stared at his patient, who was not looking in the pink of health at that moment. He quickly bent over his patient, careful not to interrupt the respirator or its attached tubing that connected with the breathing tube in the center of his neck. He noticed that both sides of his chest were moving simultaneously during respiration, and the settings on the respirator indicated that the patient was triggering the respiration. *That's good,* he thought. *At least his brain stem drive for respiration was intact.* Dr. Lund then applied his stethoscope to Benson's chest. He carefully listened to the breath sounds to determine if there were the sounds of heart failure present. He examined him for the presence of right heart failure and confirmed there was none present, because the neck veins were flat even though the head of the bed was elevated to forty-five degrees. There were no large pulsations noted in the jugular veins, which meant that there was no heart block. He remembered seeing a patient in third-degree heart block years ago. He recalled that when the atria contracted against closed ventricular valves, the pressure of blood hitting against them was transmitted into the veins, entering the right atrium as well as the jugular. This could be seen in the neck as large pulsations. Moving his scope over the heart, he listened for the presence of a third heart sound commonly heard in heart failure patients, which was also absent. He then applied pressure over the liver and watched for an engorgement in the jugular vein, which would indicate congestive heart failure. Again, there was no evidence of this.

"Well Ms. Marple, I don't believe we are dealing with a primary weak heart muscle as the cause of the drop in blood pressure and pulse. I want to do a neurological evaluation on him. Will you get me a hammer, light, and ophthalmoscope please?"

As she left to retrieve the items, Dr. Lund, who had always prized himself as being a good bedside clinician, felt good about his diagnostic acumen. Having the skills to diagnose at the bedside and not having to wait for the more exotic tests was important to him. He thought it was inappropriate that in today's medicine you were at the mercy of so many subspecialists. The interpretation of these tests by those select few specialists always delayed treatment. *Whatever happened to the physical examination?* he thought. The nurse handed him the ophthalmoscope. He leaned over Benson's face and directed the bright beam into each pupil but did not notice any constriction, although he took notice of the tiny pupils. Peering into the pupils was virtually impossible. "I don't like this," he said, "I can't visualize the retina. Will you please lower the head of the bed?"

Marple pressed the electric control, and the head of the bed approached the horizontal position. "There you are, Doctor," she announced with a sense of great accomplishment.

Dr. Lund held the breathing tube connector firmly to the neck while he rotated Mr. Benson's head. He did not want it to come loose and detach from the respirator or the patient's tracheostomy.

"Look here," he said as he gently turned the head from left to right. "The eyes remain in the center and fail to move to the opposite side. Do you know what that is called?" Lund could not help but play the professor, because his ego needed stroking, and consciously he knew that he would be admired for his knowledge by this nurse. She was dense.

"Something about doll's eyes, I think," she responded hesitantly. Lund was impressed that she knew the answer to his question.

"Yep, that's it, but it's the failure to show doll's eyes. When a patient's eyes don't rotate to the side opposite the side the head is rotated toward, it indicates that there is destruction of the nerve connections located between the inner ear and the eyes within the brain stem. This is a grave finding and correlates well with the hemodynamic instability shown by the abnormal blood pressure and pulse rate." He was immediately sorry that he had said anything about the patient's pathology, because he didn't want the nurse to record anything indicating the gravity of the patient in the chart. It might be difficult to explain the patient's sudden improvement if he was moribund. There was no question in Lund's mind that Mr. Carson would soon become a healthier Mr. Benson. "Go ahead and start some dopamine and titrate the flow to keep his pressure at one hundred and start him on strict intake and output and I'll write IV fluid orders."

Marple walked briskly to the nurses' station and gathered all the IV fluids and made some comment to another nurse that she would be tied up with her patient for a while.

Dr. Lund took his patient's chart from the nurse's desk and opened to the progress notes where he wrote, "Patient has minor changes on his neuro exam.

He is still conscious and appears to be slightly dehydrated. Will start some IV fluids now and reevaluate response."

"Dr. Bob Lund, that's a joke. It should be Dr. Bob Boob," he muttered to himself as he ran across the street and then entered the rear door of his private office with his key. He called his secretary and asked her to place a call to Dr. Kovacs. In a minute he was connected to a ringing telephone.

"Hello, Dr. Kovacs here."

"Harvey, this is Bob Lund. I've got a minor problem." Lund spent the next ten minutes explaining the recent events surrounding Mr. Benson's clinical state and assured his colleague that Benson would live until a mask could be made and placed on Mr. Carson to take his place.

"His blood pressure is now normal, and I have stopped the IV meds."

"Are you certain that Carson has no family?" asked Kovacs.

"That's been checked out thoroughly and there are no next of kin," answered Lund.

"All right then. I'll make all the arrangements for the mask to be made, and then we'll go from there. Have Carson transferred over to the acute unit tonight for a physical therapy evaluation in the Physical Therapy Department. That shouldn't raise anyone's suspicion since PT evaluations are done until 8:00 p.m. daily, and the only hospital personnel around will be on the floors and in the ER," said Kovacs, slightly irritated that his partner hadn't told him about this earlier. He hoped Alex was well enough to start the job.

"That sounds innocent enough to me. By the way, who will be our artist in this creative venture? You never told us," asked Lund.

"My son is home recuperating from a recent bout with hepatitis and is well qualified in this area. He works for an independent Hollywood studio that contracts his service to the movie industry. He is an expert in the arena of special effects and lifelike masks. Don't worry, I have cut a deal with him that is sweet for us. We'll pay twenty-five hundred per mask, and that's it. I'll call him now." Kovacs hung up the phone and dialed Alex's number.

The phone rang at least nine times before Alex picked it up. He had been napping on the couch and was immersed in a dream involving an old girlfriend where he was just about to have sex with her, when the phone rang. He was so irked at being awakened and realizing it was only a dream that he just let the phone ring. "Hello," he growled. "Oh yes, I'll go over at five-thirty to begin," he said and then hung up the phone.

Bob Lund had ordered a brain CAT scan for his patient in order to get him out of the Respiratory Care Unit and into the acute hospital. It would work out very well, he thought. He had conceived a perfect plan to get the mold of Benson's face made without any witnesses. Lund knew that his patient would be given Valium IV in the CAT scan waiting area of the radiology department, as had been previously arranged by his colleague Kovacs. He didn't have the slightest idea how such a mask was created, and he didn't really care to know. After he discussed the details with Kovacs, he reasoned that he had better set the respirator on the control mode in case the Valium caused the patient to stop breathing. He had found it rather easy to switch the respirator to the control mode when he examined the patient and wrote the orders just a short time ago.

When Alex arrived at the hospital, he went to the CAT scan room in the X-Ray Department, where he found his wife sitting at a desk behind the control panel. She called him aside and told him that his patient was behind the drawn curtains at the other end of the large room. Alex carried his bag of supplies and entered the closed area to find Mr. Benson lying on a gurney. "Hi Mr. Benson, I'm Alex and I'm going to give you a facial."

Benson stared blankly ahead without giving any hint he was aware that anyone was in the room with him. Alex called out to Erin, "Will you call Dr. Lund and have him order something to keep this geezer asleep while I do my art?"

"Right away, Alex." She was aware of the whole scenario because Alex had told her all about the deal his father had made with him. She was anxious to see Alex do his work again, as it had been a while since she had observed her husband's creativity, and they needed the money. They had already discussed the fact that if there was a conflict in Alex's schedule that would delay his starting time, she would fill in for him. Erin was also blessed with a talent for art, and with a little practice, she knew she could be very good at making masks. It worked out perfectly. Since there was so much work, the hospital had started her on a late shift from noon until eight-thirty daily. What made it even better was that she was all alone from four o'clock until she closed the department each day, except on the weekends when she would come to work to do paperwork. She was impressed with the ease that patients were moved to the acute hospital from the Subacute Unit for CAT scans and other more esoteric imaging tests that were ordered by Dr. Lund. He wasn't married, and she found him very attractive. He had also been there at just the right time to offer her the comfort and attention she needed during the aftermath of the last fight with her husband. Lund had noticed her bruises and offered her pain medication, which she readily accepted. He had invited her to his office, and she waited for him in his inner private office until his nurse had closed up for the night. After he had examined her bruised neck, face and chest, he had asked her to return the next day. He made love to her in his closed office during the day, which had been an exhilarating experience for her, and she had experienced similar follow-up performances thereafter. He had raised her self-esteem, she thought. She was now important, and moreover, she was entitled to more. Erin remembered how it was when she was a child. She lived in squalor, and her father was always drunk. As she grew older, she worked at building her defenses, so she never allowed herself to become truly involved with people. Erin became an expert at successfully blocking emotional attachment to others. She became a user of men. Now she was a self-assured, tough woman and fantasized that she was wealthy. Sometimes she even fantasized she was a queen with untold riches.

Dr. Kovacs had instructed Alex to ask his wife to go to the Respiratory Care Unit in the subacute center and accompany an orderly, as he rolled Mr. Benson through the long-enclosed causeway that connected the acute hospital to the Subacute Unit. She knew that this was the way the patient could be hidden while her husband made the mold from the patient's face. The orderly left the patient at the radiology holding area, which was right next-door to the CAT Scan Department. Erin told the orderly she would watch him until radiology was ready to take him for his CAT scan. As soon as the orderly was out of sight, she wheeled the gurney into the hall and rapidly pushed it into the door that opened into the large vacant CAT scan room. She pulled a syringe out of her desk that was labeled Valium and walked over to Alex.

"Just squeeze this IV tube," she said as she inserted the needle into the soft rubber part of the tubing and slowly pushed the plunger forward until the syringe was empty.

"Fifteen milligrams of Valium should keep him out for a few hours," she laughed.

"Where did you get that, Erin?" asked Alex.

"Your father gave me a box of Valium preloaded syringes when he was here and told me how much to use."

"But Valium can cause you to go into coma and stop breathing. That's what kills people who take these types of drugs."

"Sure, but your father told me that since these are all patients who are on respirators they cannot stop breathing, so lighten up."

Alex opened his black bag and placed his equipment on the table.

The casting of the face would only take twenty minutes to make; he had done this hundreds of times before. Dental alginate was the casting medium used by the special effects prosthetics people in the entertainment industry. This was the same material that dentists used to cast impressions for teeth. He mixed the powder with water and smeared it on Mr. Benson's face. Alex worked very swiftly, as the material would be set in three minutes. He then applied wet plaster bandages over the rubbery mask and waited for it to dry. *This is the easy part,* thought Alex. Twenty minutes later, Alex checked the hardness of the mold and found that it was ready to remove. Using a special plastic device, he slipped it behind the hair line at the brow and slowly began to lift the mold from the face.

"It's almost off now," he said in a whisper. He removed the mold and inspected it closely.

"Boy, that is perfect," said Erin.

"Looks like a winner to me too."

"Give me a hand in moving him next door to the x-ray waiting room," she said.

Erin picked up the phone and dialed the nurses' station. "Mr. Benson has finished his CAT scan and needs to be returned to the Respiratory Care Unit as soon as possible."

"I'll send an orderly right away," said the nurse.

The next afternoon, Dr. Lund made rounds on Mr. Benson. In his white coat pocket, he carried a small bottle of clear colorless fluid. Lund had devised a plan that would justify the necessity of having to use intravenous Norcuron to keep Mr. Carson totally paralyzed. In so doing, it would then be necessary to place him on continuous respiratory support. He entered the Respiratory Care Unit and saw Ms. Marple at the nurse's station.

"Would you please set Mr. Benson up for a spinal tap?"

"Certainly, Doctor, I'll meet you at the bedside in just a moment."

Lund took the patient chart from the rack and walked to the door of his patient's room.

"I have the setup for the tap here," said Marple cheerfully.

"Fine, let's roll him over onto his right side." Lund carefully opened the sterile pack containing the spinal tap instruments and then put on his own sterile gloves.

"Tuck his knees under him, please."

"Is this good enough, Doctor?"

"That'll be fine."

He prepped the lower back with a Betadine swab and drew an imaginary line from the right to the left iliac crest inferiorly, and where it crossed the spine, he wrote an "x" on the skin with a needle. Choosing a number twenty spinal needle, he applied pressure and slowly advanced it into the spinal canal. When clear fluid ran out from the needle's end, he knew he was in the right place. Marple handed him a three-way stopcock, which he attached to the end of the needle and turned it to the "off" position, stopping the flow of spinal fluid onto the bed sheets. He connected the manometer, asked his nurse to hold the tip steady, and opened the stopcock, noting that the spinal fluid pressure was fifteen centimeters of water. At the stopcock, he then collected some spinal fluid in plastic tubes for biochemical analysis and for culture.

"You can let the manometer lie against the patient." He was trying to think of a way to get rid of the nurse so he could finish what he had to do in private.

"Please go to the lab and get me a couple of blood culture bottles so I can draw them while I am here. I don't want to wait for a lab tech to do it because

Mr. Benson has bad veins," said Lund. He knew that this would take her at least five minutes to go to the lab, page the tech, and get the bottles, then return.

"I'll be back as soon as I get them," she said, leaving the room.

Lund quickly removed his gloves and withdrew a vial from his pocket. He inserted a syringe into the vial and withdrew twenty milliliters of aminophylline. Raising the syringe to the vertical position, Lund pushed the barrel to eject any air.

This will do just fine, he said to himself, as he connected the end of the syringe to the stopcock. He opened the stopcock and withdrew some spinal fluid, which mixed with the drug in the syringe, and then he slowly injected the mixture back into the spinal canal. Rapidly he stuck the syringe and the bottle of aminophylline into his pocket and withdrew the spinal needle. He rolled his patient on to his back again and straightened out his legs and then sat down. This had taken him only four minutes to accomplish, and now each second was an eternity. Ms. Marple returned in another minute and handed the blood culture bottles to Dr. Lund.

"I have a tourniquet here, if you want to draw the blood now," she said, sounding efficient.

"Good idea, hand it to me, please." Lund tied the tourniquet on the left arm and drew the blood sample into two bottles. Just as he withdrew the needle, Mr. Benson began to shake violently. His head was shaking in an affirmative gesture, and his teeth were clenched with spittle exuding from his mouth while the rest of his body jerked in a rhythmic fashion.

"He's having a grand mal seizure!" shouted Dr. Lund in an excited voice. "Get me some Valium and a tongue depressor. Quickly!"

Marple ran out of the room and returned with a syringe of Valium and the tongue depressor. She deftly inserted the plastic blade into Benson's mouth to pry it open and prevent him from biting his tongue. "He is cyanotic; I'll increase his oxygen concentration," she announced loudly.

"Give me the Valium," shouted Lund. He then injected a small amount of the Valium, pushing the plunger to empty the rest of the contents, and finally withdrew the needle. Lund was quite aware that aminophylline induced seizures and would be difficult to control, but he didn't want to see Benson die from this toxic effect, at least not now. He had calculated that five milligrams of Valium would be enough to suppress the seizures but not sufficient to eliminate them.

"It looks like they're diminishing," he said authoritatively. For the next five minutes, the patient improved, and seizure activity had been reduced to a rare twitch of the right arm and head and then it started again with a total body eruption that shook the bed.

Great! thought Lund, *this is just what the Doctor ordered.*

"Please get me the intubation tray now!" Lund said decisively

Marple arrived with the tray and quickly opened it up. Lund grasped the laryngoscope and inserted it into Benson's mouth, being careful to keep the airway patent. "Hand me a number seven tube," he demanded.

Marple responded, and Lund slipped it over the lighted blade of the scope and into the larynx. He placed his stethoscope over the stomach and listened while he blew forcefully into the endotracheal tube. This was an old trick to determine that the tube hadn't accidentally been placed into the stomach. If so, blowing air into it would cause a loud gurgle as the air passed into a stomach that always had some fluid in it. He then asked Marple to listen for breath sounds over the lungs as a further precaution and insurance that the tube was in the right place. At that moment, the respiratory therapist arrived with a respirator that had been requested by Marple earlier in the chaos. Lund waited until the respirator was connected to the endotracheal tube and then listened to the lungs himself. It was too easy to accidentally advance the tube directly into the right mainstem bronchus, thereby depriving the left lung from ventilation. He knew that the anatomy of the trachea as it led into the right and left main stem bronchi was such that the upside-down Y it formed allowed for easy entrance into the right main stem, thereby occluding the entrance to the left main stem. This would result in collapse of the left lung and severe disturbances in oxygen uptake. This complication might cause the death of a patient which Bob could not afford to let happen.

"Marple, get me some Norcuron stat," shouted Lund while he grasped the tongue depressor. Norcuron would cause total paralysis and therefore eliminate the seizure.

She ran out of the room and returned with the drug. "How much do you want to give, Doctor?"

"Give two milliliters and then titrate one milliliter every thirty minutes until the seizure stops. I'll write further orders for continuation of the drug in the chart for you."

In three minutes, Mr. Benson's seizures were in control. It was too bad, Lund thought to

himself, that he had to instill aminophylline into the spinal fluid to bathe the brain with a seizure-producing drug, but it was a very necessary part of his plan to achieve the clinical indication for Norcuron. Severe seizure control with Norcuron was an accepted mode of therapy when Valium failed. It worked very well because it paralyzed the muscles, completely preventing the seizures, but by doing so all the respiratory muscles were also paralyzed. It was this latter effect that required a respirator to breathe for the patient. This part of the plan had gone extremely well, he thought. Now he had to put part two in place, and he headed down the hallway to the chronic rehabilitation area where Mr. Carson was located.

"Well hello, Doctor," said a cheery voice.

He looked at the elderly nurse who was waving at him. Anita Pershing had worked for the hospital in its early years, and when she became sixty-five, she prevailed on her old friend Dr. Lund to let her stay on, working in the Chronic Care Unit. She could spend most of the eight-hour shift sitting at the desk reading her favorite novels. It was a very slow pace with not much care to be given by the nursing staff. She had severe arthritis and had to take at least three long-acting Vicodin for pain control, which prevented her from moving quickly. He had felt sorry for her and was aware she had no source of financial support, thus on that basis, he had convinced the hospital administration to continue her employment.

"I want to see Mr. Carson, Anita; you stay right there." He knew that she would remain at the station.

He walked to Mr. Carson's room, which was at the end of the hall. Lund had seen to it that Carson had no roommates. He walked into the room and looked around to satisfy himself that there was no one else present and then pulled a syringe from his pocket, which he had already filled with Versed, and injected it into the patient's wrist vein. When he had finished, he pressed a piece of gauze firmly over the puncture sight to prevent the blood from oozing into the tissues. Lund was very familiar with this short-acting Valium-type drug and expected the patient to show signs of slowing his respiratory rate within three minutes. It then happened just as he knew it would. Mr. Carson's breathing rate dropped to four breaths per minute, and Lund dashed out of the room and shouted, "Anita, get me an endotracheal tube, Mr. Carson is having difficulty breathing. He's in severe respiratory distress."

She limped down to the room pulling a crash cart that had an intubation tray sitting on the top shelf and ripped the sterilized seal open. "What size tube do you want?"

"A seven and one half will do. Call Respiratory Therapy for me and have them come right over with a respirator," he ordered.

He continued to intubate the patient by himself. After holding Mr. Carson's lower jaw open, he was able to identify the larynx and advanced the tube into the trachea, where he stopped just short of the mainstem bronchi. He connected the end of the tube to the ambu-bag and turned on the oxygen meter at the wall, which immediately filled the green bag that he clasped between his hands. As it filled, he compressed the bag, causing the oxygen to flow into the lungs, and observed that his patient's chest was rising with each compression of the bag. Two male inhalation therapists entered the room pushing a respirator. They were sweating and gasping while trying to speak. They had pushed the ventilator from the acute hospital through the causeway while running all the way in response to the emergency call for help. Ventilators were very expensive, and the only place there were any not in use was in the inhalation therapy department. The department was quite a distance from the Chronic Care Unit.

"Please hook him up to control with 50 percent oxygen," ordered Lund.

"What do you want the minute ventilation set at, Doctor?" questioned the respiratory therapist.

"Oh, uh, tidal volume at six hundred and the rate at ten, okay?"

"Sure thing, Doctor," responded the therapist.

Lund left the room and found a telephone in a corner of the nurses' station where he could talk in private. He dialed the number of Dr. Kovacs.

"Harvey, this is Lund and I'm at the rehab unit. It seems that Mr. Carson had a respiratory arrest and is now ventilator-dependent. He will require a permanent tracheostomy, if you get my drift."

"I understand . . . when do you want to do it?" asked Kovacs.

"I want to ship him to you now, and you can send him back tomorrow," replied Lund.

"Make sure that all the paperwork is proper and that it supports the need for the permanent tracheostomy, okay?" asked Kovacs.

"It's a done deal, Harvey, talk to you later," answered Lund as he hung up the phone.

Dr. Lund turned to the nurse and explained to her that he was sending the patient down below to another hospital for a tracheostomy because he couldn't get a surgeon from Lancaster to come over to Palmdale. He knew that she wasn't that bright and would not question his order as it was a rather common practice to transfer patients to Dr. Kovacs in the San Fernando Valley.

"Fine, Doctor, do you want me to make the arrangements for you?" she asked.

"That would be fine—just as soon as I write up the transfer."

He opened the chart and placed a new set of progress notes inside so he could back date tonight's events, and then it would appear perfectly appropriate for this patient to require a tracheotomy since the endotracheal tube would have been in for two weeks. He began by starting his first note dated fourteen days ago and described the spontaneous episode of respiratory failure followed by daily recorded observations indicating that the patient had continued respiratory depression, which was no doubt due to a small brainstem stroke. He therefore had crossed that magic time period whereby it was necessary to do a tracheostomy and avoid the complications of any longer intubation time. This was acceptable medical practice. He would remove the nurse's note from the chart after it was written by the nurse and insert one of his own, which would confirm all the events that he had just recorded in the chart.

Mr. Carson was transferred by ambulance to Valley hospital to the service of Dr. Kovacs, but not until he had received another injection of Versed with a little morphine added to it so that his ride would be enjoyable.

That day Alex went to work finishing the mask. He placed the plaster facial mold on the table and then brushed it with a medical-grade silicon. This resulted in a translucent covering. After applying the first layer, he carefully brushed it with color to add facial tones. Adding more silicon with the appropriate color was the work of an expert. Alex was just that, and he knew it. He then mixed various oil paints to accomplish the realistic appearance. When he was done, he sat back to admire his artwork. Yes, he had created a masterpiece.

The tracheostomy was done quickly, and on the following day, Mr. Carson was transported back to the chronic care facility in Palmdale on the respirator. Dr. Lund was there when he arrived and ordered that Norcuron, the muscle-paralyzing drug, be continued as an infusion along with sizable doses of Valium. He reasoned Valium was necessary to keep his patient in an unconscious state. It was his expectation that Mr. Carson would be in his new home in the Respiratory Care Unit within twelve hours, albeit with a different name and face. He had successfully convinced all the chronic care nurses that there would be a bed available in the Respiratory Care Unit shortly, and he was only to remain in this area temporarily. The nurses were nervous about caring for a respirator patient in the Chronic Care Unit but readily accepted the doctor's plausible explanation because the temporary holding of an acute patient in their area was not that rare an occurrence. Furthermore, his recent appraisal of Mr. Benson revealed his vital signs were deteriorating, but if he didn't die by the morning, he carried a syringe of insulin with him to hurry Mr. Benson's exodus. An injection of one hundred units of regular insulin would cause sustained hypoglycemia and certain brain death. Dr. Lund was not going to lose any money on a vacant respiratory care unit bed if he could help it, and help it he could.

~8~
THE ART OF ALEX

Alex Kovacs was getting nervous since he hadn't heard from his father concerning the time the mask would be needed. He knew he would have to move very fast when he was given the green light. Alex had already made the mask from the mold, and it had turned out even better than he expected. The Benson mask would now have to be applied and adjusted to the face of the recipient, Mr. Carson, and he needed time to do it, but he couldn't begin the process until the donor, Benson, died.

The phone rang at eleven-thirty that night at Alex's house. He recognized the voice of his father.

"Alex, go to the MRI Department in x-ray; your wife has a key. Mr. Benson just expired . . . you know what to do." The line went dead.

Dr. Lund had worked out a scheme in his mind on exactly how to transfer Mr. Carson to the hospital's Physical Therapy Department without arousing anyone's suspicion.

He entered the chronic care facility and asked the nurse for Mr. Carson's chart. She handed him the patient's chart.

"I am going to check on Mr. Carson. He wasn't doing all that well yesterday, and I think he might be having recurrent small strokes." He left the nurse and walked alone to his patient's room and opened the door. The room was dark except for the eerie glow of the dials on the panel of the respirator. He walked to the bedside and placed his stethoscope on the chest, just in case anyone should happen to walk into the room. He then entered a progress note in the chart:

Patient has developed a dilated pupil on the right and now the neck is rigid. A positive Brudzinski sign is present.

He knew that no nurse would ever detect these findings or record the presence of a Brudzinski sign, because it was not something the nurses knew anything about. The Brudzinski sign was elicited when a patient's neck was so stiff that you could actually lift the patient's entire upper torso by placing one's hand under the neck and lifting it. This was a positive sign of meningitis, or a subarachnoid hemorrhage, as was a dilated pupil. Feeling very sure of himself, he walked to the nurses' station and said to the nurse, "Please send Mr. Carson to the X-ray Department for a stat MRI of the brain. I will meet him in the radiology waiting room, and I'll personally call the radiologist about this case. If you will call for an orderly, I'll go to the X-ray Department right away, and by the way, I'm taking his chart with me." Lund knew that the slow pace of the Chronic Care Unit and its less-than-sharp nursing personnel were in his favor. He didn't really expect the nurse to make a note about the MRI he had ordered, but if he found one later in the chart, he would just remove the note and substitute another one that he would author himself.

After the orderlies transferred Mr. Carson to the gurney, he walked through the causeway to the radiology holding area with them.

"Do you want us to wait here until the x-ray tech shows up, Doc?"

"That won't be necessary; I'll just wait here with the patient until the radiologist shows up. I just spoke to him on the phone, and he will be here shortly."

"Okay, we'll go back to the floor now. Tell them to call us when he's ready to go back to the Chronic Care Unit."

"I sure will," answered Dr. Lund, nodding his head.

As soon as they were out of sight, Dr. Lund pulled the gurney back into the hall and stopped in front of the MRI Department. After unlocking the door with his master key, he pulled the gurney into the room and did not turn on the light. He shut the door and sat down, noticing that he was sweating profusely. He could actually hear his heartbeat and felt extremely anxious and lightheaded. Many wild thoughts ran through his mind. What if he were noticed or if someone were to find him in the room now with a patient on a respirator in the dark, just sitting there? This would look stupid and be difficult to explain. He then decided the best plan would be to leave the door open to the MRI room and turn on the television that was mounted from ceiling brackets. At least he could always say that he got tired of waiting for the radiologist to appear and decided to wait here where there was a television to kill time.

Alex got out of bed and dressed, then left the house with his black bag in hand. He arrived at the hospital grounds, parked his car, and entered the rear door of the hospital at the emergency room entrance. Knowing exactly where to go, he wasted no time in getting there. He was surprised to find the door to the MRI room wide open. Dr. Lund was sitting at the head of the patient's bed. His patient was connected to a respirator that was silently moving precious oxygen into the lungs. This was a very large room that housed the MRI and had a large area to manipulate patient beds and gurneys between the operator's control panel and the MRI unit.

"Hello Alex, good to see you again," said Lund as he pushed his chair back and stood up. "Let me close this door now that you're here."

Alex removed the mask from his bag, along with some bottles and other items, and placed them on the bedside stand. Two days ago, when he had come to see Benson to evaluate his skin color tones, Alex had painted the mask. As Dr. Lund looked on, Alex worked rapidly to apply the mask. He applied the Dow Corning medical 355 adhesive to the face and attached the mask under the chin. This was a special adhesive that was pressure-sensitive to the silicon and could never be removed unless the chemical 1-1-1-TTE was applied. He brushed the adhesive thinner at the eyelids. In order to exact the hair approximation to the brow, Alex punched tiny holes into the mask. Then he used the eye of a sewing needle that had been cut so that the eye was open at the end. It resembled two spoons that were facing each other. The sharp needle point was held by a pin vice and poked back into the needle hole. Here the man-made hooks captured hair, which was then pulled through the mask and became lodged in the silicon. It was impossible to discern that the real hair was not growing from real skin. The mask extended from below the chin, and when he finished, Mr. Carson was no more. In his place was Mr. Benson.

"Excellent," said Lund. "I can't believe that he isn't really Mr. Benson. Please excuse me while I make a call."

"Hello, this is Dr. Lund," he said to the charge nurse on the Chronic Care Unit. "Mr. Carson just expired."

He then had the mortuary called by the nurse to request a pickup of the deceased. It was the hospital's custom to hold the body in an unused storage room next to the Physical Therapy Department. When he had examined Benson earlier, he had assured the nurse that he was still alive. She had difficulty in obtaining a blood pressure, but thank goodness, there was no cardiac monitoring in this unit to demonstrate that there was indeed no heart action. It was not unusual to see patients on a respirator who gave the appearance of being alive when life had been extinguished. With the respirator attached, he had the patient transferred to the radiology holding area to await an MRI scan, where he dismissed the orderly. When he was alone again, he pulled the gurney into the hall and opened the door between the holding area and Physical Therapy with his key. This was the room that was used to hold bodies until their pickup by the mortuary. He then put the death certificate with the body and left the room.

Dr. Lund placed a call to the coroner and easily convinced him an autopsy wasn't necessary due to his long-standing illness and the age of the patient. That had always been easy to do in LA County because of the excessive workload of the Coroner's Office. Often the coroner would even suggest the diagnosis to write on the death certificate, if the doctor was at all the least bit hesitant. They were overworked and always had a backlog of cases, especially since funds had been cut from the Coroner's Office. Word was the bodies were not even refrigerated because they had run out of capacity for cold storage.

He then returned to the new Mr. Benson and asked Alex to assist him in transporting him on the gurney by guiding the respirator alongside while he pushed the patient. As they passed the nurses station in the respiratory unit, Dr. Lund asked the nurse to lend a hand.

"Mr. Benson looks better now," she said.

"The x-rays were okay. I guess he just had another small stroke," answered Dr. Lund.

$$\sim 9 \sim$$

COMPLICATIONS

Alex was not feeling well and had in fact just made another appointment to see Dr. Gaines. It had been six weeks since his last visit, when he was informed his liver function tests were becoming worse. Now he was experiencing a lot of abdominal pain, and his eyes were more yellow than ever. He stood up quickly, walked to the television, and turned on the switch to catch the six o'clock news, when he suddenly became very dizzy and had to grab on to a chair for support. Alex had never felt this weak before and was having trouble focusing his eyes. Beads of cold sweat broke out on his forehead, and he was experiencing an insatiable thirst. Erin was on the couch looking up at him.

"You really look terrible, Alex. I think you should go to the hospital now." She took his pulse, which was very rapid and thready. "Let's go now, Alex!"

"I think I can walk if I can hold on to you for support," he said. Erin placed her arm around his waist and walked slowly to the door.

"I'm getting nauseated," said Alex in a whisper.

"Wait here and I'll bring the car to the front of the house," she said as she slowly lowered him into the chair. She ran out of the house and left Alex sitting slumped over in front of the door. In a moment she returned and helped him to his feet. She assisted him in walking to the car, where she had left the passenger door open, and Alex fell into the front seat and lost consciousness.

Erin drove frantically through the streets, and although she slowed at the red traffic lights, she drove straight through them with determination. She sped into the street leading up to the hospital's emergency room and stopped the car in front of the entrance, blowing the horn in a staccato fashion to attract someone to help her. An emergency room technician and a nurse wearing green scrubs ran through the automatic doors toward the car.

"I need help! My husband is unconscious in the front seat." The tech ran around to the passenger door, opened it, and grabbed Alex around the back while the nurse lifted his feet, and they placed him in a wheelchair. The tech tipped the chair back toward him to keep his unconscious passenger from falling forward and being ejected from the chair. He ran with the chair through the automatic doors into the emergency room, where he was directed to the first bed. He again tried to lift Alex from behind by placing his arms under the arm pits and around his chest while another technician rapidly lifted his feet at the same time, placing Alex on the emergency room gurney. Alex's head was limp, and his face was white. Dr. Justin Graham was the doctor in the emergency room; he observed the activity from a short distance away while speaking on the telephone. He hung up the phone and ran to the bedside. At the same time, the emergency room nurse, Nancy Powers, placed an automatic blood pressure cuff on Alex's arm and turned it on.

"The pressure is fifty-four over twenty-eight with a pulse of 128," she said.

"Start an IV of normal saline and get a type and cross-match for four units of blood stat," ordered Dr. Graham.

Dr. Graham was an experienced ER physician, and he rapidly assessed Alex. He noticed that the conjunctiva was pale, as was his skin, and there was a putrid odor on the breath. The abdomen was protuberant, and the ankles were swollen. He then examined the nervous system. Graham took Alex's hand and pushed his fingers back toward his head then rapidly let the fingers fall back to their normal position. The hand and fingers continued to move as though the hand were waving or flapping. "Uh-oh," said Graham, as he continued his exam. He checked the knee reflexes and found them absent, as his patient began to utter sounds and thrash about. His skin had large areas of blue-green staining all over the body. He then gently palpated the abdomen, and when he pushed over the area of the stomach, Alex wretched and vomited a huge amount of blood. Dr. Graham instinctively backed up when he heard that unmistakable sound that signaled an impending vomit. The blood was projected to the end of the bed as Alex tried to sit up and then fell back on the gurney.

"Turn his head to the side so he doesn't aspirate and choke, then start another IV with a venous catheter. Now!" shouted Dr. Graham. "Somebody get me a central venous catheter line and open the IV to full." He put on a pair of surgical gloves.

"I need a large-bore nasogastric tube and ice water to stop this bleeding." The ER tech handed him the tube with a tube of K-Y Jelly. He squeezed the jelly on the tray next to the bed and with his glove smeared the end of the tube with jelly then inserted it in Alex's left nostril. When he had reached the posterior pharynx, he stopped and watched Alex's throat. "Elevate the head of the bed about thirty degrees," he ordered. Alex made a feeble attempt to swallow and at exactly that moment, Graham advanced the large tube with a steady motion. Alex coughed violently and spattered blood mixed with saliva over his chin. Dr. Graham attached the end of the rubber tube to the large syringe and pulled back on the plunger. Nothing happened so he repeated the process, pulling back the plunger of the syringe, but this time he moved the tube up and down with his left hand, and the syringe filled with deep-red blood.

"Get another large syringe and put on gloves, Nancy, I need you to help me with this."

"Where is a fifty-cc syringe?" asked Graham.

"Do you want to start Plasmanate?" asked Nancy Powers.

"Good idea, please do it right now, and what is his pressure?"

"Coming up . . . it's now seventy-eight systolic"

"Nancy, after you hang the Plasmanate, put in a Foley catheter and record the output."

"Docs anyone know who this guy is?" said the ER clerk.

"His wife is in the waiting room. Get him admitted to the unit and then call his private doctor and fill him in, if he has one," shouted Graham.

The clerk left to get the information and returned in a few minutes and announced that his doctor was Dr. Gaines and that a call was being placed to him now.

Dr. Mark Gaines ordered Alex to be admitted to the Intensive Care Unit and that he be given two units of whole blood. In addition, he asked Nancy to call Dr. Walker for a GI consultation and to go ahead with an esophagogastroduodenoscopy to visualize where the bleeding source is. Nancy advised him that Dr. Walker would be there shortly.

Dr. Walker arrived at the hospital before his colleague and quickly evaluated Alex's clinical condition. He performed the scoping and determined that the bleeding was coming from two large esophageal veins, upon which he performed a sclerosing procedure to prevent further bleeding. He was at the bedside when Dr. Gaines walked in. "Hi Mark, looks like you've got a real serious problem here."

"I'm sure that I do, since he has chronic hepatitis C and a recent bout of acute hepatitis B."

"Did his liver enzymes ever come down?" asked Walker.

"No, they didn't, and as a matter of fact, I think two weeks ago they were still rising," replied Gaines.

"Well, that explains the rapidity with which he developed the esophageal varices," explained Walker.

"What do you mean?" asked Gaines.

"Well, I wouldn't expect the development of portal hypertension so soon after the bout of acute hepatitis, even superimposed on his chronic C-induced cirrhosis, unless there was sustained liver inflammation that caused the acute increase in portal vein pressure," explained Walker.

"That makes sense, but what are our choices to prevent hemorrhage from reoccurring?" asked Gaines.

No guarantee that he won't bleed again, but I sclerosed the two bleeding veins and started him on a Pitressin drip to help control the active bleeding. In a few days, we should start him on Inderal for the same purpose," said Walker.

"Graham, the ER doc, told me he demonstrated a liver flap. Did you confirm that?" asked Gaines.

"Yes, I did." Hopefully it will disappear when his brain clears, but that will depend on how long it takes the liver to regain some function and eliminate the toxins and ammonia in his blood that are causing the flap," replied Walker.

"Have you drawn an ammonia level yet?" asked Gaines.

"Yes, and it's two fifty, which is really high," replied Walker.

"He's still out of it from what I can see, but his pressure is holding at one hundred, and the pulse is eighty," said Walker.

"He's responding as well as can be expected, especially since he was in shock for at least thirty minutes before he received any therapy," stated Gaines.

"I can see his urine output has also increased, so at least he is now perfusing his kidneys," said Walker.

Gaines looked down at his patient and shook his head. "As much as I hate his father, I don't wish this tragedy on anyone."

"It's certainly not a healthy prognosis, Mark, and I strongly doubt that he will last a year without a liver transplant. You should let him know this, when he's out of here."

~ 10 ~
Dr. Lund Finds a Way

Bob Lund had arranged for a meeting between Kovacs and himself to review the current financial state of their medical investment, and only out of a sense of obligation did he include his partner, Dr. Small. Dr. Kovacs showed up promptly at 6:00 p.m. and sat down at the head of the conference table, as was his custom. He knew psychologically his colleagues were more easily led from this position of authority. "Well, doctors, shall we begin?" he asked in an arrogant manner.

"Yes, let's start," said Lund.

"Okay by me," muttered Rick Small.

Bob Lund placed a ream of computer data sheets on the table and addressed his colleagues.

"The financial data, in a nutshell, reveals that the Respiratory Care Unit is still bringing in a monthly gross of about one hundred fifty thousand a month, and our operational costs are running only forty percent, which is less than I had anticipated it to be. So, after two months of operation, we've got one hundred eighty grand to split. I think we should split up one hundred fifty now and hold the rest in an account, just in case. Do I hear a vote on this motion, gentlemen?"

"That money will come in handy right now," said Dr. Kovacs.

"Fine by me," chimed in Small.

"I thought you'd be pleased, so I took the liberty and had the checks prepared," said Lund as he handed out the checks. Now that he had made everyone happy, he thought he had better continue. He looked directly at Harvey Kovacs. "Harvey, I don't know whether you are aware that your son is here in the hospital." He paused and waited for a response; when there was none, he continued. "Alex is in the ICU with liver failure and a GI bleed. Dr.'s Walker and Gaines are treating him."

"Who did you say?" Asked Kovacs as he sat up straight in his chair.

"Alex, your son . . ."

"No, I mean what Doctor is taking care of him?"

"Dr. Mark Gaines is his attending physician."

"Oh my God," moaned Kovacs. "I don't believe it! How long has that jerk been practicing here?"

"Oh, we hired him a couple months back," Harvey. "What's the matter? Do you know him?"

"You bet I do; he caused me a lot of grief at Valley Hospital, that bastard!"

"He's a very good internist, Harvey, and he has been very helpful to all of us, right Small?"

"That's right, I use him a lot."

"Why hasn't anyone alerted me that Alex was here?"

"I guess it was just an oversight, Harvey," said Lund, throwing his palms up in a gesture of admitted weakness.

"Well, what's his current condition?"

"He's coming along, but from what I hear, he will be totally disabled for quite some time."

"Oh great, where does that leave us with our necessity for an artist?" asked Small.

"I have an ace up my sleeve," said Kovacs, "but I need to explore it further, so if you excuse me, I will leave you now and do some investigating."

"I hate to be the bearer of bad news, but I need to tell you that we are low on replacement patients, and we heard the state is considering establishing their own Respiratory Care Unit. They are concerned because of the costs related to the care of these patients that are scattered all over the state. If that becomes a reality, we really need to find another population of respirator-dependent patients."

"If push comes to shove, Lund, I have an idea that we can explore further. But on second thought, maybe we should discuss it now before I leave," said Kovacs.

"I don't have any plans tonight; do you, Small?" asked Lund.

"No, I can stay as long as I need to," replied Small.

"Fine, then let me run this by you both. A few years ago, I was referred a patient to evaluate for shortness of breath. This was before there were any medical pulmonary guys around my area. He was a sixty-year-old fellow who was eventually proven to have myasthenia gravis. This is treated with Mestinon, which restores the connection between the neuromuscular junction, thereby improving the function of all the respiratory muscles and alleviating the shortness of breath. As I am sure you know, this is a very rare disease. I've only seen two cases in practice, so I had to check the Physician's Desk Reference to refresh myself in how to use this drug.

"The patient improved dramatically on the Mestinon, but I got a bit too aggressive in its use and pushed the dosage a bit too high. This patient came into the emergency room in full-blown respiratory failure, and we had him on a respirator for nearly a week. I learned that the therapeutic dose of this drug is close to the toxic dose, and one must adjust doses very slowly and with extreme care. This is because the toxic effects of Mestinon cause respiratory failure. You see then, one never knows if a myasthenia patient on Mestinon therapy is in respiratory failure due to his inherent disease or whether it is due to an excess of Mestinon." Kovacs widened his eyes and raised his eyebrows as if to ask "understand?"

"Yes, I got it Harvey. It's ingenious!" shouted Bob Lund.

"I don't get it," whined Small.

"Look, Small," said Kovacs, "too much drug throws the patient into respiratory failure."

Small wrinkled his forehead and cocked his head to the side and a broad grin came over his face. "Got it," he said.

Dr. Kovacs drove directly to his son's house. He had called Erin, his daughter-in-law, to see if she was home. He exited his car and walked to the front door and rang the bell.

"Oh, you're here so fast, Harvey," she said as she motioned him to come inside. "I'm glad I was here when you called." She led him into the living room and offered him a seat.

"Thank you, Erin," Kovacs said.

"Well, this is certainly an unusual occurrence. I have only seen you here once since your son and I were married," said Erin sarcastically.

"Could we bypass your personal animosities and allow me to get to the point?" asked Kovacs.

"Of course," she said, with venom dripping at each word.

"Thank you. I will proceed now." Kovacs had no tolerance for his daughter-in-law and had always viewed her as a low life who married his son with the idea that Alex had money. What a surprise she got when she eventually came to learn there existed no communication or even feelings between father and son. As a matter of fact, it was a hate relationship. He was also irked because she called him by his first name without his permission to do so, and he knew she did it just to upset him. Well, he was much smarter than that, and it would take a lot smarter woman than Erin to make him lose his temper. He would use her for his own designs, and he was here now to do just that. He would play on her lust for money.

"First, let me say, I am sorry that Alex is so ill, although I do not know any of the particulars of his case." He put on his most serious face and looked at her with empathy. He didn't really care how sick his son was because as far as he was concerned, he didn't have a son.

He continued, "From what I hear, Alex will be totally disabled for a long while, and I don't believe that he can continue to make masks for us as we had previously agreed. I also know that you have done some of this type of work, and Alex has taught you as well. Is that true?"

"Well yes, I have had some experience, and over the years, Alex has taught me as well."

"Excellent then, would you like to continue the work for us now?"

Erin now began to feel a lifting of her spirit, for earlier she had been depressed about Alex's condition. She knew in her heart that her depression stemmed from having financial stress and longing to split this scene and not from any real concern for Alex. She had become numb and had no feelings for him anymore. If it weren't for the affair she was having with Dr. Lund, she would have tried to end it all. Over the past few months, she had done everything she knew how to do in order to keep her lover interested. She knew that he was noted for his flamboyant behavior toward women, and she took advantage of that fact by wearing short skirts and tight clothing under her white coat. He had fallen for the bait, and whenever he was alone with her in the hospital, he would gently run his hand over her thigh or buttocks, depending on which was more easily accessible to him now. She was thrilled with the chase and the way it made her feel wanted, which had been sorely lacking in her marriage for the last three years. She was also now finding herself fantasizing about riches and continued to fantasy that she was entitled to be wealthy.

"Yes, I would like to do it as long as you pay me for the masks."

"That's not a problem, Erin. I think you might consider allowing Alex to make the mask, and you can make the mold and apply the mask when needed."

"Fine with me. I'll be here ready to go at the drop of a hat."

"Very well, I must be going now. I'll be in touch."

As Kovacs drove away and approached the freeway entrance ramp, he called Bob Lund.

"Bob, I forgot to ask you earlier. Would you find out all you can about Alex?" I don't want to talk to Gaines ever, okay?"

"I'll take care of it and get back with you."

Erin mixed herself a vodka and soda and sipped it slowly, letting the liquid ignite her throat as she swallowed. In fifteen minutes, she felt a glowing warmth all over, and it then became easier for her to think. She would save the money from the masks, and when she had squirreled away a bundle, she could get up and leave. She'd worry about filing the divorce papers after she relocated. In the meantime, her salary would cover her immediate expenses but no more. She felt rage when she thought about her wealthy father-in-law, who never offered to help financially. He also never had the decency to inquire whether they could manage. "He'll get *his* someday," she muttered aloud.

She turned on the television and found a movie she hadn't seen and lay back on the couch. Immediately she envisioned herself wearing a crown. *Yes, she would become a queen.*

Three weeks had passed since Kovacs had met with his partners and received the check for fifty thousand dollars. He was at his office when he received a call from Bill Hendrickson, the administrator of the hospital.

"Hello, Dr. Kovacs. How are you today?"

"Just fine, Bill, and to what do I owe this call?"

"Well, I've got some bad news for you sir."

"Okay, let's have it."

"The state has notified us that they will not be transferring any more patients to the respiratory care center because they plan to reopen their facilities at Rio Hondo, which will take care of all the Southern California area."

"When does this happen, Bill?"

"In about sixty days, maybe longer. I sent our contract to the attorney, and he said it is legal for them to do this. We can't stop it from happening!"

Kovacs felt an overwhelming depression coming on but managed to continue the conversation. "Thank you for letting me know, Bill. I'll talk with Lund and Small about this and get back to you." He hung up the phone and called his front office secretary. "Cancel the rest of the day; I'm going home now. I am not feeling well at all."

~11~

ALEX HEARS THE BAD NEWS

When Alex was strong enough, he was transferred to the general medical floor to convalesce for a few days while beginning a physical therapy program designed to enhance his muscle strength. After eight straight days confined to the bed, his muscles had become exceedingly weak because of disuse. He noticed that his abdomen was now very protuberant, and his umbilicus was now everted. His legs were also swollen and found that he could place his index finger over his shin bone and press down, leaving a large depression in the skin that remained long after he removed his finger. His entire body was covered with bluish discolorations of various sizes, and as if that were not enough, he was handed a handful of pills each morning. The coup de grace was that he had to urinate every hour throughout most of the day. He didn't care that his wife hadn't been in to see him, even though she worked in the hospital. By this time, he had accepted the fact that she would soon be leaving him, and he was totally complacent about it.

On the eighteenth day of his hospitalization, Dr. Gaines had determined he was ready to go home. Mark Gaines had been made aware by his colleague, Bob Lund, that the hospitalization charges would be written off, and since there was no insurance, he would appreciate the same professional courtesy as well for Alex. Knowing the disarray of Alex's marriage, Mark agreed without hesitation. It was common hospital gossip that Alex's wife was having a heated affair with Dr. Bob Lund. As a matter of fact, he was told by a nurse that an orderly had walked in on the duo while during a matinee performance. This had evidently taken place in the storeroom a week ago, where a body had been deposited for the mortuary to pick up. This had not been reported to administration because of the concern that the poor orderly might lose his job. Mark felt compassion for Alex and knew he would be better off in the hospital than at home alone. He pulled Alex's chart from the rack and went to his patient's room.

"Good morning, Alex, how goes it today?"

Alex was sitting in a chair next to the bed watching the television. He looked up and gazed with glossy, yellow eyes at his doctor. "I feel like crap, Doc, I told you that before. Am I ever going to get better?"

Dr. Gaines had been waiting for the right time to discuss in detail the prognosis of his patient, and it had finally come. Alex had now improved all his cognitive abilities and was thinking in a normal fashion. *No time like the present*, he thought to himself.

"Alex, I want you to listen to what I am going to tell you. Please don't interrupt me until I am finished, and then you can ask me all the questions you want, okay?"

"Do I have a choice?" Alex asked with a childlike grin.

"Sure you do, everyone has choices, Alex. If you'd rather discuss this later, we can put it off for now."

"No, Doc, go ahead . . . hit me with your best shot."

"Alex, this is a serious matter, so I want you to listen carefully. Here goes . . ."

"You bled from veins in your esophagus, which had developed from your long history of chronic hepatitis, which also led to scarring of your liver. As your liver tried to repair the injury caused by the hepatitis C virus, it healed with scars. When you developed a superimposed hepatitis B infection, it became too much for your liver to handle, and you went into liver failure. Increased pressure in the veins going to the liver caused the weak veins of the esophagus to rupture, and you went into shock. Since you have been here, we have managed to correct many of the problems you had as a result of liver failure, but some of these complications still linger on. Your spleen is enlarged and has begun to destroy your platelets, which are needed for the blood to clot. Your liver is not making adequate amounts of prothrombin and other protein-clotting factors, which are also required for normal coagulation. As a result of these abnormalities, when you do bleed, it is difficult for us to stop it. The failure of the liver to make adequate albumin, a protein, causes you to swell up throughout your body, including your abdominal cavity, and potentially any other body cavity may follow suit. To sum it all up, you have an extremely sick liver that is beyond its ability to repair itself. The only treatment available is a liver transplant."

Alex looked at him incredulously and then frowned. He couldn't believe his ears. How could he have become ill in such short time when only a few months ago he had felt so well?

"Are you absolutely sure, Doc?"

"Yes Alex, I'm afraid so. I have gone over your case with Dr. Walker, the GI specialist, and he concurs with me."

"Look, Doc, I don't have insurance. How can I ever be considered for a transplant?"

"What about applying for the State Medi Cal program?"

"According to the social worker I talked with yesterday, I'm not eligible. She came to see me to discuss my home situation and resources. Even though I am disabled and can't work, the social worker told me I won't qualify for state welfare of any type, because my wife is working."

"Alex, while that is probably true, you may still be able to go on Social Security Disability because you are now totally disabled. That's a federal Medicare program, and you need to apply as soon as possible."

"If I get around to it, I'll do it, Doc." He looked down at the floor.

"Alex, listen to me! You need to do it now because as soon as you get it, I can refer you to UCLA Medical Center, where they have an excellent transplant program. After they evaluate you for the program, and once you are accepted, they will place you on a waiting list until a donor liver is received. Will you call me and let me know what happens when you have applied?" Gaines was pleading with Alex at this point.

"Sure, Doc, I will let you know, and I want to thank you for all your care and concern."

"Call my office and set up an appointment in ten days. I'll see you then, Alex. Now go on home, take it easy, and be sure to take all your pills every day."

Dr. Gaines walked out of the room slowly and returned to the nurses' station, sat down, and wrote a long progress note summarizing his discussion with Alex. When he had finished, he sighed and wiped a wet spot from the corner of his eye.

❧12❧
MORE ADMISSIONS TO THE RESPIRATORY CARE UNIT

"**P**aging Dr. Lund, Dr. Robert Lund," blared the loudspeaker system in strong annoyance to its intended recipient. He picked up the phone at the nurses' station on the medical wing where he was making rounds on his patients. "Hello, Dr. Lund speaking."

"Hi, Graham in the ER. I've got a bad one here that I'd like to admit to you."

"Fine, what have you got?"

"A head crunch. It's a head-on auto versus motorcycle. I can't believe he is still alive. He's twenty-four years old, the CAT scan shows cerebral edema, and he is unconscious and functioning at about a midbrain level. The vitals are normal, but he has a pneumothorax of the right and left lungs. I have already intubated him and placed him on the ventilator."

"Has the front office checked what kind of insurance he has?"

"We just verified excellent coverage with Aetna. Up to one hundred thousand, 80 percent coverage. After that, it is 100 percent coverage to a limit of one million bucks."

"Sounds like he is going to need it. Send him to the unit." Lund chuckled to himself and thought how fortunate it was that this million-dollar coverage policy holder was delivered to his hospital. *Yes indeedy, that would buy a lot of respiratory care.* "Oh, what's his name?"

"Randy Wiley."

"Okay, thanks."

He finished up with his patients and went to the Intensive Care Unit (ICU) to examine his new patient. Upon his arrival to the unit, he was met by Kathy Jones, the ICU Nurse Supervisor.

"Your patient is in bed four, Doctor, and his chest films are on the view box."

"Thank you, Kathy." He walked to the bedside and saw the chest tubes exiting the chest at the same level on both sides. His eyes followed them down to the bed, where they were connected to yellow rubber tubing that ran down the side of the bed rails and into a large transparent plastic bag containing water. Each tube was below the water level, and when the chest expanded, bubbles were seen to exit from the underwater tubes, which were the trapped air in the pleural space. The respirator was delivering life-sustaining oxygen to this patient who could no longer expand his chest walls because of multiple fractured ribs. Without the respirator, the chest had sunk down during an attempt at inspiration and expanded during expiration. Lund had seen this many times before and knew that this paradoxical respiration had to be overcome by respirator support. Also, he was acutely aware this support may be required for weeks. He examined his patient and concluded from his neurological findings and of pathological reflexes that his patient had suffered severe brain damage as well. He went to the view box on the wall and put up the chest films.

What a mess, he thought, as he counted five ribs on the right and seven on the left that were fractured. Three of them were fractured in two places, revealing jagged ends, while two ribs looked like snapped popsicle sticks. There were fluid levels within the pleural cavities that were no doubt blood. The chest tubes were properly placed in each pleural space. There were also opaque densities seen in each lower lobe lung field that alarmed Dr. Lund. He had managed many patients like this before, and in many of them, the dreaded adult respiratory distress syndrome had occurred. In two out of three cases, the outcome was death. He shook his head rapidly from side to side, let out a deep breath, and replaced the films in their large brown jackets.

"What's his oximetry reading?" he shouted to the nurse at the end of the unit.

"It's running 89 percent and he's on 70 percent oxygen."

"Better start him on four centimeters of positive end expiratory pressure [PEEP] now."

The respiratory therapist standing at the respirator made the PEEP adjustment to the setting. In two minutes, the oxygen saturation rose to 94 percent, and the therapist smiled with satisfaction.

"Dr. Lund, he's in the normal range now."

"Fine, why don't you decrease his oxygen to 60 percent and call me in an hour for further adjustments." He sat down at the station and quickly wrote two pages of orders on his new patient, Randy Wiley. He handed the chart back to the nurse. Dr. Lund hurried out of the unit almost at a run through the hospital's front door and down the small incline two hundred yards to the medical building where he entered the rear door of his office.

"Peter Bunkin is here to see you, Doctor Lund. He is complaining of weakness."

He was a spry seventy-two-year-old who had been fortunate in his life to maintain good health. Every year he came to Lund's office for a complete checkup. It was more of a social visit, and he looked forward to it with enthusiasm.

"Hi Doc, another year has flown by."

"True enough," said Lund. "How have you been feeling?"

"To tell you the truth, I've been kind of weak lately."

As per his custom, Dr. Lund reviewed his patient's chart while asking questions of a general nature. He made a mental note that Peter had excellent Medicare insurance coverage, with Medicare as the primary and National Republic the secondary. Retirees from the aircraft industry always had excellent insurance like this. It was a rare occurrence to find other Medicare patients who had 100 percent hospital coverage like the aircraft workers' union had bargained.

"Have you recovered from the loss of your wife?"

"Yes, I think so, but I sure wish I had children now."

Bingo. The alarm went off in Lund's head. This would be an excellent patient to replace a respirator-dependent one if the need should arise, thought Lund. It was hard to find a patient that qualified for the program since it required excellent insurance, no family, and a trusting patient. *Peter Bunkin would qualify very nicely*. He did a cursory examination.

"Peter, I want to draw some blood tests to see if everything is normal. I'll call you in a few days and let you know the results, then maybe prescribe some medication at that time."

"I trust you, Doc, you'll cure me."

"I sure will, Peter."

Lund had been collecting the names of patients who might qualify for "The Program," and he now had five names on his list. It had been five weeks since he had spoken with Kovacs, and it was again time to set up another meeting.

He went to the respiratory care unit to make rounds on his patients. Mrs. Anna Scarzio was a fifty-year-old who had been transferred there from the county hospital. She was a permanent respirator patient as a result of severe brain injury due to a cardiac arrest suffered at the County Hospital. Her history revealed she had collapsed in the ER of County Hospital from a heart attack. This caused the heart to beat with a fatal rhythm, pumping virtually no blood to the brain. She required respiratory support. One thing that doctors all know very well is that the big mistakes always happen in training hospitals during the month of July. This was simply because all the new house officers were interns right out of medical school with no experience. These interns were thrown into the heat of battle and would eventually come to learn by trial and error. They, of course, were always assigned to the busy areas of the hospital. Anna had been very obese, with a thick neck, and it was difficult to pass an endotracheal tube into her trachea. As a result, the tube had inadvertently been placed in the stomach and remained unrecognized by the intern until the first-year resident had become suspicious by the rapid onset of abdominal distention. By that time, she had developed permanent brain damage due to poor oxygen delivery. Her stomach, however, had been well oxygenated for fifteen minutes. The brain damage had involved the respiratory center of the brain, which caused her to become respirator-dependent.

She had just recently shown signs of congestive heart failure, and Lund had ordered a portable chest x-ray to be done at the bedside.

"Are the films here, Nancy?"

"They are on the table."

Lund walked over to the table next to the bed, picked up the film, and held it up to the light.

An enlarged heart and dilated upper lobe vessels with opacities at the lung bases were immediately noted by Lund. "Nancy, give her eighty of Lasix stat and start her on five milligrams of Vasotec through the feeding tube daily. Let's repeat the chest x-ray the day after tomorrow, and in the meantime, reduce the sodium in her diet to two grams and increase her oxygen to 65 percent." He left the unit.

The next morning Dr. Lund went to the ICU to see Randy Wiley, who was still on the respirator. He was certain his patient was respirator-dependent because the neurological exam continued to show brain stem function only. Yesterday's electroencephalogram (EEG) revealed widespread injury to the higher cognitive centers of the brain. The conscious centers of the brain were gone and Randy was a vegetable, only now kept alive by a ventilator. He entered the ICU, took Randy's chart from the rack, and walked to the bedside.

"Are all his vital signs normal?" asked Dr. Lund.

"Yes, they are," answered Kathy, the ICU Nurse Supervisor.

"I am going to transfer him to the Respiratory Care Unit for chronic care," said Dr. Lund.

"Shall I call discharge planning and request they make the arrangements?" asked Kathy.

"No thanks, Kathy, I'll do it," answered Dr. Lund.

Dr. Lund knew that he had to transfer Randy into the Respiratory Care Unit. This was the twelfth day in the ICU without any change. He had to make his move now. After writing his progress note in the chart, he left the ICU and walked down to the chronic unit.

Entering the Respiratory Care Unit, he picked up the chart of Anna Scarzio and went to her room. He placed his stethoscope on her chest and heard crackles that sounded like the sound that cellophane makes after you compress it in your hand. When you open your hand, you hear crackles, just like the ones he was hearing in the lung. He detected the ominous third heart sound known as a gallop. These findings were caused by severe heart failure. Dr. Lund entered his progress note containing his observations into the chart. He noted that Mrs. Scarzio was on 65 percent oxygen, and the oxygen saturation monitor was reading 88 percent. He turned the oxygen concentration switch on the respirator to 30 percent and noted that his patient's face and lips turned blue. *She would die anyhow,* thought Lund. *I am only helping her to die quickly.* He sat by the bed and watched. After three minutes, he examined the pupils and saw that they were dilated. Soon they would be in mid-position, indicating brain death. He quickly returned the oxygen setting to 65 percent and walked slowly to the nursing station.

"Nancy, I believe that Mrs. Scarzio is on the way out," said Dr. Lund.

"Shall I call a code?" asked Nancy.

"She's a No Code, Nancy, don't bother," replied Dr. Lund.

They both walked to Anna Scarzio's room. The blue facial color was now replaced by pasty white, and the oximeter was reading 85 percent. Dr. Lund opened Anna's eyes and shined his light into the pupils. He saw no response and then rotated her head from side to side.

"Brain stem reflexes are gone; pupils are mid-position and fixed. She's gone. Turn the respirator off, Nancy," said Lund.

Something had been bothering Lund for a long time. The use of a special effects mask for their subterfuge was flawed. It had finally hit upon him. It would be next to impossible to switch a male for a female. It was the hair. How could one successfully duplicate a woman's hair? He felt a sinking feeling in his chest. No wig would ever do it.

The families, if any, only visited Respiratory Care Unit patients the first month of their admission. After that, the patients were abandoned. The Respiratory Care Unit statistics revealed two-thirds of the patients were from northern California, while one-third came from southern California. Some of the families, however, called every two months and spoke to the nursing staff.

Lund sat at his desk and doodled while he again ran these thoughts over in his mind. "Eureka!" He startled himself by his outburst. *What I have to do,* he reasoned, *is to get rid of the insured females. I'll replace them with insured males. When these males eventually die, I'll replace them easily.*

The profound sinking feeling was now gone and in its place was a feeling of exhilaration. He had solved another dilemma. He had also upstaged his pompous colleague Harvey Kovacs, God's gift to medicine. Oh, how he hated Kovacs's arrogant attitude toward others, especially other doctors. Lund had concluded that Kovacs would bottle his own bath water and sell it to poor mortals who needed an icon. He picked up the phone and dialed Kovacs's office number. A moment later he was speaking to God himself.

"What can I do for you, Bob?"

Lund mused, *as if you could*. "I just wanted to let you know that your artistic plan is flawed." He had emphasized the word artistic rather than using the word mask on the phone.

"Really?" retorted Kovacs in a condescending voice.

"Yes, really," Lund replied emphatically. "Women's hair will be the problem." The phone remained silent for a long moment.

Kovacs finally responded, "Yes, Lund, I think you have something there. Have you been able to solve the problem?"

"I believe I have, Harvey; I'll update you when I see you." He hung up the phone and was elated that he had shown Kovacs that he wasn't so damn smart. He also knew that not disclosing the solution would drive him crazy. That, at least, was some consolation.

~13~
LEAVING FOR GOOD

Alex had been in contact with the Social Security Office and had filed an application for Disability benefits. He was told he would receive Medicare coverage approval within thirty days. Because of the gravity of his clinical condition, he was eligible for a quick evaluation, and he would also be eligible for Social Security Disability benefits. The benefit was slightly over five hundred dollars a month, and he would receive that amount if he was permanently and totally disabled. Alex kept his appointment with Dr. Gaines and informed him of his pending Medicare benefits.

"That's good," said Dr. Gaines.

"Doc," interrupted Alex, "I want you to be the first to know that I am leaving California. I am moving to Colorado."

"Why are you doing that?" Dr. Gaines said.

"I can't live with my wife anymore, Doc. She's so damn hateful. It's best that I leave."

"I'm deeply sorry Alex. I don't know what to say."

"It's okay, Doc, I feel happy for the first time in years just knowing I'll be rid of her."

"Look Alex, why don't I try to get you an appointment at UCLA Medical Center before you leave. They need to evaluate you for the liver transplant program, and this takes time. When you are accepted, you can return to California to await a donor. They will place you on a waiting list as soon as they clear you for the transplant."

"Are you sure, Doc"?

"Yes, I am. They don't care where you live if you are in California when you are on the waiting list. Their real concern is that your insurance carrier will pay the bill. Medicare will approve the transplant if you are accepted for the transplant. You should be home free."

"Sounds great to me. Set it up, Doc. I can return for an appointment at any time."

Dr. Gaines examined Alex thoroughly. He found a small liver and an enlarged spleen. The lower extremities were edematous, and the abdomen was enlarged and tense. He knew that this meant the presence of ascites. When the abdominal cavity was full of fluid, it was known as ascites. This was an ominous sign. It occurred because the liver was unable to make protein. With the low levels of protein in the blood, fluid in the blood vessels leaks into all the tissue spaces. Dr. Gaines drew blood from Alex and bid him farewell.

"Keep in touch, Alex. You're going to need a doctor to follow your condition in Colorado. Call me when you're settled; I know a few doctors there."

"Thanks, Doc, I'll keep in touch."

Alex drove home, walked into the condo, and carried two duffle bags to his car. He had already packed in anticipation of his departure. He returned to the condo, and on the back side of a home delivery flier for pizza, he scribbled a note to Erin. *Moving to Colorado for good, have a good life.* He signed his name. Alex whistled as he walked out the door and entered the car. As he drove away, he thought of Martin Luther King's famous speech, and in a loud voice he shouted, "free at last, free at last, free at last!"

He felt exuberant as he headed east on Route 138 toward Victorville. At a large gas station at the junction of 138 and the 10 Freeway, he stopped to fill up with gas. Turning the pump on, he set the gasoline trigger on automatic and walked to the pay phone. He wanted to confirm his departure with his friend, Jimmy Morton. Alex and Jimmy had grown up together but parted ways after high school. He had only recently contacted him. "Hi, Jimmy, this is Alex. I'm on the way now. I'll be there the day after tomorrow."

"Fine," said Jimmy. "It will be great to see you again. You'll have to tell me how you found me."

"That was easy," replied Alex. "I ran into our mutual friend, Dave Renner. He told me that you were living in Crested Butte, Colorado. A few calls and I found you. The Marshall's Office in the Butte said that you worked for the city of Crested Butte. You're a lifesaver friend; I'll tell you more when I see you."

⁓14⁓
The Hook

Bob Lund had already decided that he really enjoyed Erin's company, as well as her body. He made every effort to wine and dine her now that she was alone. They were driving to a quaint little French restaurant in Canyon Country. La Grange was a converted stone house and garage. It lent itself to the ambiance of a rustic country farmhouse. He entered the unruly sand parking lot and chose a spot far away from other cars. His 450 SL Mercedes was without blemish, and he wanted to keep it that way. As he was about to open the door, Erin bent over and kissed him passionately. As she darted her tongue into his mouth, he became excited. She wanted to keep her catch on the hook, so she continued to explore his mouth with her tongue and then moved to his ear. Lund was extremely sensitive to this stimulation, and he groaned in response as she moved her hand to his groin and began to lightly stroke him.

"I love you, Erin," he whispered into her ear.

She knew she had him now, and now she then set the hook. "I love you too, Bob," she moaned.

They walked into the restaurant holding hands. The aroma of garlic was present in the air and permeated their nostrils. Once they were seated, Lund ordered a bottle of Kendal Jackson Chardonnay, and after sipping the wine for fifteen minutes while he gently stroked her fingers, he said, "What are your plans for the future, Erin?"

"What do you mean?" she retorted, tipping her head slightly to the side.

"Do you want to remain in the Antelope Valley indefinitely?

"God no!" she answered quickly. "I hate it here, but my job keeps me in this place. Good-paying jobs in hospitals are difficult to find these days."

"I feel the same way about this place, and I want to retire in the Caribbean."

"That sounds great Bob. Can I come along too?" she asked laughingly. "I could be your housekeeper."

"I'm serious, Erin, let me share something with you. It's very confidential." After a few more glasses of wine, he became more talkative.

"You know you can tell me anything, and it will go no further," said Erin.

"I am certain that we will sell the hospital, the whole kit and caboodle," Lund said. "I think it will happen within a year's time. When that happens, I'm history. I really care a great deal for you, and I would love for you to come with me. Please think about it, and we can talk about it later."

She didn't know what to say. This was what she wanted. She knew she had some measure of emotional commitment to Lund, but just how much, she wasn't sure. She imagined a life of lounging in the balmy Caribbean. She imagined even more that she was showered with wealth.

⁓15⁓
THE OFFER

Doctor Harvey Kovacs was only one of the sixty doctors who attended the meeting at the Marriott Hotel in Woodland Hills. These doctors had built Woodside Community Hospital in 1962. Back then, a hundred-bed hospital was large. After the hospital was built, they added medical buildings for doctors' convenience, and now US Care, a large California HMO, was about to present an offer on their hospital. HMOs were expanding and it was a good time for doctors to cash in on their investment. In the beginning each doctor invested twenty-five thousand dollars to build the hospital. Another fifteen thousand was required from each of the sixty doctors for the construction of the two medical office buildings. The presentation was made by the attorney for US Care and their CEO. They presented an attractive but simple offer to the group. US Care would pay twenty-five million for their hospital. They also would offer the same amount of money for the purchase of Woodland Heights Hospital. That hospital was their rival and was owned by an equal number of doctors. Both hospitals had been built at about the same time, and their plan was to designate one of the hospitals as the predominant managed care facility. The remaining hospital would function primarily in the private sector and would be available for the overflow of managed care patients.

Harvey Kovacs was not on the board of directors of the hospital corporation. He had found out earlier that the hospital's liabilities were about seven million dollars. He rapidly calculated there would be eighteen million dollars left to split up. This would amount to three hundred thousand dollars for each doctor's share. Since Harvey had bought out the share of a desperate colleague some years ago, he would receive six hundred thousand from the sale.

Harvey was very pleased about this, but there was a catch. US Care also intended to purchase the two office buildings. Both medical buildings were adjacent to the hospital. One was a sprawling two story structure that had thirty thousand square feet of space and housed the offices of twelve doctors, including Dr. Kovacs. The intent of the HMO was to convert that building into a staff model practice like that of Kaiser Permanente. The staff model was simply many doctors all working directly for the HMO in one facility rather than working for a medical group who contracts with an HMO. It was also important for them to have the practice next to the hospital for the convenience of their physicians. The doctors, he included, who now occupied those offices, would have to find space elsewhere.

This would be a problem for Harvey and most of the physicians because of the paucity of available office space in the area. Harvey felt pressured and left the meeting wondering if he could go through with the deal. He had occupied the same office for twenty-eight years, remembering when it had been a cabbage farm and the group of doctors had turned it into a medical complex. Kovacs was complacent in his professional life. He abhorred change and was content to remain where he had been for years. The only problem he encountered was the thought of all that money. He didn't sleep well that night and was still anxious and uncertain in his dreams.

How he wished that he had someone to confide in and seek advice. He could not bring himself to do this, because throughout his life, he had always relied on himself. He had never developed trust with anyone because of his childhood traumatic life with his father.

The following morning, Harvey received a phone call from Norman Sydney, the CEO of US Care, inviting him to meet with him for lunch at noon. Harvey agreed to meet Norman Sydney but felt somewhat apprehensive about it. He walked around his desk and began to breathe deeply. Peering out his window, he began to daydream. At ten minutes before noon, Harvey walked into the Jolly Pirate at the Warner Center. The maître d' led him to Norman Sydney's table.

"Dr. Kovacs, I'm Norman Sydney. Thank you for coming."

"My pleasure," responded Harvey.

They exchanged some light conversation, then moved into a discussion of managed care medicine. After a brief discussion of that topic, Dr. Kovacs relaxed.

"Tell me, Mr. Sydney, what can I do for you?"

"Dr. Kovacs," he said softly, "I have been asked by our board to discuss a concern we have with you."

"Certainly, please proceed," Harvey coaxed, as he was now very interested to hear more.

"As you know, Doctor," said Norman, "We have made an offer on Woodland Community Hospital. This offer includes both medical office buildings. We plan to convert the two-story building to a staff model managed care practice."

"Why is that necessary when you can just as easily assign the patients to an Independent Practice Association physician? These doctors are all practicing within their offices and provide both primary as well as specialization care for all the capitated patients."

"Because we have experienced an unexpected massive growth surge, we have more patients than doctors to render them care. There are just not enough good doctors to contract with," said Norman, gesturing with his outstretched hands.

"I didn't realize you had such a large enrollment," said Kovacs, shaking his head in agreement.

"We are the leading HMO in California, Doctor, because we strive to be the best."

"You do have a very good reputation," said Kovacs.

"The Department of Corporations mandates no more than one doctor for every twenty-five hundred assigned manage care patients, replied Norman. We have just enrolled thirty thousand new patients in the west San Fernando Valley. You might have seen the article in the *LA Times* about our acquisition of Prime Net HMO."

"Yes, I saw the article. They were forced to sell because of financial instability," said Kovacs.

"Correct," replied Norman, "but what you don't know is that they had assigned all their patients to the Benjamin IPA for medical services. That group was mismanaged and had received far too many grievances from their patients, and the Department of Corporations received many complaints from these enrollees, which were confirmed by audit. The Department of Corporations [DOC] found many other quality-care issues as well. Because the HMO did not ask the group for a corrective plan of action, it led to a full audit and the discovery that the HMO was financially insecure. They had cut back on their Quality Management Department and just let the complaints pass. Recent data show that an HMO must commit 12 to 15 percent of their capitated dollar to administration. Prime Net was committing only 7 percent. The DOC is very strict on how an HMO handles complaints and quality issues, so the HMO was given six months to divest themselves. From what I heard, the DOC went to the group unannounced and inspected records, logs, and their financial books."

"So, you don't want to leave those thirty thousand patients assigned to the Benjamin Group?" asked Kovacs.

"That is the issue exactly, Doctor," replied Norman. "We cannot diffuse these patients to other groups in this area because they are already saturated with patients."

"You mean that all the West Valley doctors contracted with Prime Net are at one to twenty-five hundred ratio," replied Kovacs.

"Yes, that's about it, I'm sorry to say," said Norman. "The growth of managed care has exceeded the ability of doctors to care for the patients in certain areas."

"So, you want to hire your own doctors to perform primary care, and you want to put them all in our medical building as well," said Kovacs, slightly irked at the idea.

"Dr. Kovacs, that building fits our needs exactly," said Norman.

"Thirty thousand square feet would easily house twelve or thirteen doctors to care for your thirty thousand patients," said Kovacs.

"Yes, it would. Your building currently has seventeen physicians in it. We would eliminate two suites on the ground floor, and after alterations, we would have administrative offices in their place. It will then be a simple task to redecorate the other offices," said Norman.

"How does all this affect me?" interrupted Kovacs.

"I was just coming to that, Doctor," replied Norman in an irritated manner. "Our HMO is very interested in expanding across all of LA county, particularly the Antelope Valley," said Norman.

Harvey Kovacs felt the irritation leave him. His interest in the conversation was now renewed. Immediately he had grandiose ideas about his Palmdale Medical Facility.

Norman continued, "Our direction is to now acquire medical groups that we will operate as well as hospitals and chronic care facilities. In this manner we will be able to enhance our bottom-line profits. Medical group ownership offers us the opportunity to profit from the practice, as well as from the hospital risk pool each group shares with the HMO. We would have it all then."

Kovacs was already aware that hospital shared-risk pools were very profitable. He had seen the claim reports from contracting HMOs before; they calculated each hospital day at one thousand dollars a day. The HMO Medicare plans calculated hospital bed usage at an average of nine hundred days per one thousand patients. If the group used only six hundred days per thousand, there would be a savings of three hundred thousand dollars. This would be split fifty-fifty with the HMO. The Palmdale group had ten thousand Medicare patients, meaning that the group would split three million dollars with their contracting HMOs at the end of the year. The HMOs had determined that the magic number of days per thousand for the non-Medicare commercial patients was three hundred. The contract with the state for the medical patients was different. They set the number of bed days per thousand patients at two hundred fifty. The profit would be less in this class of patients, but nevertheless a profit. Now he thought about the medical group's income.

The cap rate for Medicare patients for doctors was one hundred thirty dollars a month and thirty dollars a month for the commercial patients. Eight thousand commercial and ten thousand Medicare patients yielded almost sixteen million dollars yearly for the latter group and three million dollars for the former. The Medi-Cal contract was worth six million dollars between the combined amount paid to the group and the hospital. The group then received twenty-five million dollars a year, plus another three million from the private sector.

"Dr. Kovacs, I am going to be right up front with you," said Norman. "Our company is interested in the purchase of the Palmdale Medical Facility. We have done our homework and are aware that you are a shareholder in that entity."

"Mr. Sydney, everything has a price tag," replied Kovacs.

"There is a slight problem, however, which you may be able to help solve," said Norman. "We have evaluated the operation and think that it fits all our criteria for purchase except one."

"And just what is that?" asked Kovacs.

"We have looked at your reported public financial data submitted to the state. There seems to be excessive expenses that could possibly be trimmed. This would enhance the profitability."

Kovacs was impressed with the extent of the knowledge acquired by Norman about his group.

"What expenses are you referring to?" asked Kovacs.

"The figures show that you are spending a small fortune in transportation of patients to the valley for surgical procedures," replied Norman. "The costs include transportation, hospitalization, and the professional fees."

"I must confess that I have not been privy to this part of the operation," said Kovacs.

"If you would consider relocating to Palmdale to provide surgical services, we would make an offer to purchase," replied Norman.

Kovacs was now salivating. This was his opportunity to make a killing. "How many years must I commit to?" Kovacs asked.

"I think three years would be agreeable," replied Norman. "It would allow us sufficient time to arrange for your replacement here in the valley."

Kovacs didn't need to think about his answer. This was his timetable anyway. He wanted to work for three more years then retire. "I'll do it," Kovacs replied. "I'll sign a contract when we accept your offer to purchase."

"Fine, Doctor, I'll get moving on this right away," replied Norman.

Kovacs returned to his office and sat down at his desk. A minute later, he had Bob Lund on the line. "Lund, I have some really good news for you," said Kovacs.

"Shoot," replied Lund.

Kovacs recounted his conversation with Norman Sydney to his partner.

"That sounds like a winner, Harvey," Bob Lund said. "How do you feel about relocating out here for three years?"

"Not a problem with me," said Kovacs. "Lund, we must keep the revenue high so as not to screw up the sale. They will be doing their due diligence in about a month or so."

"Harvey, not to worry, we have a new respiratory care patient in the unit. This man replaced the bed of the female who unfortunately died," replied Lund, emphasizing the second and third syllable of "unfortunately."

"Good job, Bob," said Kovacs.

"Anything else we can do?" asked Lund.

"Just keep all the beds full, Bob."

"Do you have any idea what they might offer us?" asked Lund.

"Well, Bob, look at our numbers," said Kovacs. "The group is grossing about twenty-five million dollars, plus the private sector. The hospital grosses about eighteen million, the chronic care does about three, and the respiratory care is at two million. If they base their offer on capitation, they usually buy practices at three hundred dollars a head for Medicare and commercial. We have a total of twenty-two thousand lives, which would be about six and a half million. Throw in another million for the private patients and the workers comp patients, and we're talking about eight million for the practice alone. I think that the hospital, skilled nursing facility, chronic care, and the Respiratory Care Unit should be worth another twelve million dollars. All in all, Lund, twenty million plus. By the way, Bob, please put the word out for a house that I can rent for now. I'd be looking at a move in about a month."

"I sure will, Harvey."

~16~
GOT THREE MORE

The usual rule in medicine is that serious medical events happen in cycles. Over the next few weeks, the Respiratory Care Unit lost three more patients. When Dr. Lund received notice of the first death, he instructed his office nurse, Sally, to call Mr. Bunkin and have him come in for an appointment. A replacement for the unit was needed fast.

"Good morning Mr. Bunkin. How do you feel?" asked Dr. Lund.

"Still kind of weak, Doc," replied Peter Bunkin.

"Peter," began Dr. Lund, "the lab tests show that you have a disease called myasthenia gravis."

"What's that?" asked Peter.

"It's a nervous system illness that results in poor transmission of electrical impulse to the muscles."

"Can it be treated with medications?" asked Peter.

"Yes, it certainly can. I am going to start you on Mestinon, and please take it exactly as I instruct you."

"Okay, Doc, when should I come back?"

"Why don't you make an appointment for one week, Peter," responded Dr. Lund. Leaving the examination room, he started for his office.

"Doctor, your next appointment is here," announced Carol.

"Who is it?"

"Mr. Babcock," replied Carol, rolling her eyes upward.

"You mean George Babcock, the hypochondriac?"

"Youuuuu got it, Doctor," said Carol, looking askance.

"I'll see him now and get it over with," answered Dr. Lund with a forced smile as he opened the examination room door.

"Good morning, George," said Dr. Lund. "How goes it today?"

"Doctor, I am not feeling well at all," stated George in a whine. "My head hurts and I have a sore back. I'm always tired, and I'm short of breath."

Dr. Lund squinted his eyes as he gazed at his patient. He was mulling George's symptoms over in his mind.

"How is your family, George?" said Dr. Lund, with sincerity.

"The wife's getting along okay since her hip surgery, and my boys have both moved to New York State for better jobs," answered George.

Dr. Lund had already diagnosed George Babcock with chronic bronchitis. He had acquired this lung infirmity from years of cigarette smoking and had steadily continued to show deterioration of lung function. Lund knew that it wouldn't take too much to push him over into respiratory failure.

"I am writing a prescription for you, George. The medicine is Mestinon, and I want you to take it as directed."

"I sure will, Doc. I hope it will make me feel better," replied George.

"Oh, it will," replied Dr. Lund. "You need to take one pill every eight hours." Lund left the room to see his next patient.

Sam Wiener returned for a recheck on his sciatica. "Well, Doc, those pills you gave me last week are just not working. Haven't you got something stronger?" asked Sam.

"Mr. Wiener, I have a new drug for pain control. It comes as a skin patch, only you replace it every twenty-four hours."

"Will it kill my pain?" asked Sam.

"It sure will," responded Dr. Lund, in a voice of authority.

Dr. Lund thought a moment. The medical facts were that Sam had pulmonary interstitial fibrosis, and his lung function was poor. The Duragesic skin patch was a morphine-like drug that had the side effect of affecting the respiratory center in the brain. It would reduce the depth and rate of breathing; the result would be respiratory failure in a patient with compromised lung function. He wrote the prescription for Duragesic patches, one hundred milligrams, and directed Sam to apply two of them daily. This dose would achieve a continuous high basal level of the drug. It was sure to do the job.

"Mr. Wiener, I want to see you the day after tomorrow," said Dr. Lund, voicing concern.

"Okay, Doc, see you then," Sam muttered.

Dr. Bob Lund felt extremely confident now that he had started three private insurance patients on medications. In each case, they were designed to promote respiratory failure and insure rapid hospitalization. He had even covered the remote possibility that he might be discovered by writing the prescription direction to take as directed rather than the standard times to apply the patch. In this fashion, oral directions to each patient instructing them to take excessive doses of the drug would not be detected. He made a rapid mental calculation. Three empty respiratory care beds were causing a financial loss of fifteen hundred dollars a day. Those beds were what the state paid, whereas private insurance paid substantially more for the same services. It was very probable that the private insurers paid almost twice that amount.

~17~

READY FOR A FIGHT

Erin was relaxing at home on a Sunday afternoon. She was on a continuous emotional flying carpet and didn't remember the last time she felt so good. It was now three months since Alex had left, and she had not heard a word from him. *Out of sight, out of mind,* she thought. It was about time to drop the ax on Alex and get on with her life. After all, she said to herself, she now was in a secure relationship with Bob Lund, and the temptation of living with him in the Caribbean was more than she could resist. She recalled the night he had confided in her and had talked freely about his desires and hopes. She now knew that the hospital was to be sold soon and believed him when he told her that he would take her with him to live in the Caribbean. Last week she had met with a lawyer, who informed her of her rights. Karl Bixby told her that in a divorce settlement, she was entitled to half of the community property. They had no debts, which meant she would receive half interest in the condo. Since she had a three-year-old Blazer, and Alex had a two-year-old Bronco, the Blazer was hers.

Erin was angry and dissatisfied after the meeting and returned home to make a list of their possessions. She thought it very unfair that she would only receive one-half interest in the community assets. In her mind she had earned all the assets for the marriage she had to endure. She wanted to make Alex suffer, to inflict pain upon him as repayment for her many repeated episodes of pain she had suffered. How careless, she thought, that she almost forgot about Alex's rare coin collection. Alex had collected coins since he was a child. Two years ago, he had the collection appraised, and to both their surprise, it was worth about six thousand dollars. She was interested in money for certain, but also in causing aggravation to her estranged spouse and was positive that Alex would freak out when she made a community property claim on the collection. She felt happier now. Yes, she'd do it. Her mind raced—she saw herself again wearing a crown and confirmed that she deserved to be treated like a queen.

It was fortuitous that Alex had called his friend in Crested Butte Colorado from his home telephone. When Erin saw the Colorado telephone numbers, it was an easy task for her to place a few calls and find Alex. Mr. Bixby would arrange to serve him there and force his return to California for the divorce proceedings. *I'll make you suffer now,* she murmured to herself.

Alex was enjoying himself in Crested Butte, Colorado. He enjoyed the fresh, cool mountain air at nine thousand feet. It was also a welcome change from the dull, drab-brown desert of California. He had arrived in January, and it was already April. The old mining town was surrounded by mountains covered with snow. The streets were dotted with bright freshly painted houses, tiny but expensive. Three main streets spanned the small town and were cluttered with shops for the tourists, while the permanent population of the town was a booming eight hundred. This number did, however, mushroom to thousands in both the winter and summer months. The streets were now becoming ugly, dirty brown. This was the mud season, payback for seeing the sun daily. The warm temperatures coaxing the snow off the mountains produced four inches of mud throughout the streets. The skiers were gone, and the town was winding down to its basal state of boredom, but the barrooms and saloons would do very well each evening.

The daytime activity for most of the unemployed was the pool hall, and right in the center of the tiny town was the White Rock Lodge. It was one of two motels that the town boasted. The ski bum temporary employees were leaving now, and jobs became available. Alex had been lucky to arrive in town just when the Lodge needed temporary help, their day desk clerk having just been fired for drinking on the job. In reality, the clerk was sampling cocaine and was caught by the manager. Alex was eager to occupy himself during the day and easily found the work to his liking. He met all the locals rapidly since the Lodge was the only place in town that sold lottery tickets. His employer had agreed to pay him under the table, which Alex had insisted upon. He could not place his

Social Security Disability income in jeopardy. One day while he was on duty at the desk, the town marshal drove up to the Lodge.

"Got somethin fur ya," drawled Ted, the deputy marshal.

"What have you got, Ted?" inquired Alex.

"I reckon it's a subpoena," said Ted. "Sign here."

Alex took the three-page document and sat down. She had subpoenaed him to appear in court with an order to show cause. Erin was filing for divorce, and he was ordered to appear in the Lancaster California Superior Court on May seventh. Alex made a call to the local legal eagle, Tom Watson, and asked him what the consequences were if he chose not to appear. To his chagrin, he was informed that Erin would be awarded everything she asked for. He knew very well that he had to contest these proceedings, but really didn't want the hassle. He'd think about it when he wasn't so tired. Two days later, a letter arrived from Erin's attorney, which listed all the community property to be adjudicated. Alex scanned the list and froze when he saw his coin collection was listed at the end. He flew into a rage and after an hour had elapsed, calmed down and resigned himself to the fact that he must return for the hearing on May seventh.

～18～
PREPARING FOR THE AUDIT

The meeting was called to review the financial condition of the medical practice and the hospital complex. All three partners were present.

"As you all know," said Dr. Lund, "US Care will be here next month to perform their due diligence."

"What is that?" asked Rick Small.

"Let me answer that," said Kovacs. "A purchaser must satisfy their directors that the seller's representation is factual. They will send an administrator, accountant, lawyer, and anyone else that is familiar with the business to physically look over the facility, books, contracts, tax returns, deposits, and checking accounts. They will want to see all our financial statistics, and they will scrutinize it all. We will have to disclose every contract and agreement that we have with the HMO and referral consultants. They will pour over our accounts receivable and payables. For the medical practice entity, they will be asking to see evidence of how we pay the claims. They will be looking for IBNR data."

"IBNR, what the hell is that?" asked Small.

"That is the estimate of the amount of money that the group owes to outside referral consultants and providers," answered Kovacs. "It stands for 'incurred but not received,' which refers to potential professional financial obligations."

"Do we track that estimate?" asked Small.

"We do," answered Kovacs.

"About 38 percent of the capitation is used for outside referrals," said Bob.

"And we pay our providers by ninety days," added Kovacs.

"It sounds like the due diligence will take a long time to complete," said Bob.

"No doubt, but it depends upon the number of people they send to do the task," replied Kovacs. "We just went through the same stuff at Woodside Community Hospital."

"I'd guess that it will take them at least a month," stated Bob.

"Probably so," replied Kovacs, "and what do our numbers currently show, Bob?" asked Kovacs.

"Over the last eight months, the revenue has dropped on the hospital side," said Bob nodding his head.

"My take on that is because it's become more profitable for our group not to hospitalize managed care patients," said Kovacs.

"Right, Harvey," said Lund, "but it's a double-edged sword. When we don't hospitalize, the hospital revenue drops. This is compensated by the group receiving half of the hospital shared-risk pool, which last year netted us one million two hundred fifty dollars. Last year the hospital's gross of thirteen million dollars was down almost five million dollars from the year before. Our profit was 15 percent, or two million bucks. Now that's the bad news. The good news is that the Respiratory Care Unit, after only six months in operation, grossed us an average of ten thousand a day, or about two million bucks. It's a good thing we added three more beds to that unit."

"Four million a year, that's unreal," chimed in Rick.

"Let me finish, you guys," said Bob. "The profit on the respiratory care unit runs 60 percent. It's the best moneymaker we have. And by the way, the private insurance companies pay an average of seven hundred fifty dollars a day and, we get about four-sixty from the state."

"That's all well and good, Bob, but what about this year so far?" asked Kovacs.

"I'm coming to that," said Bob. "We had a 95 percent occupancy rate for the first quarter. The patient mix was 75 percent state insurance and 25 percent private insurance. The gross revenue remains between two hundred fifty and three hundred thousand a month. Which is down about 20 to 25 percent. This was all due to the death of a few of our Respiratory Care Unit patients."

"That will reduce the bottom line," said Small.

"Brilliant deduction," growled Kovacs, shaking his head side to side in disbelief. He thought to himself, what an absolute idiot Small was. He could not imagine how he had ever completed medical school.

Bob Lund continued. "I have the three empty beds covered, gentlemen. You may safely assume that they will all be occupied next week."

"I think US Care may lowball us on the offer for the hospital complex," said Kovacs. "If the Respiratory Care Unit continues like it is, we may come out okay though."

"You're forgetting one thing," said Lund. "The state has given us a termination of contract notice. They are expecting to be able to use their own facilities soon. When that happens, we will lose about half of our patients, and the gross income will take a nosedive. We must disclose the termination notice to US Care during the due diligence or we are buying a potential lawsuit later."

"Look, if that's the case and private insurance pays twice as much, why don't we try to replace the eight patients in the Respiratory Care Unit with private insured ones?" asked Kovacs.

"Exactly my plan," said Bob. He prided himself on both his business and medical acumen.

"I have three designated patients for the Respiratory Care Unit. Mr. Bunkin, Babcock, and Wiener are all patients of mine who met the criteria for respiratory failure. It shouldn't be that difficult to find eight more between Rick and myself. Rick, you can help us, can't you?"

"I just don't know that much about internal medicine to be of any help," replied Rick.

"What about referring me your patients who have severe chronic lung disease or any other serious illness for that matter. Maybe I can find the right combination of medication for them," sneered Bob. He looked up at Kovacs and widened his eyes and sighed.

"Okay, Bob, I'll keep an eye out for the sickies," answered Small.

"Gentlemen," interrupted Kovacs, "may I also offer my talents to this effort?"

"When will you be on board full time?" asked Rick.

"I expect to be up and going in one week," answered Kovacs. "I've rented a house in the Country Club Estates."

"Great, as soon as you start, we will save a ton of money by not having to refer down below anymore," said Lund.

"Did you sell your house, Harvey?" asked Rick.

"No, I didn't, but I did lease it out for two years. I was fortunate to have leased it to the new hospital administrator at Woodland Community. US Care took over last week, and I was evicted from my office."

"Oh, I bet that hurt a whole lot," said Bob.

Kovacs laughed and said, "all the way to the bank."

"Aren't you glad you became our partner in 1960? Look at all you can now look forward to in Palmdale," said Lund.

"Yes Lund, I am grateful that I had the hundred thousand to invest with you guys,"

answered Kovacs. "Who would have ever thought it would have burgeoned into a small

fortune?"

"Not so small," said Rick.

"That's right, we may all walk away splitting up twenty-five million dollars," countered Kovacs.

~19~
God's Gift to Surgery
Arrives

Dr. Harvey Kovacs took a small office in the medical building annex in front of the hospital. The annex was added a few years ago when the group ran out of medical space. The explosion of managed care contracts to the group mandated more primary care doctors, and the quickest way to fill the need was to incorporate prefab construction to create office space. In the old days, Kovacs had acquired the ability to perform many procedures. Then it was only a matter of attending a hands-on, two-day course in the state of the art, relative to the procedure. Before there were gastroenterologists, he had mastered the technique of colonoscopy. Then the onslaught of specialists hit the front lines, eliminating the need for surgeons like Harvey to perform colonoscopies anymore. He could only remember about a dozen cases he had performed over the last five years. In today's world he was obliged to refer such procedures to the GI colleagues, if he were to avoid a malpractice suit. The fact that he had successfully passed a two-day course in performing colonoscopies didn't hold water anymore. *I did them before and I'll do them again,* thought Kovacs. *They're no big deal to do. It's only passing a tube through a tunnel. It was a lucky break that Hendrickson was able to get all my privileges rubber stamped by the Credentials Committee.*

He knew that he would never have been able to get colonoscopy privileges at any other hospital because he could not document proficiency in that procedure. Hospital credentialing was scrutinized these days, and unless the doctor had current experience and training, he would never be given the privilege to perform the procedure.

Mrs. Janet Childs had been referred to him by Dr. Small. She had experienced three separate episodes of bleeding over the past two weeks. The utilization department of the group had issued the referral since she was a managed care patient of the Palmdale medical group. It had already been determined by Drs. Kovacs, Lund, and Small that all future colonoscopies would be done by Harvey. This would save the group the expense of paying for the referral to Dr. Walker for a consult and colonoscopy; his contract called for a two-hundred-dollar fee for each such procedure and consult.

Mrs. Childs sat in a chair in front of Dr. Kovacs's desk. She fidgeted with her fingers and showed signs that she was uncomfortable.

Dr. Kovacs looked up and placed her chart on his desk. "Mrs. Childs, I am writing a prescription for you. I want you to drink this tomorrow morning between six and ten o'clock. Afterward please come to the hospital at eleven and I will meet you in the GI lab. It's a total of four quarts that you must drink."

"Do I have to drink it all?" she asked.

"You sure do, dear, if I am to get a good look at your colon," replied Kovacs in his most fatherly voice. He then wrote an order to schedule her on his prescription and handed it to his patient.

"I'll see you tomorrow at eleven, and don't forget . . . nothing to eat after midnight tonight," reminded Kovacs.

The next morning at ten-forty, Janet Childs, a sixty-five-year-old mother of three and grandmother of four, walked into the hospital and was directed to the GI lab. Shirley North, RN, oversaw the lab. She handed a paper gown to Janet and pointed her to the changing room. After gowning, she was positioned on the procedure table. She looked up from the table and saw that she was surrounded by TV monitors of various sizes. At the foot of the table was a large computer, which was used to take and enhance photos. An IV was started in her right wrist and Shirley affixed an oximetry probe on her index fingernail.

"At least I don't have to play manicurist and remove nail polish," said Shirley with a slight laugh.

Dr. Kovacs entered the room and wrote a hasty entry in Janet's chart. He then sat down on the stool next to his patient and explained the procedure he was about to perform.

"I will be instilling air into your bowel as I advance the scope to inspect your colon. If I should see anything suspicious, I will take a small biopsy. You will not feel it at all. If I find polyps, I will remove them by using a snare and cauterizing the base. Do you have any questions?" asked Dr. Kovacs.

"Will I be awake, Doctor?" she asked.

"Not entirely, Mrs. Childs. I will be giving you a rapid-acting Valium-type drug called Versed. When you awake, you won't remember anything."

"That's just the way I prefer it," replied Mrs. Childs.

"Shirley, please give her two milligrams of Versed and hold," said Kovacs.

At his command, the nurse injected the needle into the IV tubing and clamped the line behind the needle. She pushed the plunger to the two-milliliter mark and reopened the clamp. The line flushed with saline, and Janet was already asleep.

"Doctor, her pulse ox is 97 percent, pulse is 80, and pressure is one thirty-three over seventy-eight," reported Shirley.

"Okay, let's begin," said Kovacs.

Shirley switched on the computer, and the video screens became active. She positioned Mrs. Childs in the standard left lateral position.

After performing a digital rectal examination, he inserted the anoscope. It was only six inches long and was meant to allow observation of the anal canal and lower rectum, which cannot easily be seen with the colonoscope. With ease he advanced the scope through the sigmoid and stopped at sixty centimeters. At this point the colon made a right angle turn to the left, as it now became the transverse colon. He then continued the advancement to the point where it made a left turn into the ascending colon. Advancing the scope further, he was now at the cecum. Kovacs was impressed with the new fiber optic scopes. They had a four-way directional control of the tip, excellent optics, and a biopsy suction channel. In addition, there were controls for air insufflation, suction, and distal lens washing. Kovacs noted two large polyps extending from the wall of the cecum. He told his nurse to administer three milligrams of Versed and to continue to inject one milligram if the patient was awakening. He had ascertained that the colon was clean of fecal matter. This was critical when you wanted to use cautery within the colon. Methane gas had caused explosions within the colon in the hands of less experienced doctors, but Kovacs was savvy in this area. He had done this procedure many times before and proceeded with confidence. With the tip of the scope situated proximal to one of the polyps, he inserted the snare and looped it around the polyp. The polyp looked like a mushroom with a small stalk or pedicle. He tightened the loop of the snare about midway on the pedicle and watched the tissue turn from pink to deep blue. Certain that the large polyp was not touching any other part of the colon wall, he applied a low coagulating current into the snare with short bursts while maintaining steady tension on the snare enclosure. The polyp turned white at the coagulation site, signaling that it could now be grasped by the long forceps inserted through the biopsy channel. The scope and forceps were then withdrawn from the colon. He dropped the specimen into a small bottle containing 10 percent formaldehyde and reinserted the scope to its previous position within the cecum. The visual inspection of the other polyp was different. This one was a large sessile polyp. It had no pedicle, so it would be necessary to create one from normal mucosa surrounding the polyp. Kovacs knew from experience that these were the most difficult to remove and were most likely to cause complications. In his earlier years, when he had seen this type of lesion, he would discontinue the procedure and opt for an open laparotomy. This would generate a nice fee, and the lesion could be removed easier. He knew that the possibility of causing a burn to the colon's mucus membrane was very real. He also realized that his job was to eliminate all unnecessary operations. Besides, he wasn't going to receive any remuneration for the surgery because Mrs. Childs was a capitated patient. He rationalized that he had better remove the polyp now. He repeated the snaring procedure but found it difficult to completely ensnare the mass. After numerous attempts, he settled for what he saw. The snare encircled most of the sprawling lesion so that he was able to create a false pedicle of normal tissue around the polyp. He tightened the snare and the tissue turned blue. Small bursts of coagulation current were applied, and he then removed the lesion with the aid of the forceps and suction. The entire procedure had taken

Kovacs almost thirty-five minutes. Janet Childs was awake within five minutes, and as promised, she had no recollection of the procedure.

Dr. Kovacs dictated his operative note and hung up the phone. "Mrs. Childs, I am going to discharge you in one hour. I'd like to see you in the office next week. I should have the biopsy report back by then. I removed two polyps, which looked benign," stated Kovacs.

Later on, that evening, Janet Childs experienced lower abdominal pain. She was awakened that night with a chill and decided to take Tylenol and go back to sleep. She saw Dr. Kovacs the morning, and he had assured her that her pain was perfectly normal. Over the next two days she again came to the office complaining to Dr. Kovacs that she had become weak and had developed profuse sweating. Her chills continued, and she reported to Dr. Kovacs that she had not had a bowel movement in three days. She was now in his office again after the third consecutive day of continuous pain since the colonoscopy.

Dr. Kovacs's nurse had written the blood pressure in her chart. Seventy-four over fifty-two. Dr. Kovacs repeated her pressure himself and recorded ninety over sixty. His note further stated, *pulses are poor, looks pale, abdomen soft, and bowel sounds may be absent.*

"Janet, I want to get a blood count now and, in the meantime, I want you to stop your blood pressure pill. The Lopressor is dropping your pressure, and you are dehydrated. Go home and take a few enemas to help you move your bowels." After more reassurance, Janet left his office.

At 2:00 a.m. the following morning, Kovacs was called by the emergency room to come to the hospital and see Janet Childs. The emergency doctor told him that his patient had awakened at 1:00 a.m. with profuse sweating and was lightheaded. She was difficult to arouse, according to Mr. Childs, and when she stood up, she fell to the floor.

Kovacs appeared at the hospital in an aggravated state. He was sure the emergency doctor had called him for nothing. He had told him that this was all due to the beta blocker Lopressor. *A little IV fluid and he could have sent her home,* he thought.

"Which bed is she in?" growled Kovacs as he stormed into the emergency room.

"Bed three," replied the ER tech.

Kovacs grabbed the chart and saw that the blood pressure was seventy over fifty and the pulse rate was one hundred twenty-six. The white blood count was forty-two thousand and the hematocrit was fifty-eight. The catheter coming from her bladder contained a few milliliters of urine and there was none in the bag. He examined her abdomen and found tenderness of the right lower quadrant and elicited the signs of peritoneal irritation.

"She's in shock!" shouted Kovacs. "Call in the OR crew stat! Start another IV with dextrose and saline and give her two grams of Mefoxin now with one hundred twenty milligrams of gentamicin." He ordered plasma to also be started. Kovacs now recognized clinical shock and the immediate need for intravenous fluids and antibiotics to be given.

The surgery on-call crew had the operating room ready to go in less than one hour. There was still no urine in the bag draining the bladder.

"Try and keep her pressure up," said Kovacs to his anesthesiologist.

"I'm not a magician," answered Dr. Martin Sharpe.

"Don't give me your smart-ass remarks Marty, just do your damn job," shouted Kovacs.

"Touchy bastard," grumbled Sharpe as he attended to his patient's vital signs.

Kovacs opened the abdominal cavity and was met with volumes of blood-tinged turbid fluid.

He inspected the large intestine at the cecum and quickly found the problem. The cecum had been perforated, and its contents had ruptured into the peritoneal space. His patient had a fulminant case of peritonitis, and now bacteria were circulating in the bloodstream, causing shock.

"Pressure dropping, now eighty over fifty," said Sharpe.

"Do whatever you think best, give her dopamine and plasma," replied Kovacs angrily.

Kovacs hurried to complete the colectomy. He had seen where the necrotic bowel was located and was now at work removing that eight-inch segment. Once he had it out, he sewed the ends of the colon together.

"I'm done," he shouted!

"I'll lighten her up," answered Marty. "Her pressure is now ninety over sixty and holding."

The surgery was concluded at 4:45 a.m., and Janet never awakened. She was pronounced dead at 7:17 a.m.

On the following afternoon, Dr. Kovacs's office was scheduled to see twelve patients. Ralph Hadley had been examined yesterday by Dr. Rick Small. Mr. Hadley was a private insurance patient who was complaining of severe dizziness and was unable to move his right arm for five minutes. Dr. Small had correctly inferred from this history that there might be a problem within the carotid arteries that supply blood to the brain. He ordered an immediate ultrasound and flow study of the neck circulation on his patient. That report was now in the hands of Harvey Kovacs, MD, as he spoke.

"Mr. Hadley, your ultrasound or echo study shows that you have severe occlusive disease of your carotid arteries, which needs to be confirmed. The next step is to do an angiogram to determine the precise location and extent of the disease," stated Kovacs in all his omnipotent grandeur. This is a diagnostic test where radio-opaque dye is injected into an artery for radiographic viewing.

"What does all that mean?" said Mr. Hadley with a crackle in his voice.

"It means that you will need to have an operation to remove the cholesterol deposits in the arteries," said Kovacs. "It's a kind of 'Roto-Rooter' job, but the fancy medical name for it is an endarterectomy. It's really a simple procedure where we remove the entire lining of the diseased artery," explained Kovacs, gesturing with outstretched hands as if to imply, *just trust me*.

"That sounds scary; will I be all right afterward?" questioned Mr. Hadley with uncertainty.

"You'll be just fine," responded Kovacs in his smug and overconfident manner. He peered over his glasses and continued as though he were lecturing a class of medical school students.

"I'll set you up for the angiogram at six o'clock tonight at the hospital. I will be injecting a dye into your arteries, and at the same time we will be taking x-rays of your head and neck," said Dr. Kovacs. "We will be looking for areas blocking the blood flow to the brain so I know exactly where to make the incision."

"Okay, Doctor, you convinced me, I'll be there tonight," said Ralph.

Kovacs enjoyed performing angiograms himself rather than allowing the radiologists to do them. After all, he thought, he had been doing them for about thirty years or so and was very accomplished in the technique. No need to have the radiologist receive a hefty fee for the procedure, when he could do it.

The radiology department had a designated procedure room where angiography procedures were performed. Mr. Hadley was already gowned and draped on the x-ray table.

Dr. Kovacs was assisted by an ER nurse and an x-ray tech. He inserted the needle into the right carotid artery and advanced the catheter to the correct position. Dr. Kovacs performed the angiogram on the right carotid artery first, where he confirmed the presence of a 95 percent obstruction. He then injected the left carotid artery. A moment after the dye was introduced into the vessel, Mr. Hadley's speech became incoherent, his eyes roamed from side to side, and his right arm became limp.

"Quick, let's remove the catheter," shouted Kovacs.

"He's stroking," said the nurse as she applied the blood pressure cuff.

Kovacs applied pressure to the site of needle entry into the carotid and asked, "did we get the rays?"

"We did get a few frames," replied the tech.

"I want to see them as soon as they are out," growled Kovacs.

He turned to the nurse and barked his orders. "Give Hadley seventy-five hundred units of heparin now and start a drip of one thousand units an hour. Get a partial thromboplastin time now and repeat it in six hours." Kovacs needed to measure the clotting activity of the blood for him to administer future doses of the anti-coagulant heparin. Without knowing the value, the patient could easily be given an overdose, which could cause hemorrhaging.

"I'll take care of it," replied the nurse. "Oh, look, Doctor, Mr. Hadley is awake."

"Can you raise your right arm?" asked Kovacs.

"I'm trying to, Doctor, but it won't move."

"All right, Mr. Hadley. A small clot in your artery has broken loose from the vessel wall and has lodged in the internal carotid; this has caused you to suffer a small stroke. I want to operate on your left carotid immediately. If I don't go in now and reopen the blockage, you might die."

"Okay Doc, do whatever you need to make me better," replied Mr. Hadley. He was resigned that his life lay in the hands of his surgeon.

"Get the OR crew and let's get this show on the road," shouted Kovacs to his nurse.

Mr. Hadley was trying to move his right arm, but when he finally realized the attempt was fruitless, he tried to move his right leg. "Nurse, I can't move my leg now," said Mr. Hadley in a whimper.

"That's all right, you'll soon be able to," she assured him.

Hurrying to the operating room, Kovacs thought to himself. *This is one hell of a start in Palmdale. My first case and the guy strokes on me.* He entered the doctors' dressing room and called Dr. Small to assist him in surgery.

The left carotid artery lay exposed, awaiting the scalpel of the surgeon. Kovacs ordered the heparin to be continued and placed clamps on the left internal carotid, then the external carotid, and finally he clamped the common carotid artery.

"Hand me an eleven blade," demanded Kovacs. He took the blade and made an incision into the internal carotid artery.

"Look at that, the vessel is plugged," he said to his assistant, Dr. Rick Small.

"There's no blood flowing in it that I can see," responded Small.

"Nurse, hand me the Penfield dissector now!" demanded Kovacs.

"See the layers of the vessel, Small?" asked Kovacs. "I've got to separate the outer layer, the adventitia, from the two inner layers. This dissector works like a charm." Kovacs proceeded to snip away the layers from each other, all the while removing plaque, debris, and clot.

The anesthesiologist was Dr. Martin Sharpe. In his preoperative examination of Mr. Hadley, he had determined that he was an extremely high risk because, among other things, Hadley still had paralysis of the right upper and lower extremities. Dr Sharpe turned his attention to the blood pressure monitor that was now chirping.

"His pressure is two ten over one thirty. I'm starting Vasotec," he announced quickly. Sharpe had many other drugs to use for this acute hypertensive crisis, but in his experience, Vasotec worked rapidly in most patients.

"Do whatever you have to do. I'll be done in fifteen minutes," replied Kovacs.

"It's unresponsive! It's now two fifty over one forty-four! He'll stroke out, if I can't get it down," shouted Sharpe.

"Add some Inderal," suggested Kovacs.

"I don't dare. His pulse is fifty and Inderal will drop it further," replied Sharpe.

"It's your call then," shouted Kovacs.

Sharpe ran through the available drug options quickly in his mind. "I'll start a Nipride drip so we can control the pressure minute by minute," he answered.

"Fine," replied Kovacs automatically. He wasn't even aware of the distress in his colleague's voice.

"The Nipride is working," blurted out Sharpe in excitement.

"I'm ready to close," said Kovacs. He finished the surgery and left the operating room.

After attempting to remove the patient from ventilator support without success, Dr. Sharpe settled for keeping his patient in the recovery room under direct observation. Many patients required assisted ventilation for hours after surgery. The inability to extubate an elderly patient immediately after surgery was not a rare occurrence, but it worried him anyhow. General anesthesia had a direct effect upon the respiratory centers of the brain, and he knew that it might take as much as twenty-four hours for some patients to breathe without ventilator assistance. The nurses were able to keep the pressure at one thirty over ninety by adjusting the rate of the Nipride infusion.

Dr. Sharpe went to the bedside two hours later and found Mr. Hadley lying motionless with his eyes wide open. He shined a bright light into his pupils and noted that they were both dilated. He then used the tip of his car key to apply pressure to the lateral sole of each foot while stroking the key in a upward motion, and the toes spread slightly and the great toes of both feet extended upward.

"Oh God, he's got bilateral Babinski reflexes also!" exclaimed Dr. Sharpe, referring to a pathological reflex that indicates large motor tracts in the brain have been damaged. He knew too well that the presence of bilateral Babinski's meant the patient had suffered permanent brain injury. This was confirmed by the presence of dilated pupils without a response to light. He lifted Hadley's right arm above his head and let it fall and it fell right on his face. He repeated the act with the left arm and observed the same response. There was no question that Hadley had suffered permanent severe injury to both sides of the brain. The insult had spared the lower centers of the brain that controlled blood pressure and other autonomic nervous system functions as well; although Hadley could initiate an inspiration, it was extremely weak. Ventilatory support was mandatory. He called Dr. Kovacs and reported his findings.

"Well that's a shame," said Kovacs. "He was a high risk from the get-go; he obviously infarcted his brain during surgery. My guess is that he had a cerebral hemorrhage as a result of his elevated blood pressure during surgery. You should have done a better job at controlling his hypertensive crisis during surgery," Kovacs hung up the phone and called Bob Lund.

"Bob, this is Harvey," Kovacs said. He filled him in on the clinical facts surrounding the unfortunate Mr. Hadley, and when he had finished, he asked Lund to take over the care of the case.

"I put him in the ICU, Bob. No doubt he will be a viable candidate for a Respiratory Care Unit bed. He also has good insurance!"

"Sounds good to me—one down and two to go," answered Lund referring to the three empty respiratory care beds.

~20~
THE IDEAL MEDICINE FOR RESPIRATORY FAILURE

The following morning Dr. Lund made rounds on his hospital patients. Mr. Hadley was still on the ventilator and had been weaned from the Nipride infusion. His vital signs were now normal. He examined his patient's eyes and found the pupils to be very small and still responsive to light. Last night the pupils were maximally dilated. When he rotated the head from side to side, the eyes remained in the midline. He knew that this sign was called "doll's eyes," but he was always irked whenever that term was used because dolls reminded him of children, and the use of the term indicated a death sentence. The two were totally incongruous to him. Children were life, not death.

"Melody, please bring me a glass of ice water and a 10-cc syringe."

"What do want with that?" Melody asked.

She brought the glass of iced water and the syringe and asked, "Mind if I watch?"

"Not at all. Ice water stimulation of the inner ear from cold water on the ear drum is a test to confirm the loss of function of the brainstem. This is the nerve connection between the middle ear and the eye muscles. If the connection is intact, the eyes will move horizontally, and it might even cause vomiting. If there is brain stem death, there will be no eye response." He emptied the syringe of iced water into the right ear and waited. There was a response. He repeated the procedure in the left ear and again observed a response.

"Would you pass Hadley's chart to me?" asked Dr. Lund.

He wrote in the chart. *Patient's pupils are in the mid position and fixed without response to light. Present calorics and doll's eyes. Bilateral Babinski's with paralysis of all four extremities. Respiratory drive today is barely present. Diagnosis. Right carotid stenosis with embolization. Left carotid stenosis. Post endarterectomy intraoperative hypertensive crisis with cerebral hypoxemia or hemorrhage. Plan transfer to resp care unit for permanent ventilator support.* He handed the chart back to the nurse and left for his office.

Peter Bunkin was but one of twelve scheduled appointments that morning, and he was waiting for Dr. Lund when he arrived.

"How do you feel, Peter?" asked Dr. Lund.

"I am having problems breathing, Doc," answered Peter, pointing to his chest with his index finger. "I'm very short of breath doing nothing."

Dr. Lund reviewed the chart and was reminded that Peter had now been on two Mestinon timespan capsules of one hundred eighty milligrams each at bedtime. In addition, he was also taking the sixty-milligram tablet three times daily. *Almost ready for the hospital,* he thought.

After listening to the lungs and heart, Dr. Lund sat down and spoke. "I want you to take four of those sixty milligram pills each day. That should help you." Lund then wrote in the chart. *He is doing fine, will hold Mestinon at current doses. Recheck in a few days. Prognosis guarded.*

"The nurse will set up your next appointment, Peter," said Dr. Lund, handing the chart to the patient.

Dr. Lund entered the next exam room and found Mr. Babcock seated next to the examination table. He glanced at the last note in the chart and confirmed that he had prescribed Mestinon on the last visit.

"My breathing has become worse, Doctor," explained Mr. Babcock. He looked exasperated.

Dr. Lund placed the flat side of the stethoscope on George's chest and had him take deep breaths. He noted that the breathing was shallow, and the rate was slow. He also heard scattered wheezes. His face was sallow, with a blue tint to his lips and nail beds.

"George, I am going to check your oxygen level," said D.r Lund with concern. He placed the oximetry sensor on the nail bed of the index finger and shook his head in anguish. "Your level is 75 percent, which is very low. I want to put you in the hospital right now," said Dr. Lund. "Oh, by the way George, take an extra Mestinon tablet now and at bedtime, okay? You still have Medicare insurance, don't you?"

"Yes, Doctor, and I also have a secondary insurance to pick up anything not covered by Medicare," answered George very confidently. Lund went to the hospital to write the admitting orders and dictate the history and physical examination.

He rapidly wrote a full page of orders. The first order stated: *Patient may take his own pills.* This was not an uncommon order to write for patients who had rare medications. Lund had to be certain that his patient's dosage of Mestinon was taken timely. His second order was for *Mestinon sixty milligrams every eight hours.* He was certain that this additional dose of the drug would have the desired effect. The admitting diagnosis was exacerbation of chronic obstructive pulmonary disease and myasthenia gravis. He felt secure using this diagnosis, as it was commonplace for patients with myasthenia to progress to the stage of respiratory failure. It wouldn't raise anyone's eyebrows, he hoped. The blood gas report confirmed that the lungs were not ventilating efficiently in that the partial pressure of carbon dioxide is normally between thirty-five and forty and George Babcock's level was seventy.

Mr. Sam Wiener returned for his checkup and complained that his leg pain was now gone, but he found it hard to breathe.

Dr. Lund performed a cursory examination and said, "Sam, I would like to admit you to the hospital for testing." The large scar over the left chest was a result of a previous surgery for lung cancer performed in another state many years ago. Left with only one lung, Sam experienced shortness of breath with any exertional activity.

"Sure Doc, I'm tired of messing with this. Let's get it over with," he said, gasping a breath after every two words.

Dr. Lund wrote orders; the first one was for pain control. *Patient controlled administration pump6 to contain morphine sulfate at the following parameters: Basal delivery rate of one milligram per hour and a maximum of seven milligrams per hour.* The pump allowed the patient to administer added doses of one milligram at ten-minute intervals.

"You better keep using the Duragesic patches while you're in the hospital. Put it on your back side so no one will hassle you about it," said Dr. Lund, stressing its importance.

Sam shook his head affirmatively. He was so short-winded that he couldn't speak.

Dr. Lund admitted Sam Wiener with the diagnosis of lung cancer with metastasis to the spine involving the lumbar nerve roots.

Upon arrival at his room, Mr. Wiener was given instructions in the use of the patient control assisted pump. He was immediately started on three liters of oxygen per minute. In a short while Sam felt better. His severe air hunger had abated. *What a great doctor,* he thought to himself.

The medication nurse made her rounds at 10:00 p.m. This time-honored ritual was practiced in every hospital. Its purpose was for the departing nurse to gather the latest information about each patient and then report to the night shift supervisor the current clinical status of each patient. She entered George Babcock's room and saw he had agonal gasping breaths, and they were occurring very slowly. She ran to the nursing station and called a code blue, then ran back to the room and took the blood pressure. The ER doctor arrived and inserted a tube into Sam's trachea while the respiratory therapist attached it to the respirator tubing. "His pressure is sixty over forty, pulse one twenty," announced the nurse. The blood gas report returned with the results of critical ventilatory failure. The partial pressure of carbon dioxide was now ninety-five. Mr. Wiener was immediately moved to the ICU.

Dr. Lund was standing at the bedside of his patient, George Babcock. The ventilator had performed its job quite well, as Mr. Babcock was now conscious and alert.

"Your lungs failed, George, you will remain on the ventilator for a while longer." He opened the chart and wrote orders: *Mestinon three milligrams IV every three hours.* He then dictated the history and physical, ending his report with: *diagnosis exacerbated COPD, myasthenia gravis end stage and ventilatory failure secondary to both diagnoses. Prognosis guarded.* Lund then wrote a brief progress note and ordered his patient transferred to the Chronic Respiratory Care Unit for long-term care. The orders further stated that all the current orders be continued. He stood up and walked out of the ICU, engrossed in thought. *That's another bed filled; only one more to* go. He turned around and poked his head into the ICU and called to the nurse. "Please write an order for Valium five milligrams every four to six hours as needed for sedation," and as he walked out of the hospital, he couldn't help but think about the wonder drug Mestinon. Myasthenia was a muscle disease caused by rapid destruction of the chemical acetylcholine; this substance was necessary for the conduction of nerve transmission to the muscle. There is in the body, an enzyme, acetylcholine esterase, that destroys acetylcholine, but Mestinon competes with it, preventing its destruction. This increases acetylcholine and inhibits muscle function.

On Monday morning Peter Bunkin was brought to Dr. Lund's office in a wheelchair. He complained that he couldn't walk and was very short of breath. Doctor Lund took one look at him and shouted to his office nurse, "Admit Mr. Bunkin to the ICU stat!" The nurse took the wheelchair from Mrs. Bunkin and scooted him away rapidly. Lund called the hospital and admitted him with the diagnosis of acute respiratory failure and myasthenia gravis. He then asked to be transferred to the ICU so that he could give orders. When the nurse answered, he quickly reviewed the case with her and asked her to call the anesthesiologist to place an endotracheal tube immediately. "Get me a set of blood gasses and notify respiratory therapy to stand by with a respirator." Thirty minutes later, the ICU nurse related that Bunkin's admitting gases revealed the oxygen pressure was forty and the carbon dioxide pressure was seventy-four.

"He's doing fine on the respirator; when will you be up to see him?" asked the nurse.

"I'll be there at noon," answered Lund as he hung the phone up with a feeling of great satisfaction.

At twelve-thirty Dr. Lund entered the hospital, walked to the medical floor, and called the ICU. He was told that Mr. Bunkin was resting comfortably. He then walked to the bedside of Mr. Wiener and checked the PCA pump: it was locked from the outside. With the diagnosis of metastatic cancer to the spinal cord and nerve roots, Mr. Wiener would require large doses of morphine to keep him comfortable. In the dictated history, Dr. Lund had stated that the *patient had his left lung removed five years ago in hopes of achieving a cure. At that time, there was no evidence of metastasis or spread. The surgery was performed in Oklahoma. The patient had remained pain-free until recently, when he presented with severe lumbosacral nerve root pain. The tumor was compressing the nerve roots.* Lund knew that tumors often reoccur years later in other areas of the body, and they may also for some odd reason lay dormant for years. He continued his lie and stated that *the tumor was encroaching upon the fifth lumbar and the first sacral nerve roots.* When his pain first began, Mr. Wiener had a needle biopsy performed at a hospital in northern California while visiting family in that area. His pain had been so excruciating that he required a Duragesic patch initially for pain control. The pain is no longer controlled by the patch, and he is admitted for IV morphine to control the pain. Bob Lund knew that this facade would never be questioned. It was a logical assumption that a patient might present with cancer that had spread to remote parts of the body five years after the lung was removed. This was a common presentation in women with breast cancer, as five years or longer after a mastectomy, cancer could be found anywhere. No one would question the diagnosis or the treatment in a patient with a large scar from the lung surgery and the resourceful history. He rapidly devised a plan to enhance his patient's respiratory failure. Lund was aware that this would be the last patient he needed to ease into a respiratory care unit bed, and he breathed a sigh of relief opening the chart and reviewing his admitting pain control orders. They were reasonable, but not very likely to cause significant respiratory depression. The orders were available for all to see, so he couldn't very well order excessive doses of morphine. The pharmacist or the nurses would have caught that *error* in any case, so he needed to change the basal rate of infusion and the patient selection dosage. He also had to reduce the delay for the patient to activate a dose from every ten to three minutes. These changes would increase the morphine in the blood and induce respiratory depression. Lund was at the nursing station writing progress notes in his patients' charts. He looked at his Rolex and saw that it was only ten minutes before the nurses took their lunch break, and he knew from experience there was only a skeleton crew covering the medical floor during the lunch hour. He also knew from experience that the key was kept at the nurse's station and that obtaining the key would be a piece of cake. For the sake of convenience, the key to the PCA pump was kept in the top right drawer at the station. This way any nurse who received an order to change a PCA medication dosage could do so immediately, rather than trying to find the elusive nurse who had the key. This procedure had always worked nicely in the past. Lund checked the medication cards to confirm there were no other patients on the floor with a PCA pump and the floor nurse would not need the key for another patient, then he waited until the relief charge nurse was at her desk. She was speaking to another doctor on the phone, and as she hung up, she reached over to shut off the irritating sound emanating from the speaker console. He watched as she answered the call from the patient.

"What is the problem, Mr. Caldarone?" she asked cheerfully.

"I need help in getting to the toilet," answered Mr. Caldarone in a demanding voice.

"I'll be right there," she promised and left the station in a run.

Right then Dr. Lund seized the opportunity. He moved to her desk and picked up the phone in his left hand and, at the same instant, put his right hand on the handle of the top-right desk drawer and opened it about six inches, inserted his hand into the draw, and felt the single key hanging on a hook. Someone was coming down the hall. Lund removed the key and slipped it into his shirt pocket, and as a nurse appeared at that moment, he hung up the phone.

"I think I'll see Mr. Wiener now," Lund said, directing his statement at the nurse.

"Fine, Doctor, is there anything you need?"

"Nothing thanks." He quickly walked away with perspiration soaking his armpits.

He entered Sam Wiener's room and noticed him staring at the ceiling.

"How is the pain, Sam?" asked Dr. Lund.

"Pain is mostly gone now," replied Sam.

The PCA pump was fastened to the IV stand. Dr. Lund walked over to it and moved the stand so that his back was to his patient, and as he spoke, he quickly unlocked the pump cover, being careful to conceal his actions from Sam. First Lund increased the basal infusion rate to ten milligrams an hour, then reduced the delay to three minutes and increased the demand dose from one to five milligrams. Now in addition to the higher basal rate of morphine, Sam could activate a delivery of five milligrams every three minutes. Dr. Lund calculated that in eighteen minutes, it was possible that Sam could receive a total of thirty milligrams of morphine. In a little over a half hour, he could receive sixty milligrams.

He turned toward his patient and said, 'Sam, I want you to press the dosage button every three minutes or so. This is very important—even if you are not having pain, you must press the button, okay?"

"Why do I need to push the button if I don't have pain?" asked Sam.

"Because I am trying to evaluate the correct dose for your condition, Sam. I will be converting this medicine to a pill form so the new drug will keep you pain-free at home," explained Dr. Lund, in a solicitous manner.

Sam Wiener was in awe. *My Doctor really knows his business. I haven't felt this good in months.* He replied, "Okay, Doc, will do."

Dr. Lund exited the room and went to the nursing station. He opened Sam's chart to the progress notes and wrote: *Patient doing well on PCA.* He glanced at his watch and noted it was quarter of one. He calculated that by one thirty Mr. Wiener should be far gone. Lund sat at the station and read the newspaper and noted that there was an article about US Care that hinted they were interested in acquiring Palmdale Hospital.

At 1:20 a.m., Lund walked to Sam's room. Sam was breathing about four times a minute and very shallow at that. A quick look at his pupils confirmed that the morphine had done its job. They were pinpoint, so he removed a small bottle of eye drops from his pocket labeled Cyclogyl and placed one drop in each eye. Then he unlocked the PCA pump and reset all the dials to their previous settings and then relocked the pump. A quick recheck of the pupils told him they had begun to dilate; he knew now that no one would ever suspect morphine was the cause of the respiratory failure. He left the room hastily and headed for the nurses' station.

"Cheryl, I need you right away," he said anxiously. "Mr. Wiener looks like he needs to be intubated." They both ran back to Wiener's room. Cheryl applied oxygen by mask to his face.

"Call a code blue," shouted Lund, "I'll hold the mask."

Dr. Sharpe appeared in response to the emergency. He was carrying the intubation tray. "What's going down?" he asked while gasping for a breath.

"Wiener's gone sour on us, Marty. He's got terminal cancer of the lung with metastasis and only one lung. I guess he couldn't handle the morphine. It was set very low."

Dr. Sharpe looked at the PCA pump's digital readout. The levels and rates were indeed set low. He rapidly passed a tube into the trachea and attached the end to a rubber bag. He compressed the bag rhythmically and watched it fill with oxygen between compressions. "Let's get him to the ICU and on a respirator."

Dr. Lund walked into the ICU and ordered that Mr. Wiener receive five milligrams of morphine every three hours and a Valium-type drug along with it. Three hours later, Lund was informed by the ICU nurse that Mr. Wiener was having difficulties.

"What is the problem, Rona?" asked Dr. Lund.

"Your patient, Mr. Wiener, is now waking up and thrashing a lot," said Rona anxiously. "Can I have an order for something?"

"How bad is he thrashing about?" asked Lund in annoyance.

"He almost pulled the endotracheal tube out with his hands," she replied.

"Okay, put him in hand restraints and start a Norcuron drip. You can stop the Ativan but continue the morphine. The Norcuron will paralyze his muscles, but I also want to keep him pain-free. That should prevent any more thrashing, but it will also paralyze his diaphragm." He then gave specific doses for the morphine and Norcuron. He hung the phone on the receiver, rocked back on his large red leather soft chair, and placed his hands behind his head. *If I continue the Norcuron for a few days, I may be able to show the need for a tracheostomy. After all, I must give ventilatory support since he only has one lung. When he's ready, he can go to the Respiratory Care Unit on continuous morphine and Valium. That should keep him quiet permanently.*

Two days later, without having to convince D.r Kovacs of the necessity for it, the tracheostomy was performed, and right then Dr. Lund admitted to himself that he was in dire need of a vacation. He was approaching burnout, was feeling uptight, and was having insomnia, accompanied by many nights having nightmares as well.

~21~

ANOTHER SURGERY GONE BAD

Hello Harvey, can you see a patient?" asked Small.

"Sure, where's the patient?" asked Kovacs in a flat affect.

"In room twenty-two. She has a distal esophageal lesion, and I think she needs surgery."

"Fine, does she have a name?" asked Kovacs, expressing hostility.

"Sorry, Harvey, her name is Nelda Johnson."

"I'll be right over."

D.r Kovacs slipped his Litman stethoscope into his jacket pocket and started out the door of his office. He entered the front door of the hospital and turned right down the long hall to the X-Ray Department, and after reviewing the barium swallow films of the esophagus, he was positive of the diagnosis. He took one of the films with him and walked over to the medical floor, examined Mrs. Johnson and, when he was finished, sat down in the chair at her bedside.

"You have a tumor at the end of your swallowing tube, the esophagus," explained Kovacs. He held up the x-ray to the light and pointed to the lower part of the esophagus. He was careful to indicate the ominous mass and its crater. "The esophagus transports the food to the stomach. I will make an incision so I can reach the area where the mass is located, and then I will take a small piece of tissue for a frozen section. The pathologist will be able to give me a diagnosis in minutes. If it is malignant, I will have to remove the area with the mass and reconnect the esophagus to the stomach. This is an extensive procedure, but I promise you an excellent result."

Mrs. Johnson wiped the tears from her eyes and asked, "How long will I be here?"

"About one week," replied Kovacs. "Because of the pain after the operation, large doses of narcotics will be necessary. These medicines often impair the lungs from working efficiently, and so, my dear, you will be on a respirator for a while after surgery to help you breathe."

Mrs. Johnson voice trembled, and the tears rolled down her face. She whispered, "Okay, Doctor, I am in your hands." The next morning, she was taken to the operating room. She was placed on the OR table and positioned on her right side. Dr. Martin Sharpe adeptly passed the endotracheal tube and had her connected to the anesthesia machine in ten minutes. He was sitting behind the protective barrier set at the patient's head. With her chest laid barren, the circulating nurse prepped the lateral chest with a brown liquid. Large, green, sterile drapes were applied, and the surgical field was ready. Dr. Kovacs began the operation. All had gone well, and he was ready to biopsy the esophageal lesion. He cut a piece of the angry-appearing tissue and placed a clamp on it, then he removed the biopsy and dropped the clamp with the specimen into a sterile stainless-steel bowl. The circulating nurse handed the bowl to Dr. Wayne Spector, the pathologist. Spector had watched the operation and saw the large amount of bleeding ebbing from the biopsy site and was sure it was cancer. The OR crew was at a standstill as they awaited the biopsy report. The answer came in eleven minutes and confirmed cancer of the esophagus.

"Okay, folks, let's get on with the show," barked Kovacs.

Over the next two hours Kovacs operated with intensity and passion and finished the surgery at 5:20 p.m.

"Give her two units of whole blood now and get a hemoglobin and hematocrit in four hours," said Kovacs to Dr. Sharpe.

"I'll write the orders," said Sharpe.

The chest tube was draining blood from the operative site, while two IV lines were carrying blood into Mrs. Johnson's veins. Her endotracheal tube was attached to the ventilator, and a drain exited from her chest. A urinary catheter drained her bladder into a clear plastic bag hanging on the bed rail. Dr. Kovacs studied his patient. *I hope this isn't an inverted string sign.* He recalled the time he had first heard this mentioned years ago when he was a resident. A professor of his had first called this sign to his attention. The more strings that a patient had, the less likely the patient would survive. The definition of strings was loosely applied to any and all tubes, drains, catheters, or lines of any type that were attached to the patient for any purpose. This was a simple direct proportion issue. The more strings, the graver the illness, and therefore, the more likely the patient would never recover. He congratulated himself on a job well done but was convinced that she would recover. He had promised her a good outcome.

He left for home. There were many financial documents that he wanted to review in anticipation of the forthcoming offer to purchase the hospital and group practice; however,

at 8:00 p.m. that evening, the first of many calls arrived from the ICU.

"Doctor, this is Jan in the ICU. Mrs. Johnson's pressure has dropped to ninety." Her chest tube continues to show gross blood."

"Did you get her H and H?" asked Kovacs, annoyed at the interruption.

"Hemoglobin is six and hematocrit is eighteen," answered Jan.

"What were her values at the end of surgery?" inquired Kovacs.

"Seven and twenty, Doctor," replied Jan, sounding very efficient. "She received two units of whole blood after surgery."

"She's lost three units then, so give her three more of whole blood," instructed Kovacs.

At 11:00 p.m., Jan called to report the values of six point five and nineteen, and she informed Kovacs that the blood pressure was still eighty-five.

Kovacs ordered four units of blood this time and fresh-frozen plasma. Between the hours of 11:00 p.m. and 7:00 a.m., the ICU nurses continued calling Kovacs to report that Mrs. Johnson was continuing to bleed. They also informed him that there was excessive bleeding from the chest tube. Despite transfusions of a unit of blood every hour, the pressure continued to hover at eighty to eighty-five. Kovacs was also made aware that her pulse remained at one thirty and that her urine output had declined to zero. Dr. Kovacs slammed the receiver down and told the nurses not to bother him anymore because he had done all he could. The last call was made by the night nursing supervisor, who suggested to Kovacs that just possibly Mrs. Johnson might be bleeding from an untied blood vessel missed at surgery.

"Look, Mrs. King, don't you dare tell me how to practice medicine," he screamed at the top of his voice. "Why don't you just take care of the bed pans." Dr. Kovacs was now threatened—he had been challenged, and by a woman yet, so his ego had been injured, and now he searched for a way to convince her he really did know what he was doing.

"Furthermore, Mrs. King," he continued, "Mrs. Johnson has been on large amounts of Motrin for her arthritis—she is bleeding because non-steroidal anti-inflammatory drugs and aspirin cause bleeding. Isn't that correct?" he hastened to add.

"Yes, Doctor," the supervisor retorted sarcastically. "I will, however, write up my notice of concern on this matter. Good night!"

How can I help it if a patient decides to bleed? Kovacs would and could never accept the premise that his lack of surgical skill was at the root cause of the bleeding. Finally, at eight-thirty in the morning, the great healer and God's gift to surgery made his grand entrance. Just as he approached the bedside, he witnessed Mrs. Johnson's departure from this world. She had requested a no code before her surgery, because she knew she had cancer. A no code would guarantee that she would not receive any cardiopulmonary resuscitation if her heart were to stop beating. Her wish was honored, and no resuscitative measures were instituted.

Dr. Kovacs took the chart and read the nursing notes. He counted the number of blood transfusions that were given. From 5:30 p.m. until 7:00 a.m., twelve units of blood and ten units of fresh-frozen plasma were administered.

Mrs. King, the night nursing supervisor, submitted a three-page notice of concern to the Quality Assurance Department. The case was assigned to Dr. Mark Gaines for review. Dr. Gaines served as a member of the QA Committee of the Medical Staff. Members of this committee were frequently asked to review cases that resulted in high-risk complications or medical care issues. All deaths were reviewed in accordance with accreditation regulations and guidelines.

It had been a week since Mr. Bunkin and Babcock had undergone their tracheostomies. They were both in the Respiratory Care Unit, dependent upon respirators for life support. Sam Wiener was also there and equally dependent. Bob Lund felt satisfied with the results that all the respiratory care beds were generating daily revenue, and he could now ease up on himself. Plans had been made to travel to the Cayman Islands. Erin was ecstatic about the trip and today received her passport in the mail. She daydreamed almost daily about the trip but always ended up feeling anxious. No amount of rationalization could conceal her real passions. Erin was only after Bob Lund for his wealth. She kept telling herself, *after all, I deserve* it. She was thirty-four years old and had nothing but was acutely aware that Lund was soon to become extremely wealthy, and she could just taste it. Erin conjured up the fantasy of being a queen in her mind. *I deserve it*, she thought.

~22~

GOOD NEWS FOR ALEX

It was already March 29, and Dr. Gaines was alerted by UCLA Medical Center that Alex had been provisionally accepted into the transplant program. The Center advised him they were unable to contact Alex and thought that he might know his whereabouts. Mark assured the program director he would give the message to Alex. Alex was then given an appointment for ten days, at which time the final selection process would occur regarding his liver transplant. All the blood testing and the ultrasound testing and CAT scans to determine patency of the veins of the liver and liver pathology, as well as the psychological test results, had been reviewed by the transplant team. The final step was the second evaluation. The transplant program was very efficient. Whenever a recipient was approved, they were subjected to random drug and alcohol testing because they had found out by bitter experience that their patients sometimes resorted to their former drug or alcohol habit. The random sampling program increased the possibility that the patient remained sober. When a patient was finally accepted as a recipient, he was given a pager to carry so that when a donor liver became available the patient was paged to report to the medical center immediately, and there were always fifty patients who carried pagers at any one time. This insured against the remote possibility of multiple donor availability when notified recipients failed to respond within the allotted time, as well as pager failures. Each recipient was assigned a number commensurate with their place on the list. If a potential recipient was ill or couldn't be reached, the next one in line was contacted. The last one on the list usually had a two- to three-month wait. This was faster than most places in the country because Los Angeles had a rapid donor rate due to its gangs causing frequent murders.

Dr. Gaines placed a telephone call to Crested Butte, Colorado.

"Alex, this is Dr. Gaines."

"How are you, Doc. What's going on?" asked Alex.

"UCLA called and told me they have placed you in their program. You have an appointment in ten days, Alex."

"Great news, Doc. Have you spoken with Dr. Marino in Gunnison?" inquired Alex.

"Yes, I have. He sent me your last lab results," replied Gaines.

"Well, how were they?" asked Alex somewhat hesitantly.

"Let's just say that it is a good thing that UCLA called," replied Dr. Gaines.

"I can believe that; I feel bad. My skin has black and blue spots all over, and I look pregnant," replied Alex.

"Sounds like your belly is full of fluid again. When will you be here?" asked Gaines.

"I'll leave in a few days," said Alex.

"Okay, Alex. Call when you're in town."

Alex was on a cloud. He knew his liver had become worse in the months since he'd left California and now could dream of living rather than dying. Life was being offered again. *Couldn't have timed it better myself.* He remembered the court date set for the divorce hearing and realized he'd be there in time for that hearing as well, so he picked up the phone and called the few friends he had in town to let them know he would soon be returning to California.

～23～

CAYMAN ISLANDS

Bob Lund and Erin Kovacs boarded the Delta shuttle at Palmdale Airport, where there were only two flights a day. The airport was small and was shared with Lockheed and Northrup Grumman Aircraft Corporations. They parked their car in the empty parking lot and walked one hundred feet to the terminal, where they found there were only three other passengers awaiting the shuttle flight to Los Angeles International Airport. They soon heard the drone of airplane engines as the small propeller craft taxied to the terminal and quickly were airborne, flying toward the San Gabriel Mountain range in a southwestern direction. The small craft was climbing, and when it had achieved the proper altitude over the tallest peak, it encountered turbulence. Erin was terrified and clutched Lund's arm while burying her face on his chest. "I'm scared," she cried. "Oh God, please make it stop!"

"We'll be over it in a few minutes," replied Bob in a soft, soothing voice.

Just as quick as it had begun, the tempestuous weather ceased. The announcement to fasten seatbelts was made, and they landed at LAX without further incident. They quickly made their way to the ticket counter and confirmed their seats. Two hours passed quickly, and they were again airborne and headed to Miami.

Their island flight was a Cayman's Airways plane that would deposit them in the Caymans in two hours. The connection was made easily; they retrieved their luggage and were now on the way to the Grand Cayman Resort. The weather was ideal, with temperatures in the eighties, but the air was saturated with moisture, and just sitting in the cab without air conditioning caused them to perspire. They drove through the narrow streets for thirty minutes, seeing an abundance of green everywhere. Bob had been in the desert so long that he was experiencing flora shock, stemming from having been continuously exposed to all shades of desert brown for many years. The lush vegetation seemed to impart a sense of coolness to their skin. There were flowers everywhere, growing on the ground and hanging from nearly every tree. This was a picture-perfect paradise, and they both sponged up the landscape with their eyes.

When they arrived at the hotel, they walked slowly through the massive portals, with the scent of floral bouquet thick in the air. After registering at the desk, they were shown to their room. Their quarters faced the pool and was surrounded by lush tropical trees and plants, but since they had been traveling for the better part of twelve hours, they were now exhausted, so they unpacked their luggage and laid down on the bed, and within five minutes they were both in deep slumber.

The next morning at 8:00 a.m., Bob awakened as it was his California set biorhythm that caused him to open his eyes. After putting on a pair of shorts, he left the room and walked to the front of the hotel. He then jogged about three miles, and when he returned, he was dripping with sweat. Crossing the narrow road, he found himself on Seven Mile Beach. He ran to the water's edge and quickly waded up to his chest. The water had to be eighty-eight degrees, and the surf was gently caressing the white sand with sparkling clear water. The ocean was emerald green, and the sky was royal blue with an occasional cloud here and there. As he swam, he could not help but feel that it wouldn't take much to convince him to stay here.

He walked from the water and felt the warm sand radiate the soles of his bare feet. The air was warm, with a hint of a breeze that stirred through the palm trees dotting the beach. Bob returned to the hotel across the road and met Erin at the pool, and they ate breakfast in the garden patio flourished with trees, plants, and blossoms. She had already avidly read all the tourist material in their room as well as what was available in the lobby. Next they discussed their itineraries and then headed off to visit the turtle breeding grounds that contained a hatchery for sea turtles. Driving up the coast, they noticed large cruise ships heading to port. Erin had already made plans earlier to go to Sting

Ray Village and was excited over the possibility of swimming with the sting rays tomorrow. In the meantime, they explored all the dead ends and out-of-the-way roads on the way to the turtle hatchery. They spent the better part of the day driving around the island after their visit, then upon arrival back at their hotel, they made plans for dinner that evening.

They arrived at the Sunset Restaurant on the north part of the island shortly before seven o'clock. Gaping at the spacious eatery that was located on the beach sprawling over three levels, they entered on the first level and were led to their dinner table. The entire dining area was outside and looked out upon the sea. The bar was situated on the first level, and tables were spread over the second level, which also contained a dance floor. Each level was separated by four steps. They followed the hostess, who made her way toward the left side of the third level, and eventually they found themselves seated at a table facing the sea. In front of them was a small pier on which a crowd was gathering. "Feeding the fish will begin in one minute," blared the speakers. Interested in seeing the activity, Bob and Erin ambled over to the pier, where an employee of the restaurant was standing with a large overflowing bucket of food scraps next to him. He had just begun to reach into the bucket, announcing to all the crowd that he was about to serve the "entree" to the aquatic diners, then he dropped a scoop of food into the water. The water was crystal clear, and the surface was calm, and immediately it became alive with swirls and splashes, with glimpses of large groupers as they dined on their feast. There were thirty fish weighing fifteen to forty pounds competing for each morsel of food.

After the frenzy was over, Bob and Erin returned to their seats and were treated to a dramatic sunset, with the backdrop of the sunset in radiant oranges and blues serving only to highlight the ships anchored in the foreground. They sipped a bottle of local white wine and remained silent for a long time while watching the changing tones of the setting sun. After they each had a glass of wine, they talked. The beauty and majesty of the sight was awe-inspiring and appeared surrealistic. The rays of golden light peered through the clouds on the horizon, and as the sun sank further, purples and blues became interwoven into the fabric of dusk, making the evening exquisitely memorable while they spent most of their time talking to each other.

"I think I could really be happy here," remarked Bob in a whimsical manner.

"You wouldn't have to break my arm either," replied Erin with a smile. She fantasized about the life of the rich on the islands. Yes, she was ready for it. It was long overdue her.

"It could happen real fast now, Erin," said Bob.

"I know, Bob, I've been following all the publicity about the sale in the newspaper."

"I think we will have an offer by the time we return, and if we accept it, we will have our money in a month or so."

"What then?" Erin asked, reaching out for his hand. "What are your plans?"

"Erin, I told you before, I want you to come here to live with me."

"Yes, Yes, Yes," replied Erin. She was flying high. *I can taste it*, she thought.

He leaned across the table and kissed her softly on the lips. She responded by brushing her tongue across his, which promptly led to his suggestion that they take a walk on the beach. He paid the check and they exited the restaurant and strolled toward the white, sandy, shore, removing their shoes and walking hand in hand along the beach while the warm Caribbean waters caressed their feet. They found a secluded cove and took their clothes off. Their lovemaking was intensified by the excitement of all that had transpired between them during dinner. Bob was planning a new life here with Erin, but she had her own views on the matter. She wanted the life of royalty and now she really had access to it.

They spent time together on the beach and exploring the island while each dreamt of a future life in this paradise.

～24～

DR. MARK GAINES REVIEWS DR. KOVACS CARE

Mark Gaines went to the medical records department and asked for the hospital chart on Nelda Johnson. He took the chart and went into the medical staff library across the hall, where he knew it would be quiet. He opened the chart and made notes of events. After his review, he was shocked. Kovacs had turned away from his patient's dire call for help, despite the intensity of phone calls from the nursing staff. There was no question in Mark's mind that Kovacs had been wrong. He had failed to come in and evaluate his patient's hemorrhage, and more so, Kovacs had ordered fresh-frozen plasma in an attempt to control the bleeding that was obviously due to the Mrs. Johnson's use of Motrin. This was inappropriate treatment and indicated how little Kovacs knew about the treatment of bleeders. Motrin was a nonsteroidal anti-inflammatory drug that was a well-known cause of bleeding. It directly affected the response of the platelets, which were necessary in the formation of a clot. The inability for these tiny cells to adhere to each other was the problem that caused continuous bleeding once bleeding began. The real issue here that Mark honed in on was that Kovacs refused to come in and evaluate his postoperative patient. It was axiomatic in surgery that when bleeding occurs postoperatively, a blood vessel wasn't tied off somewhere. Moreover, once bleeding started in a patient with Motrin in their body, it rarely stopped without tying the bleeding vessel. This, of course, meant the patient made an unanticipated return visit to the operating room. Had Kovacs examined his patient, she might have made the return visit to the OR. Gaines dictated a report of his findings and returned the chart. Upon returning to his office, he called Gerry Walker, who was now the newly elected Chief of Staff, and after relating the salient points of his review, Mark then continued.

"Gerry, Kovacs is that bad news guy I told you about before. I left the San Fernando Valley and relocated here because he is worse than incompetent, and he's a butcher as well. This patient could probably have been saved, if he had opened her up and tied the bleeder that he obviously missed the first time," said a distraught Mark.

"All right, calm down, Mark. I want you to meet with me when your report is completed. We will both go to administration and discuss the issue. In the meanwhile, I wouldn't discuss it with anyone else," stated Walker emphatically.

"Fine with me, Gerry, but we've got to get this before the QA Committee so they can kick it up to the Executive Committee," responded Mark.

"We can't do that yet. It must be referred to the Surgical Committee," said Walker.

"What Surgical Committee? We don't have any more general surgeons here," replied Mark.

"But we do have surgical subspecialists—don't forget the urologist, orthopods, ENT, and gynecologist. They are dedicated good surgeons and won't be led astray as to the gravity and stupidity of Kovacs's actions. These guys are not going to let him get away with this. Just cool it until the meeting, Mark. All right?"

"I'll cool it. I hope Mr. Johnson files a malpractice suit against that egotistical moron."

~25~

ALEX COMES HOME

Alex said his goodbyes and headed south on Route 136 to Gunnison. The mountain peaks were still capped with snow, and the meadows alongside the road revealed last year's pasture. A doe with her fawn darted from the protection of the pines into an open meadow, and at the state's fish hatchery, a bald eagle sat alone atop a dead Douglas fir that had succumbed to beetle infestation, awaiting the arrival of her new fingerlings. He turned west on US 50 and drove at the posted speed, because he was in no real hurry to leave Colorado, where he had just spent three wonderful months in bliss away from Erin. He was now, however, feeling slightly uneasy over the prospects of the looming liver transplant. His abdominal swelling had become much more severe, and now he was experiencing more nosebleeds, which were difficult to control. Confusion was a daily event with him as his liver function continued to deteriorate, and his skin showed evidence of bleeding, with large, blue-and-green areas spontaneously occurring over his extremities, and his face was now extremely pale. Shortness of breath and headaches were now also daily occurrences in his life, but after mulling these changes over, he felt much more assured for the need of a new liver.

Colorado was certainly a state with diverse beauty, he thought as he drove past Blue Mesa Reservoir, and when he reached Montrose, he decided to turn south on US Highway 550 to take in the scenic drive rather than to continue north on 50 to Grand Junction. He so hated the desert and was well aware of the long, boring, desert-laden drive from Grand Junction to Palmdale. This was depressing to him, and that was what he really didn't need right now.

Approaching the town of Ridgeway, he was thrilled with the spectacular view of the mountain range at Telluride. The magnificent steepled crags jutted proudly out of the range in defiance to its neighboring mountaintops. In the town of Ouray, he stopped his car to take in the view. One might think they were in the Alps, thought Alex as he gazed upon the mountain splendor. He drove on to Durango and continued west to Cortez, then driving from Cortez to Flagstaff Arizona, he found himself in Navajo desert country. Alex pulled up at the McDonald's in Kayenta, and after a short trip to the men's room, he made his way to the serving counter, where he ordered a cheeseburger and fries. Anxious to make up lost time, he decided to eat while driving.

Spending the night in Flagstaff, he arose at 6:00 a.m. the next morning to get an early start, since he was now only a bit more than four hundred miles from his destination. The desert was boring and the drive between Kingman and Victorville was monotonous, so he stopped at the same gas station in Victorville that he had stopped at when he left California three months earlier. After filling his car with gasoline, he headed west on Palmdale Road. This road was known for its poor visibility due to large dips in the road, which were specifically placed for the runoff during flash flooding. The difficulty was that when you were in the dip, your vision was impeded by the rise in the road directly in front of the car. Needless to say, oncoming drivers had difficulty in visualizing traffic when they were in the troughs as well. Alex was growing weary behind the wheel, and as he passed the town of Phelan, he began to doze for seconds but would awake quickly as the car jerked coming out of the dips. He was about one mile from Route 138 when his eyes were just too heavy to keep open.

∽26∽

Dr. Gaines Sees His First Case of Myasthenia Gravis

Bob Lund had signed out to his partner, Dr. Rick Small. In particular, he had instructed the nurses on the Respiratory Care Unit that Dr. Small was on call for the unit and would also be making weekly rounds on the ventilator patients in his absence. Two days ago, on the first Monday that Dr. Lund was gone, Dr. Small had made rounds on those patients in the respiratory unit, but today he called in sick to his office, explaining to his nurse that he thought he had the flu and went on to describe his myriad of symptoms, which included shortness of breath, chest pain, muscle pain, cough, and fever. He told his nurse to refer any ill patients to the emergency room for care, and since the only patients he had in the hospital were two post-ops, he instructed his nurse to call Dr. Kovacs's office and inform him that he would not be in to see his patients.

As luck would have it, Mr. Babcock spiked a fever of one hundred two point four degrees and had a drop in his blood pressure, and when the unit nurse called the emergency doctor to examine him, he refused to do so.

"I am contracted to work in the emergency room," stated Dr. Spence. "I am not paid to take care of any hospitalized patients."

"Fine, Doctor," replied the nurse, "I'll call administration."

The administrator, Mr. Hendrickson, was not available, and his secretary referred the call to the Chief of Staff, which was standard in matters concerning physicians since this was the appropriate referral for a solution to the problem.

∽145∽

Dr. Walker was very busy seeing patients in his office when he received the call. He listened patiently as the nurse related her problem.

"Well, to tell you the truth, Dr. Spence does have a point," stated Dr. Walker. "His contract with the emergency room physician group excludes the delivery of hospital care unless it is a life-threatening emergency. All ER docs refuse to see hospitalized patients because of the medical liability involved. Malpractice suits in California have been responsible for their position. I will, however, get someone to see Mr. Babcock right away."

He placed a call to Dr. Gaines and asked if he could see Mr. Babcock as a special favor to him and explained that he was already running an hour and a half late in his office appointments. Mark agreed to go to the Respiratory Care Unit and examine Mr. Babcock.

"Hi, I'm Dr. Gaines, and I'm here to see Mr. Babcock," said Gaines. "I have been asked by the Chief of Staff, Dr. Walker, to evaluate and treat Mr. Babcock. Evidently there seems to be some confusion as to who is responsible for his care currently."

"You can say that for sure," responded the nurse sarcastically. "He's in room seven," acknowledged the nurse as she handed him the chart.

Mark had never attended a patient in this unit before. All the patients here were attended to by Drs. Lund and Small. He read the chart and noted that rounds were made once a week on these chronic patients. The patients were looked after primarily by the respiratory therapists and secondarily by the nursing staff, and nursing notes were sparse, as only one per shift was required. He examined the patient and heard coarse rales in the left lung base. A chest x-ray was already done and waiting at the nursing station for him because the nurse had anticipated the x-ray would be requested and she wanted to have it on the unit for the doctor's evaluation. After reading the chart, he became aware that the patient was suffering from myasthenia gravis, as well as chronic obstructive lung disease. Mark looked for the order sheet and found it curiously absent from the chart.

"Where are the order sheets in this chart?" he asked in a nonthreatening demeanor.

"We keep the orders on the nursing station," she replied, handing them to him.

Mark reviewed the ongoing orders and then wrote an order for one of the newer classes of antibiotics and also dictated a consult stating that the chest x-ray was consistent with his clinical findings of left lower-lobe pneumonia. As he left the station, he told the nurses to call him regarding any problems that might occur, and he would be back tomorrow to follow up on Mr. Babcock. Leaving the unit, Mark thought, *that's the first case of myasthenia I have ever seen.*

∽27∽
POOR ALEX

Alex was startled awake by the blast of a semi's horn. He shook his head and felt the beating of his heart and the blood rushing through his body as the adrenaline rush served to stimulate his brain. He was trying to remember how to get to his friend Mike's house. He had made provisions with his friend to live with him for the time being. Ten minutes elapsed, and Alex again felt drowsy. His eyes felt heavy, and then they closed. He was awakened by a loud noise, and for a split second, he saw the tree coming at him and then lost consciousness as the car rolled over on to the shoulder. The front end had met with a tree while traveling at fifty miles per hour. The car then bounced off the tree and rolled over on its roof.

Alex did not move as he hung in the car seat upside down. The left side of his head had met with the door frame and was bleeding profusely. The paramedics removed him from the car and transported him twenty miles to Palmdale Hospital where, upon his arrival to the emergency room, he was found to be in shock.

"What's his pressure?" shouted Dr. Raymond.

"Seventy over forty," responded Marla, the ER nurse.

"He's lost a lot of blood—start two IVs and run Ringer's in one and dextrose and saline in the other." He did a quick neurological exam and determined that there was brain injury. Alex remained unconscious while the ER crew worked on him. The ER clerk found that Alex had been a patient before, and Dr. Gaines had been the attending.

"He has severe liver disease; that's why he bled so much from the scalp wound. He might have internal bleeding as well, in his head," explained Dr. Raymond to his crew. He ordered blood transfusions and a battery of diagnostic tests, and when his pressure was stable, he admitted him to the ICU to the service of Dr. Mark Gaines. The ICU nurse placed a call to Dr. Gaines to inform him of his patient's arrival.

"How bad is he?" asked Gaines.

"Bad," replied the ICU nurse, Judy. "His pressure is holding at ninety, pulse is one twenty. The scalp wound has been sutured but is still oozing a lot. Pressure dressing won't stop it."

"Is he conscious?" inquired Gaines.

"No, and his pupils are very dilated," replied Judy.

"I'll be right over," said Gaines.

Thirty minutes later Mark Gaines walked into the ICU.

"Where is he?" Gaines asked.

"He's in bed eight, Dr. Gaines," replied Judy as she accompanied him to the bedside carrying the chart and a verbal report on the CAT scan of the head done earlier that evening.

Dr. Gaines scanned the handwritten report. It said *normal without evidence of subdural hematoma.*

"I just can't believe this," said Gaines, confiding in Judy. "He was returning here for a liver transplant." Gaines took a bright light from his pocket and shined it into the pupils. There was very little response. He noted that when he touched his extremities, they went into spasm. Saddened by this physical finding, and the normal CAT scan, he thought about the ominous clinical significance that since there was no bleeding under the fibrous membrane covering of the brain, surgical release of pressure was not an option.

Concluding his examination, he then wrote a page of orders. Mark surmised that the extensive blood loss had been the result of the inability of Alex's blood to clot caused by the liver's failure to make clotting factors, and upon further thought, he realized that the shock from the blood loss had caused the central nervous system to be deprived of oxygen and thus the present state of brain damage. He ordered intravenous barbiturates, as this had been reported in the literature to enhance healing injured brains such as this.

The gravity of his diagnosis was confirmed by the presence of pathological reflexes. Mark walked to the nearby desk, began to dictate his findings and, when he had finished, wrote a longhand progress note, stated his diagnosis, and concluded with "prognosis guarded." After completing an exhaustive list of orders aimed at restoring hemodynamic stability and brain function, he started to leave the unit, but as an afterthought, he turned to the nurse and spoke.

"Judy, will you call his wife and let her know he's here?"

"Ah Doctor, may I speak to you privately, please?" she replied.

"Certainly," he answered and walked to her desk and sat down. "What is it?"

"Doctor, it's common gossip in the hospital that Alex's wife Erin went to the Caribbean with Dr. Lund. They are having an affair; didn't you know?"

"Oh my God, I forgot all about that!" replied Gaines.

"Well, what do you want to do?" she asked.

Mark remembered the admonition that Alex had given him about his father, D.r Kovacs. He had been instructed not to give him any information about his health.

Mark Gaines was examining Mr. George Babcock the next day and was pleased to see he was responding to the antibiotics, fever was gone, and his vital signs were now almost normal. Satisfied with the improvement, he told the nurse that he would be back daily.

The week had come and gone, and Mark found himself depressed over the fact that Alex had not responded. The hospital administrator had been notified of the gravity of Alex's condition and had taken it upon himself to notify Dr. Kovacs about his son. Kovacs thanked him for the call and promptly went to the ICU to see Alex. He wasn't quite prepared for what awaited him when he saw Alex attached to a respirator, and a catheter connected his bladder to a collection bag that hung on the bed railing, while a central IV line entered his left chest just below the collarbone and from it were multiple ports, all connected with tubing that led to the plastic bottles hanging from the IV pole. There was IV tubing that ran from the left mid-arm directly to the video monitor. Overhead was a video, digital, and graphic display of blood pressure, central venous pressure, electrocardiograph, and pulse oximetry.

He asked the nurse for Alex's chart and, after staring at Alex for less than a minute, sat down at the nurses' station and read the chart, and when he concluded, he was forced to admit that Mark Gaines was indeed a fine young doctor. He was impressed with Mark's treatment and assessment of the clinical problems his son had presented, but despite his admiration for his medical skills, Kovacs still harbored hate for Gaines over the incident at Woodland Community Hospital some months ago. He didn't feel any emotion for Alex but was angry that Erin had not been notified.

"I'm very sorry," said Anne Rogers the ICU shift supervisor.

"Don't be, he was probably drunk and deserves what he got," replied Kovacs with hostility.

Anne Rogers just walked away, stunned at his response. She couldn't believe that a parent could respond in such an uncaring and vicious manner, but after considering the source, she shook her head and tried to quell her anger.

Dr. Small remained at home all week, and on Monday, he again called his office to report that he was still very sick. He had gone to his own physician, who had diagnosed pneumonia and felt that he wouldn't be able to return to work for another week. Dr. Walker again passed this information on to Mark and convinced him to make the weekly rounds on the Respiratory Care Unit for Rick Small, so Mark agreed and promised he would get to the unit sometime that day.

Later that afternoon, Dr. Gaines presented himself at the nursing station of the Respiratory Care Unit and asked Roxanne, the unit nurse, to accompany him on rounds. They went to the first room, and Gaines reviewed the patient's status with the nurse and was shocked to discover that the nurses were pretty ignorant when it came to the patient's care plan and that the care of these patients was assigned to the respiratory therapists. The only time the nurses became involved was when a patient developed an acute problem, and that was a rare occurrence. The respiratory therapists wrote all the ventilator orders, and Drs. Lund and Small signed them without question. The motionless bodies lay in beds and remained in this world through the continuous oxygen delivery accomplished by machines.

Gaines was informed by Roxanne that the state had transferred their patients to one of their own chronic respiratory care facilities and that currently, most of the fifteen patients were paid for by private insurance. Roxanne was impressed with the degree of thoroughness Dr. Gaines demonstrated in each patient. He came to the bed of Mr. Peter Bunkin and read his chart, but his perusing stopped abruptly at the end of the physical examination report, where at the bottom of the page, the diagnosis of myasthenia gravis jumped out at him. Astonished that this was another patient with this very rare disease, he rubbed his brow while he considered the possibilities. The diagnosis was so rare that the possibility of two patients with this disease on this unit would be remote, or the diagnosis was incorrect.

He reviewed the data in the chart with a special eye toward the medical evaluation. It was a medical fact that the illness was found more frequently in women than in men by a ratio of three to two, which also mitigated against the reality of two men with this illness in the unit. The patient's history, as recorded by Dr. Lund, made mention that the patient had the illness diagnosed many years ago. Since it wasn't a recently discovered illness, there would not be the necessity to perform any special tests or procedures to confirm a disease that was chronic. Obviously, the workup had been done years earlier at the time the diagnosis had been initially established.

Gaines then reviewed the chart of George Babcock and, after he had finished his review, became intrigued in the similarities of both patients. Something was gnawing at Mark as he closed the chart and handed it to Roxanne. He was exhausted since he had been working since five that morning and thoughts were racing around in his head, but none would remain still long enough for him to focus on them. He walked out of the unit and welcomed the cool early evening air as it stroked his face gently, while at the same time it served to clear his mind.

In the days that followed, Mark Gaines stood hopelessly by while Alex progressed deeper into coma. One EEG confirmed the diagnosis of permanent brain injury due to poor oxygenation suffered as the result of hemorrhagic shock, but two EEGs had confirmed the diagnosis. Alex was now in a vegetative state and would probably remain that way until his liver failed completely. He had come so close to having a new life through a liver transplant. Mark felt that Alex's accident might have been the result of disturbed brain function from his cirrhotic liver, as this happened frequently as a result of a rising ammonia level, which is toxic to the brain.

He blamed himself for not insisting that Alex obtain liver function tests before he left Colorado. If the tests were extremely abnormal, he would have convinced Alex to fly home or at least have someone else drive. In seeking to diffuse his own guilt, Mark thought about the UCLA transplant program and how long it took to get a final interview for acceptance into the program. He had undergone the initial medical evaluation some three months or more before they ever informed him of the need for a second evaluation.

If only they had done it earlier, perhaps Alex would already have undergone the liver transplant. He was really frustrated with all the red tape in the system. It seemed paradoxical that the very institution that held out hope was the same one that might have contributed to Alex's present state of hopelessness. Mark was very aware that Alex's liver had very little time left.

∼28∼

US Care Makes Purchase Offer

Bob Lund was already back to work and in the process of catching up with the latest happenings. He was shocked to learn of Alex's grave condition. He had been weaned from respirator support and was now ready for the skilled nursing unit, which was part of the chronic care center, so Mark placed a call to Bob Lund.

"Glad you're back," said Mark. "We were pretty busy while you were gone."

"Really. How so?" replied Lund with interest.

"For openers, Rick Small has been out for almost two weeks now with pneumonia. There was no one to make rounds on the Respiratory Care Unit or to attend to emergencies either, so I was drafted by the Chief of Staff for that assignment."

There was a prolonged silence on the phone while Lund sat in shock. He never counted on the possibility that Small wouldn't be available to look after these patients. He felt a sense of panic, his heart was pounding, and he could feel every heartbeat. In a short time, Bob was breathing rapidly, but soon he brought his reflexes under control and finally responded.

"Ah, did everything go all right?" He was afraid of the answer and cringed as Mark responded to his question.

"In general, yes, but I do have a few issues that I'd like to speak to you about in person. I thought that maybe we could get together over lunch and discuss them," said Mark.

"Sure, Mark, just give me a chance to catch up on things around here, okay," pleaded Lund.

"Sure thing. Why don't you give me a call when you are free."

"I'll do that, Mark. Catch you later," replied Lund as he hung up the phone.

Bob Lund paced in his office as he replayed the conversation again in his mind. He didn't know what Mark had seen in the unit, but he was certain that whatever it had been was the reason he wanted to meet with him. It was not knowing that was driving Lund crazy. He tried to think of appropriate answers to Mark's questions that he conjured up in his mind. After ten minutes, he decided that he should set up a meeting with his partners to discuss this new development.

The common gossip on the hospital grapevine was that Dr. Kovacs was under investigation by the Quality Management Department and the QA Medical Staff Committee, and Mark Gaines had completed his review and had submitted his written report of the death of Mrs. Nelda Johnson. Dr. Kovacs was not well-regarded by the hospital staff. They all found him to be very arrogant as well as self-centered, not to mention that his surgical skills on the scale of one to ten were rated by the OR personnel to be five.

The QA Department nurse manager was a fiery woman short in stature, with an uncanny ability to see through the standard barrage of subterfuge and smoke that many doctors were expert in producing. As a result of her candor and cut-to-the-quick approach, she was feared and revered by most of the medical staff. They were aware that Peggy Drew could always find the missing link that had been cleverly hidden by the doctors.

It was her insistence that the mandates of the Joint Commission on Accreditation of Healthcare Organizations be followed to the letter, and her vigilance over the hospital's QA department had come to be appreciated by the administration as well as the medical staff. This became more apparent each time they were awarded their three-year accreditation by JCAHO. One of the many criteria that was monitored was complications occurring during or after procedures. This meant that the case must be reviewed by a physician of the medical staff and then referred to the QA Committee, where the reviewers were usually those doctors who were assigned to the QA Committee and others who were to testify.

The computer had identified Ralph Hadley because of the stroke during the angiogram and the poor outcome from surgery. Mrs. Janet Childs and Mrs. Nelda Johnson were also on the list because they had expired after surgery as well. The death of Nelda Johnson had already been signed out for review because of the notice of concern that was filed by the nursing supervisor. She shook her head when she scanned the report. In the last month, Dr. Kovacs had three serious complications. She knew that this was well above the complication rates for all the hospital medical staff combined, and now with great concern, she pulled the medical records and reviewed them. When she finished, she was convinced that there was evidence of serious error and called the Chief of Staff to discuss her suspicions.

Dr. Walker listened to Peggy's summary of the deaths; he was appalled to hear what she had to say. In no uncertain terms she attributed the deaths to the incompetence of Dr. Kovacs. After digesting the data and asking questions, he instructed Peggy to ask Dr. Gaines if he would review the two charts. He knew that it would be impossible for her to obtain an unbiased and competent review from most of the doctors on staff. They were too involved with their own practices and would never devote the time necessary to properly review a case, and who knew who Dr. Kovacs's alliances were, but he had also fought with some many times before. It was always those physicians that never contributed to the functions of the medical staff that complained the loudest about medical staff obligations. The medical staff work was done by three or four doctors, and all the others eternally griped about every issue.

Walker felt an uneasiness that crept into his soul. There was something about Kovacs he had disliked from the first time he had met him. His intuition did not evolve from what his friend Mark had told him; it was his attitude that had always been present that, given enough rope, a bad doctor would hang himself. He had also been fond of telling his colleagues that a leopard doesn't change its spots.

Gerry Walker took his position as Chief of Staff very seriously. State and federal law mandated that the Chief was responsible for all the patient care rendered by the medical staff, and he knew that he had to get to the bottom of this, and fast. Peggy assured him she would stay on top of the investigation, and if she had any problems, she promised to notify him. Feeling very disturbed about it all, Gerry took solace in the fact that these problems had not gone undetected and indeed they were now in competent hands.

The meeting had been requested by US Care for the purpose of making a presentation to the three doctor owners. Mr. Norman Sydney made the presentation.

"Thank you, gentlemen, for allowing us to make this presentation on such short notice," said Sydney. "Our due diligence has been concluded, and we wish to present our offer at this time. As you know, you will have three days to accept or reject our proposal. Our offer is as follows: The private practice is valued at three hundred fifty dollars per head, and there are twenty-two thousand patients. This amounts to seven million seven hundred thousand dollars. We value the acute hospital, chronic care, skilled nursing unit, and the chronic respiratory care unit at fourteen million dollars. The total is twenty-one million seven hundred thousand dollars.

"That is the net figure to us, right?" asked Bob Lund.

"Yes, with some minor adjustments," answered Sydney.

"Now this will all be cash at the closing, no stock, no options, or notes, correct?" asked Lund. He wanted to be very certain that this dream was for a real.

"All cash deal," answered Sydney.

Dr. Kovacs was deep in private thought. While he saw his partners excited over the offer, his enthusiasm was dampened by the thought of having to remain in practice another two years. He was aware he was being reviewed for his quality of care and was not happy about it at all; even though the thought of seven million dollars wasn't enough to elevate his spirits.

"Doctors, if you decide to accept our offer, we will want to see this transaction closed in thirty days," said Sydney.

"Thank you for coming, Mr. Sydney. We will have our attorney contact you." The meeting was then adjourned.

Erin Kovacs found out about her husband the morning after she arrived home, when Bob Lund called her to break the news. She went to the hospital immediately to visit Alex, and when she saw him, she fainted. Recognition was almost an impossibility. Alex looked grotesque—his face was bloated and now golden-yellow in color, and his skin had large blue, yellow areas dispersed throughout his body; in addition, there was a tube exiting from almost every orifice.

The ICU nurse administered smelling salts, and after she awoke, Erin sat and wept. Guilt had found its mark and now was exacting its toll. She never thought she would be affected in this manner, and after a while she got up and quietly left the ICU. Dr. Gaines had informed her that he didn't expect Alex to live much longer than a few months—he was still in deep coma from the accident and his liver wasn't any better, so it was only a matter of time.

The following morning, she called her attorney and told him about Alex. He suggested that she file for a conservatorship so she could then execute all documents she might have to sign for Alex. In addition, she would be able to cash her husband's disability checks. She authorized him to file the request with the court. After receiving an affidavit from Dr. Gaines that Alex was in a permanent state of coma, the court acted favorably upon the request, and Alex was eventually transferred to the skilled nursing unit.

Erin quickly got over her brief episode of grief for Alex and tried to put him out of her mind. She had more important things to think about.

~29~

ANOTHER QA PROBLEM

"**D**r. Gaines, this is Peggy Drew in QA."

"Hi Peggy; what's going on?"

"We have a real problem physician in our midst, and I need your help," responded Peggy.

"Uh-oh, I smell a rat, and its initials are HK, right?" asked Gaines.

"You are very perceptive, Doctor," said Peggy.

"Let me guess. You want me to review another chart," said Gaines.

"Almost, but not totally correct. There are two charts," said Peggy.

"You've got to be kidding. I know about one through the grapevine concerning a lady who died after some type of bowel surgery," said Gaines in a voice of condemnation.

"The other one is Mr. Hadley, who stroked once while the good doctor was doing an angiogram and then stroked again during surgery," said Peggy with disgust.

"Can you get someone else to review at least one of these charts?" pleaded Gaines.

"I wish I could, Doctor, but tell me, who should I ask to do it?" she begged.

"I know what you're saying. There is no one that can be trusted to do the job and let the chips fall where they may. Since Kovacs is one of the major owners here, no one wants to take him on, and everyone is running scared, right? No one wants to lose their referrals, and if they report the truth, Kovacs will make sure they never get any more referrals."

"For only being here such a short time, you are extremely perceptive," replied Peggy.

"I have run this course before with Kovacs. He will say that I am biased against him when these cases come to committee. What will we do then?" asked Gaines.

"I wouldn't worry about that now, Doctor. We need to get your detailed reviews on each case. If your reports confirm they are as bad as I think they are, we may have to do something quick to stop this maniac," said Peggy.

"What do you mean by 'quick,'" asked Gaines.

"Well, we must determine if he represents an ongoing danger or threat to patients. I will bring your reviews to the Surgery Committee right away. If they fail to act, then the Chief of Staff will have to hold an Executive Committee meeting to decide whether his privileges should be summarily suspended. At that time, you would have to deliver your findings in person and, of course, Dr. Kovacs will be there to defend himself. Thank God that Dr. Walker is the Chief of Staff this year. He won't be influenced by administration to soft pedal the issue. He is a well-rounded experienced physician who takes his position seriously and will do the right thing," stated Peggy.

"The medical staff also holds him in high esteem, and they all know his ethical standards and honesty govern his leadership," said Gaines in support of his friend.

"Will you please do the reviews?" asked Peggy.

"Okay, Peggy, I'll do them, but I won't be able to get to them until next week," replied Gaines.

"Fine, Dr. Gaines. I'll have the charts pulled for you when you are ready. Please call me the day before you want them."

"I'll do that, Peggy. I've got to go now. Bye," answered Gaines, and he hung up the phone.

Well, it looks like it's time for Kovacs to pay the piper, thought Mark.

～30～
ERIN'S AND BOB'S PLANS FOR THE FUTURE

Bob Lund picked Erin up at her condo and drove to Ventura to spend the day. The weather had changed rapidly, and now at the end of April, it was over eighty degrees. They drove north on the Antelope Valley Freeway and noted the exquisite display of orange, blue, and yellow flowers that covered the low hillside along the freeway. It was as if someone had brushed the area with paint. It was poppy season; the rains had been generous throughout the winter continuing right up to March, and a good display was usually seen in the Antelope Valley about every three years. This was the desert's response to the winter and spring rainfall and the reward to those who endured life in "Brownsville."

A carpet of bright orange gleamed in the morning sun, with an occasional patch of golden yellow. The blue, purple, and white flowers clustered amid the poppies were so spectacular that Erin asked Bob to stop the car so she could take pictures. She got out of the car and pointed to a dirt road that wound its way up the small mountain.

"Look, Bob, isn't that someone with a white horse over there?" she asked, pointing to the mountain.

"Let's walk over and see," he answered.

They walked to the path and followed it to the place where they saw the white horse, and when they got there, they noticed a large horse trailer parked off to the side. There were four beautiful Arabian horses tied individually to the trailer. A young, attractive blonde woman was riding the white stallion through the orange poppy fields while a photographer was taking pictures. When he had finished his photo shoot, she repeated the process with each of the other horses. They watched while the still photos were taken, and when the shoot was done, video camera filming began. The horses pranced and loped through the orange fields, snorting all the while. Their tails were held high in the air, calling attention to the fact that they were the aristocracy of all horses—a proud breed born from the spirit of the wind with the heart of a champion and the splendor of graceful motion. They were indeed the exotic Arabian horse. Bob and Erin gazed upon the sight for a long while and finally returned to the car.

"You know Erin, I never realized what a cheapskate Kovacs is," said Bob out of the blue.

"How so," she answered. *I will have horses like that*, thought Erin.

"Well, during our discussions about our partnership, Rick Small and I tried to get Kovacs to agree to a buy-sell agreement," replied Bob, shaking his head slowly from side to side.

"What is a buy-sell agreement anyhow?" asked Erin.

"It's an agreement whereby an insurance policy is purchased on each of our lives and the owner and beneficiary of the policy is the partnership. That way, if I die, the insurance company pays the partnership the face value of the policy and that money can be used to buy out any family or relative that might make a claim against the two remaining partners for an interest. None of us want to ever have a relative as a partner, and this would prohibit that from ever happening. Money has a way of solving those problems fast."

"Okay, I follow that so far," Erin said.

"Well, not only did Kovacs refuse to go along with us and buy insurance, but he gave us his reason, which proves he is nuts as far as I'm concerned."

"Tell me; I can't wait to hear this. I think he is a pompous egomaniac anyway," she said with a smirk on her face. She thought of the money she might have had some day, if Kovacs had only been a real father to Alex.

"He said he has no family, and that he had disowned his son. That's not all," he continued. "He hates all lawyers and would never trust any of them. He despises them so much that he doesn't even have a will and doesn't care if the state gets his money when he dies. As you are probably also privy to, he hates charities and thinks they are all rip-offs. This man is a sick puppy," said Bob. He took her hand and led her back to their car.

Bob drove on in silence and exited at Route 126, which took him through Canyon Country and placed him on the 5 Freeway northbound. He drove a few exits past Magic Mountain and then exited to continue 126 to Ventura. They passed orange groves and soon were past Fillmore and on the Ventura Freeway headed west. Lund found the right exit and he pulled into the parking area for the beach, and they walked to the beach and spread a blanket on the white sand. The sun was high in the sky and there was a light breeze; here the temperature was seventy-five degrees, but in the direct sunshine it felt like ninety.

Erin began to read a novel that she had started a week ago and Lund attempted to read a medical journal. After ten minutes, Bob spoke.

"Erin, I've got some news for you."

"What's that, Bob?"

"Well, for openers, we have accepted the offer for the purchase of the hospital and practice. And we should sign the papers in sixty days or so," said Bob proudly.

"That's great, what then?" she asked coyly.

"I would like to kick back for a while, then plan to move to the Caribbean. Are you game?" he asked.

"I certainly am. I can't leave until Alex dies. I feel I owe him that." She paused in silence. "You look concerned, Bob."

"I am worried about something, Erin. Do you know Dr. Gaines?"

"Yes, he took care of Alex when he was in the ICU," said Erin.

"He's a bright, good doctor, and I think he may be on to something," said Bob.

"What do you mean?" asked Erin.

"Remember what I told you about some of the patients in the Respiratory Care Unit?"

"Yes, you told me about some of the patients you had in the unit when we were in the Caymans," replied Erin.

"Gaines might be trying to stir up a hornet's nest now. He wants to talk to me about some problems in the unit," said Bob.

"So what?" replied Erin.

"He may be too smart for his own good, and I'm worried that he might start to suspect things," said Bob.

"Well, you won't be there, so don't worry," she replied.

"I sure hope you are right about not being there," said Lund with some uncertainty in his voice. She extended her hand and placed it on top of his with a squeeze. "I'll bet your sale will be final before sixty days," said Erin with confidence. She looked into his eyes and smiled.

"I feel much better now that we've talked about these uncertainties," sighed Bob. He leaned over and kissed her lightly on the forehead.

"Are you definite about the move to the Caribbean?" she asked.

"Not only about the move, but listen to this idea, Erin," he answered with excitement. "I want to lease a yacht and crew to sail all over the Caribbean for a few months. Are you willing?"

"I love it," cried Erin with joy. "What a blast sailing to all the islands where we can swim and fish or just do nothing all day long."

"You got it, Toyota," replied Bob with a laugh. He was at ease and no longer felt threatened about the future.

"Let's get something to eat; I'm starved," said Bob, getting up and extending his hand to help Erin.

"Thanks. Let's go find a restaurant," Erin said as she took his hand and stood up. She shook out the blanket and they walked to the car hand in hand. They decided to drive to Santa Barbara and spend the night. Checking into the Franciscan Inn, they were pleased to find their room charming, and as an added plus, they were within walking distance of the beach. They walked down Bath Street and turned to the right on Cabrillo Boulevard. It was almost six o'clock, and the dinner crowd hadn't overwhelmed the restaurants yet. The temperature had dropped to the high seventies, and the wind was still.

They found themselves standing in front of Ernesto's, a small Italian restaurant, which was confirmed by their nostrils when the door was opened by exiting patrons. The aroma of garlic stimulated their hunger to inordinate proportions, and they entered the Bistro salivating. The meal was superb, and the wine equally as great. They talked about the future, and although Erin had her own designs, she let him think she was in complete accord.

The next week found Erin in a state of indecisiveness. She had watched a news broadcast that was reporting the death of a wealthy gentleman who left no will. The only son and heir was given the inheritance, since California law recognized the next of kin as the lawful heir. She suddenly began to think about her own financial situation and wished she could be an heiress. The only problem with that, she thought, was that she had no rich relatives who were about to die. Or did she? She wished that Alex at least had an insurance policy naming her as the beneficiary, but it just wasn't the case.

She fantasized about what it would be like to be wealthy and never have to work again, then she could travel and live anywhere in the world. Maybe even have a few homes so as not to get too bored in one place. *After all, I deserve it*, she said aloud and was surprised to hear her voice expressing her innermost thoughts. As her mind played out her fantasies, she became caught up in them and allowed her emotions to take over. She saw herself surrounded by servants and expensive cars, clothes and jewelry, and she visualized herself as a woman much sought after by handsome elegant men, then she fell asleep with her mind crammed with delusions of grandeur.

After a refreshing nap, she awakened and poured herself her favorite mixed drink, The Godfather, aptly named in that it ruled the consumer after a few minutes. It was two parts Chivas Regal Scotch and one part Amaretto Liqueur on the rocks. She swirled the drink with her finger and then sipped the cool liquid. The first sensation was the cold, that was immediately chased by an intense warm glow produced by the alcohol. It was this contrast that appealed so much to Erin. After two sips, she began to think about her fantasy again. She could not get it out of her mind and was consumed with the thought of money. For years she had wrestled with that deadly sin, but never did succeed in its conquest. Erin had always been jealous of anyone who was wealthy or who owned expensive clothes or cars.

～31～
Erin Revises the Plan

Erin was now feeling anxious about Alex and about Bob. Although she had come to the realization that she would do anything in order to endear herself to Bob, she still wasn't sure he would ever consider marriage. She wanted that more than anything because of the financial security it represented. What if he threw her over for someone else? He had a reputation of doing just that to many unsuspecting women over the years.

She sighed to herself and let her mind wander. Before long she recalled the recent news story about the son who became an heir to a fortune by virtue of California law. The law provided that when a deceased left an estate without a will to indicate the heirs, the state defined the heir. When there was only one live family member, the choice was easy. Suddenly her mind began to race as she considered various possibilities. If her husband Alex had inherited a fortune, she would get it all as soon as he died. That shouldn't be long from now, according to Doctor Gaines.

She rapidly shifted her thinking toward Alex's father, Dr. Kovacs. That bastard was about to become very wealthy when the hospital was sold, and Bob had told her that Kovacs, Small, and himself were going to make about seven million dollars each on the sale. She also had learned from Bob that Kovacs had also made a small fortune when the Woodland Community Hospital was sold a few months ago. *That jerk is a millionaire,* she thought aloud. *He has no family or living relatives except Alex. God, isn't that just my luck. I have a rich father-in-law and a pauper for a husband.*

It hit her like a lightning bolt. An idea that was beginning to unfold in her mind was now flashing like a neon sign. *If Kovacs died, Alex would be the heir to his estate.* When Alex died, she would inherit it all. Now there was excitement in her very being, now feeling more alive than she had felt in years. It was possible that she might yet become that lady of leisure. There was something wrong with this scenario—in the recesses of her mind something wasn't just right, but she just couldn't put her finger on it. The more she tried to seek the solution, the more confused she became about her entire fantasy.

The next morning, she was still uncertain about something, but she still could not identify what was bothering her. Erin placed a call to her attorney and asked him a few questions. "Yes," he had told her, "If her husband died, she would inherit all his estate according to state law." He asked her if Alex had a will, and she told him that he didn't. Then it suddenly was clear. The missing piece of the puzzle that had remained so elusive was staring her in the face. She thanked Mr. Bixby and hung up the phone.

Of course, Bob had given her the answer and she hadn't seen it. Her father-in-law hated lawyers and did not have a will. Bob had told her Kovacs had said that he would rather that the state gets his money than give it to anyone himself. Kovacs was a loner and a miser—no wonder he didn't have any friends. He had amassed his wealth by working his entire life and was one of those people who relished counting their money more than enjoying the life of luxury that it could provide. *Well, let's see if I can't help you in that area.*

Dr. Gaines informed her that Alex was holding his own but that many times things looked better before they became worse. She felt a twinge of panic when she heard him say that. Her mind turned to the thought of at least seven million dollars and quite possibly more. If Alex were to die before his father, she would not inherit a dime, but if she were to inherit anything at all, it would have to come from her father-in-law. This meant that Dr. Kovacs must die before Alex, so that his son would inherit his father's estate, and thus in this manner, she would inherit the estate from Alex, since she was his wife. Suddenly she recalled that Kovacs had an insurance buy-out policy that enabled the remaining partners, Bob and Rick, to buy her out also. She did not want to mention this now to Bob, because there was a good possibility that he could easily influence his partner, Rick, not to mention this to Erin; therefore, the two of them could share the policy seven-million-dollar amount. She would wait for a time and then decide whether to get her lawyer involved. If she did this, she would lose Bob—of that, she was certain—but if she could get another seven million from the insurance, since she was the only Kovacs survivor, it would be available to pursue. After all, she was the queen, and all that was rightfully hers.

She shuddered to think how close she came to obtaining the divorce, and she understood very well that she almost blew the whole thing. Fate was on her side, and now she had to figure a way to help fate complete its course. She didn't have all the time in the world to develop an elegant plan because Alex was about to die, and she needed a way to help Kovacs get there first. The race was on, and the clock was ticking.

There must be someone she could trust to kill Kovacs. There had to be people that could be hired for that purpose.

<h1 style="text-align:center">~32~
It All Comes to Roost</h1>

Mark Gaines called Peggy Drew in the QA Department and asked her to get the charts of the two patients he was to review. She told him she would have them in her office that afternoon, and he could review them right there. The next day he entered Peggy's office to find her deeply immersed in chart reviews herself. She was involved with assisting the quality action team design a study. The new buzzwords were now quality improvement, and the teams were designed to identify problem areas within the hospital, define the issues through a specific plan of study, collect the data, and propose a solution to the problems by instituting specific measures and actions with appropriate monitoring.

American medicine had finally come to realize what the auto Japanese industry had understood fifty years ago, when anything made in Japan was laughed at by Americans, because the Japanese products were made poorly and cheaply. As a result of the failure of the Japanese market to compete in any meaningful fashion, they sought ways to improve. At about the same time, Mr. Edward Deming, a US citizen, had attempted to sell his ideas of continued quality improvement to American automobile manufacturers, because America was becoming very wary of the auto manufacturers. The cars were mechanical nightmares with planned obsolescence, which they continued to sell to the US consumers.

There were no other competitors at that time, so the CEOs in Detroit asked why they should change anything when their sales were booming? When Deming presented his plan to improve the quality of the American-made automobiles, he was laughed at by Detroit, but eventually he presented his quality-improvement plan to the Japanese industrial society, and they hired him as their consultant. His ideas were readily incorporated into all their industry, with the results that are apparent today.

The Japanese manufacturers appealed to the consumer, and by orienting manufacturing in that direction, they gained immense proportions of the US and world markets in a variety of competing manufacturing areas. The Japanese products were of better quality, lasted longer, required fewer repairs, produced much fewer complaints, did not have the American incorporated planned obsolescence, and were competitive in price. American automobile sales fell as the imports took their market share.

American medicine has come to realize the importance of quality management, and eventually the Joint Commission on the Accreditation of Healthcare Organizations—JCAHO, as it is called—mandated that every hospital demonstrate quality of care through active performance-improvement principals. This has now become the focal point of the American hospital and private medical practice. The quality management department has awesome responsibilities within each institution because they are involved in every area of hospital function. The medical staff must now look at all aspects of hospital activity and determine those areas that are problem prone, high risk, or high volume and ascertain ways to make them better.

Peggy handed the charts to Mark and said, "Here you are, Doctor; I hope you enjoy these novels."

"Thank you. I'll get out of your way now and use the desk in the corner," said Mark.

He opened the first chart and began to make notes. He read the history and looked at the physical findings of Janet Childs. He kept moving between the nurses notes and the orders and wrote furiously on a legal pad. He read the emergency doctor's dictated report, which included an extensive history of the patient's present illness. Mrs. Childs said she had undergone a colonoscopy with biopsy of polyps three days ago and had seen Kovacs in his office daily, complaining of pain. She told the ER doctor her blood pressure was in the seventies earlier that day in Kovacs office, and he assured her that if she stopped her Lopressor blood pressure pill, her pressure would improve. She also told

Kovacs she had had no bowel movement for three days, and she was also experiencing sweating with chills and fever. Mark was in shock when he read this. How could that idiot have missed what was going on? Why hadn't he admitted the woman then? Further reading of the chart upset him greatly. This patient had obviously suffered a necrotic burn injury to the wall of the cecum (the first portion of the large intestine). It was a well-known dictum that the cecum had a very thin wall, and perforations easily occur in that area. He read the operative report that described exactly what had occurred. Kovacs reported he had met with difficulty in attempting to isolate the stalk of the polyp and elevate it from the wall of the cecum. The large, flat polyp was electro-coagulated, and the current also burned the cecum. This led to symptoms of bowel injury that were all overlooked by Kovacs. The bowel then ruptured and spilled its bacterial contents into the peritoneal cavity. She died of sepsis that could have been avoided if the patient had been admitted and treated two days earlier. Mark couldn't believe Kovacs was so stupid that he fixed blame on the low blood pressure to her blood pressure medication rather than to the spreading infection. Of course, Kovacs had a bad case of the Jehovah Complex, which precluded him from ever being the cause of a problem, since God is perfect. He closed the chart and closed his eyes. *Kovacs has got to be stopped.*

With renewed fervor, Mark rapidly reviewed the chart of Ralph Hadley. Anyone could develop an embolus to the brain while undergoing a neck angiogram, but since Kovacs was performing the procedure, Mark suspected there might be other factors and was critical of Kovacs's decision to operate immediately on Mr. Hadley's carotid in the face of an acute stroke.

The damage was already done. A piece of clot had left home and found its way into a peripheral arterial structure where it lodged, causing an obstruction to the further passage of blood. The brain tissue dependent upon blood supply from that vessel had died. There was nothing further to be gained by doing a bypass on the carotid artery at that time. Kovacs's judgment was flawed. This was not the standard of practice for this emergency, but the administration of the anticoagulant heparin was. In addition to the lack of appropriateness for performing the endarterectomy, Kovacs had subjected Hadley to the complications of general anesthesia. Central nervous system dysfunction was already evident by virtue of the embolus, but it had been amplified by the anesthetic.

Mark briefly discussed his findings with Peggy. "This guy is nuts," said Mark.

"I told you we were dealing with a bad one," said Peggy.

"I can't believe anyone can be this bad. Stupid is probably a more appropriate term," Mark hastened to add.

"Two deaths and one vegetable in the chronic respiratory unit," said Peggy.

"That reminds me . . . what do you know about that unit?" asked Mark.

"Not much. We don't get involved with the chronic care facility."

"I have a lot of questions about it, and I'm not getting any answers," said Mark.

"Getting back to our problem at hand, I will bring these issues to the Surgical Committee next week. Hopefully, the surgeons will do a decent job and come up with recommendations to deal with Kovacs," said Peggy.

"I sure hope so," replied Mark as he started to leave the office.

"If they don't deal with it appropriately, we still have a chance," said Peggy. "The minutes of their committee must go to Quality Management Committee. We will deal with it there, if need be."

The meeting was held in the small conference room located in the chronic care facility. This area also housed the medical records department, a dictating office, and a small, comfortable staff library. Busy doctors always held their meetings at noon because the surgeons were busy operating in the mornings. Lunch was provided, and the attendance was 100 percent. The grapevine had spread the word that the committee would be reviewing the work of the new surgeon on the block.

Dr. Kovacs had rapidly managed to alienate most of the hospital employees, nurses, and staff doctors. His pompous attitude toward the nursing staff, as well as his colleagues, alienated them all. His surgical technique had also been the subject of the hospital gossip. It was recognized by everyone that he was devoid of empathy and showed little insight as well. He continually refused to respond to the pleas of his colleagues when they tried in vain to communicate with him in writing through various committees. It had become so bad that he had difficulty in finding a physician to assist him in surgery. No one wanted to be brow-beaten any longer by this monster.

He had received notice that he was to attend the committee for the purpose of defending his clinical decisions pertaining to Nelda Johnson, Janet Childs, and Ralph Hadley. The committee was composed of five physicians and the hospital Administrator, Bill Hendrickson. Hendrickson was a nonvoting member, as was the director of nurses and the operating room nursing supervisor. All medical staff meetings were attended by Peggy Drew, who, in most of the meetings, was the only one who spoke armed with the facts. This aggravated many of the doctors, who were usually influenced by friendship and economics. They would not do anything that might jeopardize their referral patterns. Status quo was their game, and it took real guts for them to depart from this norm. They reveled in the same old cliches such as "let's trend this problem," or "this complication is expected."

The committee members were Drs. Wayne Spector, Pathologist; Sam Atari, Urologist; Ben Carton, Gynecologist; Gil Horton, Ophthalmologist; and Raymond Bell, Orthopedist and chair of the committee. The meeting was also attended by Dr. Kovacs, who resented being there. When he had been notified, his first reaction was to rip up the notice. He called everyone he could trust to ferret information about the issues that were on the agenda, but since he had no real ties with anyone because of his recent arrival at Palmdale Hospital's medical staff, he was confined to calling his partners and Bill Hendrickson, the hospital administrator, for information.

He was furious, and we'll let it be known to all that he was above this sort of thing. Kovacs was used to the old buddy system that worked so well over the years at Woodland Community Hospital. That was now history, and he had begun a new professional life at Palmdale. Here, even though he was an owner of the real estate and the medical group, he had to abide by the medical staff bylaws and its rules and regulations, and he hadn't been there long enough to establish a network of supporters who sat in high places on medical staff committees.

The surgeons here were all subspecialists, and the hospital needed them more than they needed the hospital and its source of referrals. They were all assigned to the emergency room backup call panel, which was a constant source of aggravation to them. They were tired of being called in to see patients all night long. Many of these patients were without insurance, while others were managed care whose fee schedule agreements were low.

There had been talk among the specialists of forming an official group among themselves who would then negotiate a fee arrangement with the hospital to cover the ER backup schedule. When the administration got wind of that, they made a supreme effort to be very nice to these doctors. It would have been a financial disaster if the hospital had to foot such an arrangement.

The leaders of this group were sent on cruises, or to Hawaii for a two-week vacation with all expenses paid. The hospital wrote off the expense as "medical staff business and education." It was amazing to witness how quickly their discontent disappeared and the number of calls that were received by the administrator asking when the next "education and staff business meetings" were scheduled. It appeared their interest in these "education and staff business meetings" piqued when set in exotic places.

Dr. Wayne Spector was a serious man who viewed his function as the great teacher and mentor to his colleagues. He was a very bright and knowledgeable physician who liked to help his professional comrades in arriving at a quick diagnosis, and his interest in clinical pathology was recognized by all as a great asset to the staff. Whenever a laboratory test was abnormal, it was brought to his attention. If he thought it was crucial, he would call the doctor who ordered the test and offer suggestions to help him make the diagnosis. Thus he was held in high esteem and courted by all the medical staff.

Dr. Sam Atari was an American-born Japanese man who was only five feet five inches tall. He and Dr. Ben Carton were very close friends, which stemmed from the fact that they were both incompetent. Whenever one of their cases fell to the scrutiny of a committee, the other one saw to it that the issue was resolved with no consequences to either practitioner. This relationship worked well between them, and their strength together was difficult to overcome.

Gil Horton, on the other hand, was an individual who, like Italy during the second world war, was influenced by whoever pushed him the hardest. He would often change his opinion at the last minute and side with the one who had the most influence. After all, he did have his own practice to be concerned with, now that there was more competition in the area, and he had lost patients to managed care.

Dr. Raymond Bell, the Chair of the Surgical Committee, had started his orthopedic practice twelve years before, after having spent fifteen years with the US Air Force. He was a large man; orthopedics seemed to attract many with large stature for some unknown reason. Ray was also soft-spoken and had difficulty dealing with staff problems in the arena of today's medicine. He enjoyed referring to the past when attempting to draw analogies to the present. It never worked, however, but it caused others to be irritated with him. His knowledge of current medical state of the art was limited to his field alone. This eliminated him from being an effectual leader of the committee. He also experienced great difficulty in decision-making and agonized over issues that were unimportant and peripheral to the point, which caused his meetings to be very lengthy. This also did not sit well with committee members.

"The meeting will now come to order," announced Bell.

The room became quiet, and he acknowledged the presence of everyone and asked that the last minutes be accepted.

"Now then, we will be devoting this meeting to a review of the three cases of Dr. Kovacs, and then we will allow Dr. Kovacs to respond with his side of the story," said Bell softly.

At that point of the meeting, Peggy Drew passed out the reviews of each case done by Dr. Mark Gaines. The end of the report bore no signature; therefore, the author of the review remained anonymous. This was standard procedure for all hospital committees in order to induce the reviewer to be as candid as possible. Each doctor read the reviews, and then Dr. Bell requested that Peggy read each one aloud to the committee. Because of the sensitivity concerning the issue of competence, all non-physicians' attendees at the meeting were excused, including Dr. Kovacs.

"Dr. Kovacs, would you kindly wait outside while we review the cases? We will call you back when we have concluded."

Kovacs couldn't believe he was asked to leave and responded. "I think I am entitled to be here during this session. It is an insult that you are attempting to excuse me from this meeting. I demand that I be allowed to stay."

"I am truly sorry, Dr. Kovacs, but that is the way we do it here. It is important that all the members here feel they can speak freely. If you were to remain in our midst during our discussions, it might very well hinder our ability for an effective discussion."

"I am not going to leave," replied Kovacs with anger, "and I will sue you all if I am forced to leave."

Dr. Spector spoke next. "Dr. Kovacs, you have only been on our medical staff for a few months, and none of us really know you well and vice versa. I, and the committee, realize you must feel threatened by this meeting, but let me assure you that it will be impartial. All we ask you to do is wait until we have deliberated. In the meantime, you can read the reports and then be ready for our questions."

"I will leave, but I want it noted that I do so only under extreme protest," shouted Kovacs as he shoved his chair against the table and left the room. Everyone looked at each other with odd expressions upon their faces.

Peggy read the first patient review of Dr. Gaines and sat down. After she read the other reviews and some discussion took place by the members, Dr. Kovacs was asked to return to the meeting. He was interrogated by the members on all three cases, and true to form, Kovacs waltzed around the issues and strayed from the facts. He tried shifting the blame onto the nurses and denied that he had done anything wrong. As a matter of fact, he informed the committee that given the same set of clinical circumstances again, he would not do anything differently. When the committee had exhausted their questions, Kovacs was again excused and told he would receive the committee's findings and proposals in writing within one week. Kovacs again left, red-faced and fuming.

Dr. Atari said, "You can't hold the surgeon to blame for the stroke at the time of the angiogram."

"I would echo those sentiments also," chimed in Ben Carton.

"Wait a minute, how do you explain Kovacs's decision to do the endarterectomy at that time when the patient was most vulnerable?" asked Horton.

"That's not a black-and-white fact," said Bell.

"Well, I think it is," answered Horton, slightly irritated.

"It seems to me there are two issues here," said Spector. "The first involves clinical judgment and the appropriateness of the procedure. The decision to put the patient under general anesthesia, which would further depress the central nervous system is one issue. The other issue is whether Kovacs had the obligation to call in a neurologist or internist on the case to help make the right decision. Embolic strokes should be treated with heparin, which was done, but the question that remains is, should it have been done at the onset for a longer period as the treatment of choice?" The room was silent. No one spoke for a long time.

"Let's take a vote on this issue now. How many of you feel that the patient should not have gone to surgery?" asked Bell.

Only Spector and Horton raised their hands.

"How do you vote on whether there should have been a consultant in medicine or neurology requested?" asked Bell.

All the members raised their hands.

"Next case please, Peggy," asked Bell. After the case was read, Bell opened the meeting for discussion.

"I did the pathology on the patient," said Spector. "It was an adenomatous polyp and was very sessile, which is commonly the case. There was no malignancy on either of the two polyps, which were removed by electrocautery."

"The reviewer states the cecum is a thin-walled area and perforation is a known complication," said Atari.

"All the more reason to be very careful in that area," said Horton.

"If you refer to the operative report, Kovacs does say he had difficulty in grasping enough of the polyp to cauterize," said Bell.

"If I may, gentlemen," interrupted the pathologist. "There are two facts that should be known by surgeons. One is that the polyp without a stalk may not be able to be removed for exactly that reason. If the surgeon cannot elevate the polyp away from the wall of the cecum, he runs the risk of transferring electrical current into the wall of the cecum at the point of attachment of the polyp. He is burning the thin bowel wall, and the result is a localized piece of dead bowel. This will lead to a hole in the bowel and peritonitis will follow, which is exactly what happened here. It seems to me that when Kovacs saw the polyp was without a good stalk, he should have opted for open surgery later.

Secondly, the wall of the cecum was very thin and easily damaged. If the burn had occurred anywhere else throughout the colon, the burn would have been superficial, and the lining of the bowel would have regenerated without problems. My take on this is that Kovacs should have been aware of these issues and his ignorance is malpractice."

"What you are telling us then is that Kovacs has impaired judgment, which is related to a deficit of knowledge," said Horton.

"Maybe that knowledge has only been available recently," offered Carton to downplay the surgeon's responsibility for acquiring the knowledge.

"Not true," interjected Spector, "these facts have been known for years. The ER report documents the patient had signs of a bowel problem right after the polypectomies were done. She saw Kovacs for three consecutive days, and he never picked up on her symptoms. Was it a bad judgment call or plain stupidity? I vote for the latter."

"What about the comment Kovacs made about attributing the low blood pressure to Lopressor?" asked Horton.

"That was foolish of him to assume that a blood pressure would be affected without a similar effect on the pulse rate," said Bell. "Does anyone here think the patient should have been referred to a GI doctor or internist? What about the failure to admit the patient over a three-day period of progressing and worsening symptoms?" asked Horton.

"Any other comments?" inquired Bell. Failing to arouse any further discussion, Bell called for a vote. Bell, Spector, and Horton voted that Kovacs had demonstrated an error in judgment and that he also demonstrated a lack in fundamental knowledge of the procedure. They also found that in failing to recognize the postoperative signs and symptoms of a perforated bowel in a timely manner, Kovacs had caused the death of his patient.

The final case of Nelda Johnson resulted in a heated debate. The case did not involve the surgery per se, but rather the failure of Kovacs to respond to the crisis of his postoperative hemorrhaging patient.

"How can a surgeon not realize that the most common cause of a postoperative bleeding patient is that he overlooked tying off a blood vessel?" asked Atari.

"Why wouldn't he come in to examine his patient?" asked Carton.

No answer came forth from the members, and the room remained silent. No one had ever heard criticisms from Atari and Carton before, and they were all stunned.

"Well, I guess that says it all," said Bell. "Let's take a vote."

The committee voted unanimously that Kovacs had failed to respond to a crisis and failed to recognize and act on the cause of the patient's bleeding. There was strong concern by all that Kovacs had a real knowledge and judgment problem. They further agreed that the following actions be instituted immediately:

1. Immediate suspension of all staff privileges until Kovacs submitted documentation that he had completed a two-week review course in clinical aspects of general surgery.

2. Privileges would be reinstated when the committee received evidence that he had completed the course. ALL cases would be reviewed concurrently.

3. All cases done in the past would now be reviewed by a member of the committee.

4. Appropriate consultants must be requested in all cases where there were clinical issues other than surgical.

5. Review of all cases would continue for one year, at which time the committee would determine whether he should be advanced from provisional to active staff status.

Bill Hendrickson, the hospital administrator, was unable to do anything. These doctors had seen fit to curb their colleague's privileges in order to safeguard the patient population. He knew he had to impart this information to his bosses, Drs. Small and Lund. He would let them deal with their partner. They could decide whether to tell Kovacs of the outcome or let him wait until he received notice of it in the mail.

❧33❧
NEW RULES FOR THE RESPIRATORY CARE UNIT

Erin and Bob met in his office early in the morning because she wasn't feeling well.

"What are your complaints, Erin?" asked Bob in concern.

"I am very anxious, and I've lost about eight pounds in two weeks," she replied.

"Please sit up here," Bob said and pointed to the examining table. When she was comfortably sitting on the table, Bob walked behind her and placed his hands around her neck.

"Please swallow, Erin," he said as he let his fingers palpate her thyroid gland as it moved upward during swallowing. "Please hold your hands outstretched with the palms down," he continued as he demonstrated the position with his own hands. Bob took a sheet of paper from his desk and laid it on her right hand and then repeated the procedure on her left hand. "I am looking for a tremor, Erin, and I think that you do have a slight one. See how the paper trembles as it rests on your hands?" She nodded her head in agreement with Bob. "I want you to relax and let your legs hang free. Bob then removed his neurological rubber hammer from his white coat pocket and tapped on her knee and ankle to examine her reflexes, then, after he concluded his examination, he sat at his desk and took a more detailed history from Erin. When he was finished, he told her that she might have hyperthyroid disease, and he would like to run some blood tests. Erin was in total agreement. He asked his office nurse to draw the blood. Bob

Lund remained sitting at his desk, disturbed about Erin's symptoms. *She could be thyrotoxic or it might be run-of-the-mill anxiety,* he thought and considered all her symptoms again. He entered a written note in her chart and wrote down the blood tests he ordered, then he picked up the phone and asked his nurse to request that the lab call him with the results as soon as they were available.

Bob had made plans to meet with Mark Gaines at noon in the medical staff library to talk about Mark's concerns with the Respiratory Care Unit. He finished up with his morning appointments and headed over to the Doctors' library shortly before noon. He had only been there a few minutes when Mark entered and sat down across the small table from him.

"Well, what's the problem, Mark?" asked Bob, somewhat annoyed that he was sort of on the carpet.

"Bob, I noticed that there were two patients with myasthenia gravis in the unit, and I find that very unusual," answered Mark, looking Bob in the face.

Bob didn't wait for him to continue and quickly said, "That's not unusual at all; I have seen several Myasthenia patients over the years. It isn't as rare as you think it is."

"I guess that we have a difference of opinion, but no matter the frequency of the disease, I'd like to explore another related issue with you," replied Mark.

"Please, go right ahead," said Bob.

"I have concern about the nursing competence, and I am equally concerned about the respiratory therapists writing the ventilator orders that you countersign without ever looking at them closely. I found serious errors of respiratory care management in a few patients, and you had countersigned the orders."

Bob breathed a sigh of relief and now felt less threatened. For a moment, he thought that Mark had uncovered his overdosing of Peter Bunkin and George Babcock with Mestinon. He had almost panicked when Mark had started to speak about his concern. He had placed too much confidence in Mark's clinical abilities for a moment, but Lund now felt in control—after all, he was a much superior physician to Mark Gaines, and more experienced to boot. "Well, some-times they make a mistake, but we have had no mortalities that I am aware of. I can't be there all the time, and I'm only required by law to make rounds once a week. We must cut the therapists some slack, since they are on the unit twenty-four hours a day and are able to make immediate adjustments."

"That may all be well and true, but the direct responsibility for ventilator care right now is that of Small and yourself, and it's not right that a patient's medical care should be managed by a respiratory therapist, especially in view of the evidence that the nurses are bad," answered Mark.

"I think it is totally legal for me to sign the orders that they write in the chart as though they came from me at that time," said Lund.

"Bob, I'm trying to tell you the therapists are not licensed to do that, and I have evidence of some real screwups while you were gone. If I hadn't been there, there would have been a death or two because no one pulled arterial blood gases to monitor the carbon dioxide levels. I found that one patient had a level of seventy and a bicarbonate of forty. This caused a chloride deficiency and severe metabolic alkalosis. He would have died in ventricular tachycardia if it hadn't been corrected. I am going to take this to committee," he stated in exasperation.

"What do you intend to accomplish there?" asked Bob.

"I am going to ask the medical staff to become responsible for the care of the respiratory care patients and that we ride hard on the care that is rendered there," said Mark.

Bob turned pale as he thought about the possible consequences of Mark's proposal. If he and Small lost the ability to render the care, their misguided intentions would no doubt soon surface. They would be ruined, and what was even scarier, they could spend time in jail. "Mark," he spoke slowly, "give me a little time to see if I can correct these problems."

"How much time will you need?" asked Mark.

"Well, by the time we hire new nurses and institute changes in the way the therapists will have to do things, I would guess ninety days," answered Lund.

"Okay, that's reasonable," Mark said. "I really don't want to take on this problem but when patient care is affected like this, I feel I must." He extended a handshake to Lund, who was eager to respond as he felt it indicated a sign of acceptance by Mark.

~34~

HIRING TONY

Erin visited Alex in the unit and noticed that his eyelids and conjunctiva were swollen. He now was more jaundiced, and his abdomen severely protuberant. She questioned the nurse about his clinical condition but was unable to get any meaningful information. After the nurse placed a call to Dr. Gaines, she handed the phone to Erin. She expressed her concern about Alex and then asked Gaines if Alex would soon be out of his misery.

Gaines told her that it was in the hands of God and that Alex might last months or days. She feigned sorrow to convince the nurse of her feelings and wiped a phony tear from her eye as she hung up the phone. When she got outside, she was overcome with frustration about what to do and who to call. Driving home, she had an idea. She remembered the drug pusher that Alex had owed a lot of money to. She also recalled the story of Alex being paid a visit by Tony's messenger, Scar Face. Once inside the condo, Erin found Tony's telephone number and placed the call.

"Tony, this is Erin Kovacs, Alex's wife."

"Oh yeah, how is Alex doin?" replied Tony.

"Not real good, Tony, not good at all. I would like to talk to you about something,"

"Sure thing, what can I do for you?" he asked inquisitively.

"I would like to talk to you about a business proposition, but I'd prefer to do it in person, if you don't mind."

"Why don't we meet tomorrow, say lunch at the Desert Hotel in Lancaster," replied Tony.

"What time do you want to meet?" asked Erin.

"Noon will be fine; I'll make a reservation. See ya tomorrow."

Erin thought about how she would make the business proposal. She was aware money talked loudly, but there were still options to consider. She could offer to pay a large sum of money, but she would not be able to pay it all until she inherited the money. This was unacceptable because if perchance she became unable to pay, the consequences would be severe. She did have three thousand dollars saved, and she could also sell Alex's car. His Bronco had been repaired since the accident and was worth about eight thousand dollars; they owed nothing on it. She opted for offering three thousand dollars to Tony for the work.

Promptly at noon, she entered the Desert Hotel and was met at the reservation desk by Tony.

The hostess led them to their table, and they made small talk while deciding what to order. The waitress took Erin's order for a Crab Louie Salad with a side of bleu cheese instead of the Louie dressing. Tony ordered a Monte Cristo sandwich and a Bloody Mary and settled back in the deep, comfortable, leather lounges. The busboy returned with a steaming loaf of pumpkin bread, which was a specialty of the house. He cut the loaf and offered Erin the first piece, which she quickly devoured.

"Well Erin, here I am," said Tony.

"Tony, I need a favor, but I am willing to pay for it," she said while tapping her long nails on the tabletop. "I want somebody killed," she said, shocked to hear the words from her own mouth.

"What makes you think that I can get that done?" answered Tony.

"Alex has told me many stories about you, Tony. You had some guy threaten his life when he was having a hard time coming up with the money he owed you," she answered nervously.

Tony smiled slightly and shook his head. "Maybe I have connections, and maybe I don't. Now if I did know someone, it would be expensive."

"How much?" asked Erin with uncertainty.

"Twenty-five hundred ought to do the trick," answered Tony while taking a bite out of his sandwich. Erin breathed a sigh of relief. She was not sure that the price would have been prohibitive, but this was right in the ballpark.

"That's fine, Tony," she said.

"Okay, tell me who it is and where he lives and works," said Tony. "I get half now and the rest when the job is completed." Erin identified her father-in-law, Dr. Kovacs, as the target and proceeded to fill in Tony with all the particulars of Kovacs's daily routine. When she had finished, Tony called for the check, and they left the hotel. She had made it clear to him the deed must be done quickly, and he had agreed to see that it was accomplished with haste. He was eager to please, especially since Erin had promised him an extra five hundred dollars if it was done within three days.

Bob and Erin met that evening for dinner. They drove to a quaint Italian restaurant in Quartz Hill, about ten miles away. Over dinner, he told her that her blood tests were all normal, and he thought she was just stressed out. What he didn't tell her was that she looked gaunt and sick. He convinced her she should take a week off and they would go to Hawaii together. After weighing the pros and cons, she agreed. Erin thought it would be a good idea if she weren't around when Kovacs was killed. Bob planned to make all the arrangements the next day, and they could leave the day after that. She wished she could leave right now, but it was impossible. Tomorrow she would have to notify Tony that she was leaving. If she were to pay him all the money now, she wondered whether the deed would be done or not. On second thought, she would call Tony later tonight and discuss it. Bob kept gabbing about the sale of the hospital and told her about his meeting with Mark Gaines. His attitude then became hostile, and she knew enough not to offer any suggestions when he was in this type of aggravated mood.

Inside the condo, she kicked off her shoes and called Tony. She told him that she intended to go to Hawaii with Lund and that it was a spur of the moment decision. Tony confided in her that the plan was already set in motion and that the money had to be in his hands if she were to leave. The people he did business with did not look kindly on anyone who did not live up to their obligations. She convinced him she would pay him, and as she spoke, she had an idea. Erin didn't trust anyone, especially a guy like Tony. He wasn't above trying to cheat her out of twenty-five hundred dollars by calling off the hit man and pocketing all the money. The plan was foolproof. An envelope with the cash would be placed in a luggage locker at the bus depot in Lancaster, and she would hide the key. She would call twice a day from Hawaii, and when Kovacs was dead, she would tell him where to find the key and location of the locker. Erin figured that the murder could easily be confirmed by calling a friend back home. The financial arrangements were mutually acceptable to both parties.

Dr. Lund was really upset now. Not only was the potential for discovery of heinous acts looming, but he was on edge because the closure of the sale was dragging. He placed a call to Kovacs at home and filled him in with the latest developments. Kovacs then told him that the Surgery Committee had voted to suspend his staff privileges until he completed an acceptable current medical educational program of eighty hours in surgery. It was probably fortunate that Bob never got to continue the conversation to inform him of the rest of the restrictions, because Kovacs immediately went into a screaming rage. He wailed on and tried to justify his position in all the cases. Then he threatened to sue based on a conspiracy to prevent him from practicing.   After a lengthy period, Lund finally told him it was a fruitless effort for him to act out. Kovacs was feeling very vulnerable and threatened. He had never been in this type of a predicament before. Kovacs had always been the one to cause others' problems and had never been one to endure the wrath of others. The situation was out of control—he had now lost control of his destiny. *He would show them*, he said as he slammed the receiver down.

They were staying at a large condominium on the Wailea Shores of Maui. The condo was set at the cliff's edge, with three levels of terraces beginning at the road. The spacious unit looked out upon the rugged lava rocks, which were set in contrast to the white sand. Many tide pools were formed by the rock formation directly in front of the condo. To the right was a small beach that was cradled by lava rock, where large waves broke and spread their foam. They walked out onto the lawn and headed toward the beach. The temperature was a balmy eighty-seven degrees, with very little humidity. On the horizon was a large cruise ship that lazily made its way to the west.

It was almost noon, and earlier Erin had packed a lunch for them. She opened a bottle of chilled white wine and poured a glass for each of them. They drank half the bottle slowly and talked about their dreams and desires. Lund was like a broken record. He carried on about the hospital sale and the anticipated move to the Cayman's. He was so struck with the thought of having all that money that he became manic in his thoughts and almost in his speech.

Erin listened in silence while in her own mind she was thinking about her soon-to-be inheritance. She was torn with indecision. The money she would inherit was more than anyone could use in a lifetime, yet she couldn't control her desire for more. Her greed was ravenous and uncontrollable. Why shouldn't she try to get Lund's money too? She knew that he loved her. Her women's intuition told her so. All she had to do was get him to marry her, and then it would be community property. She was confident she would be able to exist in a marriage with Bob because she would have both her money and his money to spend. The thought came to her that it would be better if Lund never found out that she inherited any money. *Why not live on his money and save mine for a rainy day,* she thought.

After they ate lunch, Bob took notice that her face was gaunt, and she looked tired and very sickly. Making light of it, she admitted she had now lost fifteen pounds. He saw her eyes were sunken and her cheek bones appeared prominent. In the outdoor light, he thought that he saw a slight yellow tinge to her eyes. This alarmed Bob, and his mind raced through the myriad of possibilities that could cause her illness. Erin had been extremely tired, with loss of appetite and rapid weight loss. There had been days when she had a fever as well.

Suddenly, just as if a light had been turned on in a dark room, the answer loomed in front of him. Hepatitis He felt panicked and began to hyperventilate. He made a conscious effort to control himself, and the dizziness abetted. Now that he was able to think clearly, he fit the pieces of the puzzle together. She had contracted the hepatitis from her husband. What a fool he had been not to have thought of the possibility of sexual transmission of the hepatitis virus. He had been blinded by his lust and had thrown caution to the wind. He was now thinking of his own health and the possibilities that he might have been infected by her. Because she had told him that her tubes were tied, he had not feared the possibility that he might get her pregnant. Like an idiot, had never taken precautions and was now lamenting the fact that he had unprotected sex with her. He felt deep compassion for Erin but fear for himself.

How could the blood tests he just ran on her be normal?

There was only one answer that was plausible. Someone had performed the tests on another person's blood. He was now angry and quickly excused himself and returned to the condo and called his office.

"Hello Anne, this is Dr. Lund," he said softly.

"Yes, Doctor, are you enjoying yourself?" inquired Anne, his secretary.

"I am, thank you. Is Sally there?" he asked with uncertainty in his voice.

"Why yes, I'll get her for you."

"Hello, this is Sally," said the voice on the other side of the Pacific Ocean.

"Hi Sally. Remember the other day when you drew blood on Erin?" rattled Lund.

"Yes, I do, Doctor," replied Sally.

"Will you call the lab and verify that the results they reported as hers are truly hers?" he asked.

"I knew there was a problem," she answered in excitement.

"What do you mean?" inquired Lund.

"I was about to call back Mrs. Elliot to give her the lab results when I noticed they were all very abnormal. I had drawn her blood right after Erin's that day. I noticed Mrs. Elliot's tests done the week before were all normal except for the renal function test you were following her for. There was a phone call between the patients, and I remember I returned to label the tubes. I must have confused Erin's with Mrs. Elliot's. I am so sorry," she pleaded.

"Isn't Elliot the one that had the mild rise in creatinine that was due to ibuprofen and reverted to normal two weeks ago?" asked Lund.

"Yes, she's the one," answered Sally.

"Well, why did you request a whole chemistry panel when I only ordered the one test?" asked Lund.

"Mrs. Elliot asked me if it would be okay for us to check her cholesterol and calcium. She has been taking calcium tablets and had heard a news report that said calcium levels should be tested frequently," answered Sally. She quickly added, "I didn't think you would mind so I asked for the whole panel since it is cheaper than ordering individual tests."

"Don't you label the tubes before you draw blood?" asked Lund.

"Usually I do, but when the call came, I quickly wrote an E on the tubes, and when I returned, I guess that I forgot that the E stood for Erin. I made the mistake of completing the label with Elliot's name," replied Sally, very apologetically.

Lund was now experiencing anger over the mix-up in names as well as the fear and anxiety the abnormal results indicated. "Read Mrs. Elliot's lab results to me, Sally," insisted Lund with coldness in his voice.

Sally read the results of the abnormal tests slowly to Lund, who then began to shake his head in disbelief. Suddenly Lund became fearful. He had diagnosed Erin with hepatitis but forgot to think about the source responsible for her disease. *My God,* thought Lund, *it's Alex. He's the source of the hepatitis.* He instructed Sally to order blood tests on Alex. He would see the results when he returned.

When she finished, he asked her for the telephone number of the laboratory. Lund took one of his business cards from his wallet and wrote down the telephone number on the back side. He knew that the lab always saved the blood of abnormal patients for two weeks in case the physician wanted a recheck or to request further testing. The next call he placed was to the laboratory. He spoke to the head technologist and explained the error in that Erin's blood had been sent as Mrs. Elliot's and requested that Erin's blood tests be repeated, and they perform an additional test. Lund scribbled Erin's name under the telephone number and wrote something else. He then placed the card back in his wallet under his credit cards.

~35~

A Very Rare Chest X-Ray

Laura Maple was sitting alone having lunch in the hospital cafeteria when Mark Gaines approached.

"May I sit here?" he asked. He had been working very hard all morning and was famished.

"You sure can, Doctor," she replied with a big smile.

Mark sat down, ate his lunch, and listened in silence as Laura talked. Eventually she got around to asking about Dr. Kovacs. "I hear by the grapevine Kovacs is in big trouble," she said with a frown on her face. Mark attempted in vain to avoid her question. He didn't want to disclose anything to her since it was such a sensitive medical staff issue. In addition, he hated hospital gossip with a passion. After a moment of painful silence, she continued.

"Well, as far as I am concerned, he should be suspended from practicing forever! I hope the Medical Board pulls his license. He is an incompetent," she spewed with venom.

"Don't prejudge him, Laura, you don't know all the facts."

"I know all the facts I have to know!"

"I'd rather not discuss it, if you don't mind."

"That's okay, I was just letting off steam."

"Tell me," asked Mark, "how do you find the patient care in the chronic care respiratory unit?" He was hoping to learn more about the medical care in the unit, since he had discussed his concerns with Lund.

"I haven't noticed any difference. As a matter of fact, Anita Pershing has been trying to get Dr. Small to see Mr. Benson, but he refuses to do so," she said with hostility in her voice.

"What reason does he give for his refusal?" asked Mark.

"You know how he is. He says he is too busy to do everyone else's work. I guess he is miffed at Dr. Lund because he is in Hawaii. It is so unprofessional, and the patient really does need to be seen, because he is spiking a fever to one hundred two, and all we do is give aspirin."

"That is plain criminal and malpractice!" Mark was furious to learn about the neglect of the patient. "I will call Dr. Walker and let him know about it."

"Oh, please don't do that. I will get in big trouble if you do," she pleaded.

"What do you mean?"

"Look . . . Anita is very close with Dr. Lund and has always covered his butt. If he ever found out she called anyone other than Dr. Small when he wasn't around, he would have her fired. You should have heard him bitch when you covered for Small when he was sick! You know his ego; he wouldn't be able to handle it at all."

"I can't stand idly by and watch a patient go down the tubes because his idiot doctor failed to respond to the nurses' call for help. That's his job, damn it," said Mark with conviction.

"Please don't tell anybody about this," she said fervently, looking into his eyes, then suddenly seeing the solution to the dilemma. "Why don't you see Mr. Benson? We will document that Dr. Lund was out of town and Dr. Small refused to come," she said excitedly.

Mark felt pressured. He was trapped and knew he was on shaky ground, if he were to see a patient that wasn't his or wasn't requested to do so by the attending physician. On the other hand, there was an ethical matter at stake, and he had never run from those before. He thought for a moment.

"Go back to the unit and when the temperature rises again, call Small again, then record in the chart that he again refused to come and see the patient. Immediately report this to Peggy Drew in Quality Assurance, and she will notify one of the members of the QA Committee. I have a feeling I shall be that member. This way everyone will be protected, since the QA Department is charged with the oversight of quality care throughout the hospital, including the chronic care facility. Anita doesn't ever have to worry; she will be protected as well." What Mark didn't tell her was that he also felt a sense of great relief. Now he couldn't be reprimanded for acting on behalf of the QA Committee, and having its cloak of authority would give him new confidence. He was certain Lund would understand this fact and realize Mark had not overstepped his bounds.

Laura thanked him and left the lunchroom. Trying to think about the last ten minutes of conversation, Mark slowly sipped a cup of black coffee. He let the aroma fill his nostrils and breathed a sigh of relief while he focused all his attention on the aroma and taste of the coffee. He immediately felt relaxed and quickly progressed to that mental state somewhere between oblivion and the first stages of sleep when anxiety gripped him. He recalled that the QA Committee's resolution to establish control over all the chronic care facility still needed to be confirmed by the Medical Executive Committee. They had their meeting last week, but he didn't know the outcome. Had he been too premature when he suggested this plan to Laura? Mark was now evaluating his available options just in case the Executive Committee hadn't confirmed the QA Committee's request. The choices were meager, and he sat for another ten minutes slowly sipping the hot brew. Finally, he left for Peggy Drew's office.

Walking through her open door, he greeted Peggy and witnessed her usual state of tumult as she attempted to accomplish five different tasks while the phone rang incessantly. Someone was always calling to report something serious. Mark often thought this office must be what the CIA was like, reports from spies filtering in from everywhere. Some were culled and some required immediate attention. This was her world, and she managed it with extreme efficiency and great intelligence to boot. And if that weren't enough, Peggy did it with humor and was always in control.

"Well, what do I owe this unexpected pleasure to?" she asked with a twinkle in her eye.

"I need your help, Peggy." Mark relayed the conversation he had with Laura Maple concerning Mr. Benson.

"That is horrible!" said Peggy adamantly. "I'll call you as soon as Laura or Anita call me. By the way, I am delighted that you brought your concern about the quality of medical care in the Chronic Care Unit to the last QA Committee."

"What do you mean?" asked Mark with curiosity.

"The request for immediate action from the Executive Committee was approved last week. They deemed that all the Chronic Care Unit is now responsible to all the acute hospital's committees. We can now insure the delivery of quality medical care to all those long-term patients."

"Boy, that was certainly timely," said Mark. "Until only last week, I had forgotten the chronic unit was governed by their own set of rules and regulations, which were a big joke."

"That's right, Doctor, we now have complete oversight of the facility, and you will have the honor of performing the first case evaluation," she said as she turned her head and looked askance at Mark.

"Great. Call me when you hear from the unit," said Mark as he walked out of the office.

He had no sooner returned to his office when Peggy called to inform him that he was to review the medical care of Mr. Benson immediately and intervene, if appropriate, in the care of the patient. Mark's heart skipped a beat. He was anxious to comply, so he quickly examined all the patients that were in his waiting room and instructed his nurse to cancel the rest because he had a hospital emergency. He then literally ran out of the office and entered the rear door of the Chronic Care Unit. Walking with a brisk stride into the Respiratory Care Unit, he asked Laura for the chart. She handed him the chart and winked at the same time, offering a look of relief.

Mark walked to Mr. Benson's bedside and sat down to begin his review of the chart. Rapidly he read all the nursing entries that were written in the last three days. It was all there in the chart exactly the way Laura had told him. He went to the patient and examined him with care, hearing the sounds in the left-lower lung field, indicative of pneumonia. A chest x-ray was ordered to be done immediately, and Mark walked over to the radiology department to await the results.

The film was exiting the processor when the technician snatched it up and placed it on the view box in the reading room. Mark looked at the x-ray and satisfied himself that Mr. Benson did indeed have pneumonia in the left-lower lobe. Just then, Stan Richards, the radiologist, walked in.

"Stan, will you take a peek at this chest for me?" asked Mark.

"Sure Mark, let's take it into my office." After positioning the chest film on his office view box, he asked Mark about the clinical history of the patient, and Mark told Stan his findings.

"This portable chest film is poor," said Richards with disgust. "They even forgot to put the name of the patient or the date on the film." It always aggravated Stan when sloppy work was done. "You can't get competent people for any price," he continued. "It was taken with the patient flat in bed rather than at the proper forty-five degree angle, so it shows a good part of the upper abdomen as well. There's a definite infiltrate in the left-lower lobe that looks like pneumonia." He stood motionless with his hand on his chin for a long moment, as if he was trying to remember something.

"You look like you want to add something else," said Mark.

"I do. Look at that stomach air bubble!"

"I see it now; it's on the right side instead of the left," said Mark with a look of amazement.

"Exactly, and that means the patient has the rare congenital anomaly of situs inversus," replied Richards. The stomach is in the right upper-abdominal quadrant instead of the left."

"That also means the liver is in the left upper abdomen, and the spleen is in the right upper abdomen, if I remember correctly," said Mark.

"I have seen only one other such patient since I have been here," said Richards. It is an extremely rare anomaly."

"What are those five irregular densities to the right of the spine?" asked Mark.

"Those are pieces of shrapnel. He was obviously wounded in the war years ago, I guess."

Richards again assumed the posture of a man in deep thought. He scratched his head unconsciously. "Wait a minute; I remember now. See the way the shrapnel forms the letter 'V'? I know I have seen this film before. I'm positive of it!" said Richards emphatically.

"How can you be so sure you have seen this same x-ray before?" asked Mark. "You read so many x-rays."

"Because of the presence of two extremely rare findings on the same film. The situs inversus coupled with the shrapnel in the abdomen in a 'V' configuration. It would be impossible to have both rarities on the same film. You wouldn't see that in a thousand years. I'll show you. I have a teaching file I use for lectures to the medical staff and nurses at the Sepulveda Veterans Hospital where I teach part time. My x-rays are all filed by diagnoses."

He went to the computer on his desk as Mark watched. Richards punched a few keys and an information grid appeared on the screen. In the box that asked for the diagnosis, he entered the words "situs inversus" and pushed enter. In a mini-second, a name and medical record number flashed on the screen.

"Your patient, George Carson, is sixty-five years old, and his medical record number is 24584379," said Richards with a proud look of great accomplishment.

Mark looked confused. "You must have another patient with situs inversus."

"I don't think so, Mark. I would have entered all patients with rare or unusual findings into my computer database. Let me get the actual x-ray. I have them right here in this file cabinet." He opened the top drawer and began to sort through the x-rays. In less than a minute, he had the film jacket in his hand and withdrew the x-rays. Mark watched intensely as the films were positioned on the view box. He felt his heart pound as he looked at the film. Richards placed the current film of Mr. Benson next to the one he took from his file. "Look here," he pointed to the stomach air bubble and the liver shadow. It was identical to Benson's. Mark had already noticed the film had the exact same V-shape shrapnel in the abdomen also.

"This is the same chest!" shouted Mark with excitement. "There can't be any question about it."

"I'd bet my life on it," agreed Richards, "but Benson's chart says he is seventy-two years old, and he also has an entirely different medical record number. How many patients with situs inversus are there who also have five pieces of irregular shrapnel shaped like a V in their abdominal cavity as well?" He didn't have to supply the obvious answer.

"I cannot believe it! Something is rotten in Denmark, and I've got to find out what it is," said Mark with desperation. There can only be one answer, he thought: *Mr. Benson must be Mr. Carson. But how and why could this happen?*

$$\sim 36 \sim$$

THE MASK OF THE MASKED REVEALED

The QA Committee listened intently to Mark's report regarding the discover of identical x-rays that were labeled with two different patient names. They all agreed there was something sinister about the coincidental findings on the chest x-rays. They concluded that since Mr. Carson's x-ray was dated seven months ago, Mr. Benson had to be Mr. Carson. The Executive Committee ordered two physicians to examine Mr. Benson again and report their findings to the Chief of Staff Dr. Walker.

Dr. Raymond Bell and Dr. Wayne Spector went to the Respiratory Care Unit to examine Mr. Benson. They reviewed the medical chart and then went to the Radiology Department to discuss the x-rays with Dr. Stan Richards. Since Spector was a pathologist and Bell, an orthopedist, their knowledge of clini cal medicine was somewhat limited. Neither doctor had examined a patient's heart or lungs in many years and was not impressed to do so now. They peered at Benson and looked at his body after removing his blanket so they could honestly state they had examined him. They well knew that a physical examination comprised inspection, palpation, and auscultation, but they settled on the visual inspection only because they feared this problem would become a legal one and wanted to be as far removed from it as possible.

After they had done their examination, and their findings didn't add anything new, Dr. Walker called the authorities. The Sheriff's Department referred him to the Medical Board of Quality Assurance for assistance. They informed him they require a letter detailing the concerns of the Medical Staff before they would act.

Since the establishment of stricter guidelines for the care of all the long-term patients in the chronic care facility, the nursing performance dramatically improved. It was the old adage at it's very best. People do what is inspected and not what is expected! The nurses were examining their patients each day in accordance with newly instituted nursing care plans. No longer were they relying upon the respiratory therapists' evaluation. That morning, Laura Maples was at Mr. Benson's bedside when she noticed a scaly-appearing skin abnormality on his face. She placed her finger over the area and was immediately taken aback by the abnormal texture. *Oh my God,* she thought, *this can't be true.* Laura ran to the nurses' desk and dialed the extension of Peggy Drew, the Quality Assurance Coordinator.

"Peggy, you won't believe this!" she spoke with rapidity and excitement. "Mr. Benson's skin on his face is phony!! You must come over right away, and please notify Dr. Gaines."

"I'll call him, and we'll be right there," she exclaimed. *What now?* she thought.

Within fifteen minutes, Peggy and Mark arrived at the unit out of breath. Laura took them both to Mr. Benson's room and pointed out the facial tear in the "skin." Both Peggy and Mark felt it, and were in total agreement with Laura's conclusion. It was not real skin. Mark sat down at the bedside. He was feeling dizzy. *This was something out of a science-fiction flick*, he thought. He ran through the possible causes and could only come up with one. The skin was artificial . . . but why had it been put there?

"Do you have a twenty-gauge needle handy?" asked Mark.

I'll get one for you," replied Laura. She left the room and reappeared in a flash with the needle. "Here it is."

Mark took the needle and removed it from the casing. He then gently pricked Benson's face, repeating the act numerous times. "There isn't any bleeding from the pinpricks."

He pushed the needle deeper into the cheek and then released it. "Well, look at this. The needle stands upright all by itself. He then pulled the needle to the side and let it go abruptly. The needle sprang back to the perpendicular position. "This is amazing," shouted Mark. "This isn't skin at all. It's some type of a mask, but unbelievably real-looking."

"I think we should call the police," said Peggy, wide-eyed.

"I'll call," offered Mark eagerly. He picked up the phone and asked the hospital operator to connect him with the Sheriff's Department. Quickly, Mark related a summary of the events leading to the discovery that Mr. Benson was encased in some type of mask. He also told the detective about his discovery of the similar chest x-ray findings seen in both Benson's and Carson's films. He hastened to add that Mr. Carson had died at the Chronic Care Unit about seven months ago. He told the detective that the x-ray was that of the respiratory care patient who they knew as Mr. Benson, meaning the x-ray done seven months ago had to be Mr. Benson's. Gaines explained his theory that Benson was probably Carson, and, likely, Benson had to be buried with a death certificate that had Carson's name on it.

"The death certificate should be easy to check out," said detective Morrison.

"If you find one for Carson, you can bet it will be Benson who is buried in his place," said Mark.

"I'll be right over with our forensic experts. Please don't touch anything until we get there."

"We'll get an order to exhume the body and get an autopsy as well as an x-ray of the chest to confirm the absence of shrapnel.

Sheriff's Detective Sergeant Morrison arrived with a team of four forensic experts. After questioning Peggy, Mark, and the entire respiratory care nursing staff as well as the respiratory therapists, they photographed Mr. Benson's face and took his fingerprints. They were unable to remove the mask from the face of Mr. Benson, but Mark demonstrated the lack of bleeding after a needle insertion. He then showed them how the needle could be pulled down to the horizontal and then spring to the vertical position.

Detective Morrison placed a call to his headquarters and requested that they obtain assistance from Universal Studios makeup department to assist them in the removal of the mask. Shortly thereafter, he received a call back informing him a mask expert had been dispatched to the hospital. Everyone grew weary of waiting and retired to the hospital cafeteria for coffee. One hour later, a sheriff's car arrived with the expert carrying a bag of supplies. He used a chemical known by the acronym 111-TTE to remove the mask. The substance was carefully applied with the use of a Q-tip, and, after a time, the artist was able to latch on to a small segment of the material under the chin. The application and tedious removal of the mask took more than an hour to complete while the entire procedure was videotaped. Mr. Benson's face was bright red and in places the skin was broken. Many areas of coalescing white, cheesy material were present on the face. Mark ordered the face covered with a light gauze soaked with Nystatin, the anti-fungal drug. More photos of the face were added to the collection by the forensic team. Mark concluded that Dr. Lund had to know about the fraud and patient switch and, after checking with the billing office, surmised the motive was financial. He conveyed his suspicion to Detective Morrison. Just then, another call from the Los Angeles Coroner's Office was received, informing Morrison that a James Carson had indeed been buried seven months ago and that they had obtained an order from the court to exhume the body for an x-ray of the chest and autopsy. He asked everyone to keep the incident quiet for now, as this would take them years to investigate.

~37~

KOVACS MEETS HIS MAKER

That evening, Dr. Kovacs received an emergency phone call from the ER. There was a young man about to be admitted who had abdominal pain, and the ER physician had made the diagnosis of acute appendicitis. Kovacs was asked to come in to evaluate the patient and confirm the diagnosis. He was in a foul mood over the Surgical Committee's condemnation of his clinical abilities and was having an extremely difficult time in acknowledging that he might have some flaws. No one had ever questioned his judgment before.

And then it hit him. Mark Gaines was the cause of this!! He was certain of it. Recalling the committee meeting at Woodland Community Hospital almost a year ago when Gaines had tried to cast aspersions on his ethics, he became angered. Suggesting by the committee that he, Harvey Kovacs, had made a serious error in judgment was a difficult pill to swallow. His paranoia level continued to rise the longer he thought about it. Now he was condemned by his peers, and Kovacs was certain that Gaines was behind it all. This was a plot to get even with him.

Harvey Kovacs immediately saw all the pieces to the mystery, and he flew into another rage. He rushed into his bedroom and removed a 357 Ruger from the drawer. After placing the weapon in his tennis bag, he left the house. His anger continued to seethe as he formulated a plan in his mind. He would convince Gaines to see him somehow after the surgery and kill him. He had to settle the score. He drove to the hospital but was oblivious to the car that followed him from a distance.

It took him fifteen minutes to get to Palmdale Hospital. He parked in the doctors' area in front of the hospital and walked inside. The large dark sedan parked at the end of the general parking lot a short distance away from the medical building.

After he examined the patient, he summoned the OR crew and performed an appendectomy without incident. Kovacs went to the doctor's lounge and dictated the operative report. He then called Mark Gaines and explained that he needed to talk to him immediately about certain issues in the Respiratory Care Unit that had been brought to his attention. Kovacs summoned great control in speaking with Gaines. He told Mark that he had information that was very sensitive, and he couldn't trust anyone with it but him. Kovacs was able to convince Mark that he hadn't been there long enough for him to make any friends. Mark was the only one that he knew except for Bob Lund and Rick Small, and of course, he surely knew what a blooming idiot Small was. Furthermore, he said that Small would never comprehend the issues, and Lund was screwing around in Hawaii and therefore unavailable. Mark finally became convinced of Kovacs's sincerity and agreed to come to his office to meet with him in one half hour.

Kovacs had planned to hide in the bushes near the rear entrance of the medical building. He knew that Gaines had to pass directly in front of the shrubbery in order to enter the medical building. It was perfect for an ambush. Kovacs replayed all the issues again in his mind, but it only served to fuel the flames of paranoia and irrationality into an inferno. After retrieving the gun from his tennis bag, Kovacs sat in his car for a moment. He quickly checked the cylinder and determined that it was fully loaded then slipped it into his coat pocket. He then walked to the rear door of the medical building. He was observed by the lone occupant of the car that had parked out of sight at the end of the medical building. Slouching in the shadows, he knelt on the ground behind the bush to await his prey. Unseen by Kovacs, a sinister shadow approached from the other end of the building and was carrying something in his hand. The figure walked toward the rear of the bush, and when he was within ten feet of Kovacs's back, he fired five rounds into the back of his head.

The only sounds that were heard were a series of muffled thuds. Kovacs never heard a thing. The assailant picked up Kovacs's 357 and placed it in his pocket.

~38~

MARRIAGE, BORA BORA, FIJI, AND TURTLE ISLAND

Erin waited until Bob left for his jog on the beach. She placed a call to Tony. It was eleven a.m. on their third day in Hawaii when Tony told her that Dr. Kovacs had been found shot to death at the medical building. The news report said that the motive was robbery. She then told him that the key to the luggage locker 111 was in the Railway bus station in Lancaster. The key was in a magnet box under the rear bumper of her car that was parked at the hospital's employee parking lot. She gave him the license plate number and described her vehicle in detail to him. Tony thanked her and hung up.

Erin never disclosed the news about Kovacs to Lund, because she thought he might want to return home the next day. She did not want to cut her vacation short because of it, but a call came from Lund's office relating the news. They returned to California on the following day.

When the medical examiner finally released Kovacs's body, the funeral was held at Forest Lawn Cemetery in the Valley. The murder made the front pages of the *LA Times* as well as other major papers. The hospital switchboard was overwhelmed with inquiries regarding the incident. The day of the funeral came and went, and most of Kovacs's valley colleagues were at the funeral. The Surgical Committee breathed a sigh of relief that they didn't have to go. Erin put on a somber act for the crowd while secretly planning how she would spend the money that she would eventually acquire. It was now a reality and all that stood in the way was Alex.

She visited him the day after she returned home and didn't recognize his features anymore. He was a brilliant yellow, and his entire body was bloated with fluid. Dr. Gaines asked her to sign a request for a no-code, which she did gladly. He told her that although he was now severely anemic, he would not transfuse him because it would be a waste of blood. Alex's kidneys had now failed, and it was only a matter of days before the end.

The following week US CARE finally closed the purchase of the hospital and medical group. Lund was excited and had forgotten all about the items of concern that Mark had raised. He canceled his office appointments indefinitely and told his secretary, Anne, to reschedule all his patients with some of the other doctors in the group. He had all the symptoms of short-timer's syndrome. As a matter of fact, Lund hadn't been to his office since before he left for Hawaii. He thought of the accumulation of junk and regular mail that he would have to wade through and made the decision to put it totally out of his mind.

Karl Bixby filed the notice of intestate with the court in behalf of the estate of Alex. It asserted that Harvey Kovacs had only one living relative and that was his son Alex. Alex was certified as remaining in coma with no chance of survival and that he was not expected to live more than a week. Two days later, Alex died; the funeral was quick. Erin was in an emotional state of euphoria, however, physically she still did not feel very well. She decided to seek the advice of her lawyer as to what she should do if anything at this point. Karl Bixby informed her that he would draw up the necessary papers and have them ready for the court. She was now the sole heir to her husband's estate. Lund told her that each of the three partners had received seven and one half million dollars. Mr. Bixby had discovered that Dr. Kovacs had almost three million dollars in certificates of deposit and in other negotiable securities. He had asked a CPA to assess the tax liability on the recent cash the estate received and was told the seven and one half million would have to be split almost in half between the federal and state owed taxes. When she heard that, she expressed her anger at having to give up half of the proceeds to the tax man. *It was grossly unfair!* she screamed at Karl. He laughed and reminded her she would still inherit six plus million dollars, plus all the real estate, including a large mansion in Encino and many other income-producing properties that were located all over southern

California. Erin couldn't share her excitement with anyone for fear that Lund would find out that she was the sole heir. She feared this might put a strain on their relationship. She found herself unable to sleep and her appetite was still poor, but she had gained weight.

Bob had almost completely forgotten that he wanted to have his own blood tested for the presence of abnormal liver function as well as for the presence of the hepatitis virus. He had his office nurse draw the blood and told her he would take care of the specimen. The first thing he did was to substitute another name for his. He strongly suspected that the tests might return positive, and he didn't want anything about his health status known in the hospital.

Bob couldn't believe he was now very rich and could retire. Before making a permanent move to the Caymans, however, he wanted to do some traveling. After repeating a second set of liver function tests, he then informed Erin of her diagnosis. He told her she had hepatitis type B and C, but the tests showed much improvement over the past three weeks. Erin was angry that he had not informed her of this when he first became aware, but eventually, she forgave him. He convinced her that he wanted to protect her from mental anguish. Hepatitis usually improves over time, and he felt it would be better to know the tests revealed improvement before telling her. He asked her if she would like to go on a trip for two or three months, and then return to pack and move to the Caymans. She was very amenable to his proposal but added one of her own.

"Bob, I want to tell you something," she began hesitantly.

"Sure, Erin, what is it?" replied Lund.

"I . . . I want us to be together always. I love you," she said softly.

"I feel the same about you, you know that," Bob replied.

"Yes, but I want to feel secure, Bob." He remained silent and braced himself for he had been expecting this for a while now.

"I want to go to Las Vegas and get married," Erin said in a pleading voice. Bob had already resigned himself to this and surprised her with quick agreement. "Yes. I do too, Erin. When do you want to leave?" She thought of all she would gain financially from the marriage. Her mind raced with delusions of grandeur. She would have to play her cards right with Bob. Perhaps she would sit down later and develop a written plan to acquire the desires of her heart.

"I will turn in my resignation at the hospital tomorrow. Let's leave on Thursday and fly back here on Saturday. We can pack on Sunday and leave on Monday," she answered. "Oh, by the way, where are we going for the next few months?" she asked.

"I have always wanted to go to Tahiti. What about Bora Bora? To tell you the truth, I would like to visit the South Pacific before I finalize my plan to move to the Caymans. I just want to be very certain I am making the right move. I hear it is a lot cheaper to live in the Fijis than anywhere in the Caribbean, but I want to see for myself." There was also the possibility to practice in the Fijis without new license requirements, and that generated an interest in Bob. He was still enamored with the Caymans but felt uneasy about a permanent move without looking at other possibilities. Bob was always very careful to the point of compulsiveness. He evaluated all aspects of any situation so he could always have a contingency plan. Erin thought to herself, *What a miser; he'd live anywhere if the price was right. He doesn't realize I am worth much more and should be treated better.* "I think I can get accommodations at the Club Med. We can spend a few weeks there and then go to the Fiji Islands for a while."

They flew to Las Vegas and got married, then returned according to plan and packed their suitcases. Lund had instructed his secretary, Anne, to make the flight arrangements on Air France for Bora Bora. Despite the recent acquisition of millions, Lund was still cheap. Erin had taken notice of that fact from the beginning. Early in their relationship, Bob had suggested they dine in the hospital cafeteria on two different occasions. She finally had told him she wouldn't go near that food unless she were starving to death. After his second attempt to change her mind, she became angry, and he never again brought up the subject. She knew he was very tight with money, and she wasn't surprised to find that they made the long trip in coach class. She thought she could easily overcome his character flaw, if she had his money to spend.

Their flight was scheduled to leave Los Angeles International Airport on Monday at midnight. They packed light, cramming all their combined clothing into three suitcases. Lund did not want to pay extra charges if they were over the allowable weight. At first, Erin was miffed over the restricted luggage, but after a while, she accepted the fact it was probably a good idea, even if it seemed to her that her husband's total concern was the potential few bucks more that he might have to pay the airlines. They arrived at the airport and checked in at the ticket counter. Their passports and tickets were checked, and they walked to the departure gate, where they promptly boarded. The flight took ten hours, and when they landed in Papeete, Tahiti, they were met by local musicians, who played vibrant and lively Tahitian music. The time in immigration passed quickly, and within minutes they were collecting their luggage.

After checking directions for the Tahiti Air Terminal, they boarded the train for the Bora Bora terminal and exited in two stops. People from all nations were in the airport departure area, wearing bright-colored short-sleeved shirts and a variety of interesting head gear. The flight was full and left on time, putting them in Bora Bora at 9:00 a.m. The aircraft was a gleaming, white, twin-engine turbo-prop ATR 72 with a capacity of sixty-six seats. The tail and fuselage of the plane were brightly designed with Tahitian strokes of orange-red that stood out in bold relief.

It was then necessary to travel from Bora Bora by ferry to the Club Med. The ferry was a modified hydroplane vessel that skimmed the water's surface at twenty knots. The glass enclosed area of the deck had seating capacity for one hundred people. It was hot and humid with no cross-ventilation available, so Bob and Erin went upstairs to the outer deck and enjoyed the beauty of the French Polynesian countryside, snuggling against the sea.

After claiming their baggage, they boarded an old school bus and made the short trip to the Club Med. The narrow, winding streets were edged with red, purple, and yellow flowers hanging from bushes and trees; the air was thick with the fragrance of their blooms. They arrived and received a song as their welcome, and each was handed a tropical drink. Shortly after the orientation they were shown to their bungalow, where they napped until lunch. She dreamed she was shopping for clothes and jewelry. While shopping, the price of the item was mentioned by the salesclerk, and Erin told her that price was not a consideration. She paid for the purchases with his credit cards. When she returned to their bungalow, Bob became upset that she had purchased ten pair of shoes and an equal number of hats. She dismissed his anger because he was a man and just didn't understand.

Bora Bora was a lush tropical forest, and the Club was carved out along white sands. Dazzling red and orange flowers hung from bushes that grew along the pathway to the bungalows. The dining area was a large, open-air thatched structure enclosed by rain shutters at the sides to keep the diners dry during a tropical rain.

At 4:00 a.m. the next morning, they were both awakened by the dance of raindrops on the roof. The rain grew more intense as the morning approached noon. They were issued large, white umbrellas that they used when walking to the dining area from their bungalow, which was situated a short distance from the beach. The rear porch faced the water, revealing many small, white boats bobbing in the lagoon. Tall, slender palms stood straight as arrows, while others looked as if they had been broken and then began an upward climb to the sky. The storm was gone now, and they watched as the clouds were parted by the sunlight piercing through the palm trees.

Bob became concerned about Erin's intense anger with the rain. She told him that this was her vacation, and she deserved better weather. Her reaction to this minor inconvenience was much more than one would normally expect. Sometimes Bob observed Erin talking to herself after their discussion was completed. On more than one occasion he noticed she seemed to be having a real conversation with an imaginary person. She would become very loud and scream an obscenity or two, which embarrassed him immensely.

They spent every morning on the beach and made side trips that were scheduled at the Club. Feeding the sharks was an attraction that virtually every vacationer wanted to see. After a forty-minute trip to the outer reef, the boat anchored in green blue clear water. The captain set a hemp line between two stumps in the water and asked everyone to stay behind the line while he fed the sharks. The depth of the water was less than five feet, and that was the unusual character of the Bora Bora seas. The entire island was surrounded by a large reef about one-quarter mile wide. The waves broke upon the reef and flowed into the vast lagoon, which always remained shallow. The temperature of the water hovered at ninety degrees and varied between aqua, blue, and shades of green, depending on the intensity of the sun. On the shore at the hotel, the tide's variance was never more than four inches daily. Bob and Erin put on their diving fins and remained with the group while the captain removed pieces of fish from a large bag and chummed the water. In a flash, large darting shadows attacked the food. The reef sharks were white and weighed about one hundred thirty pounds. They were about five to eight feet long, and after a while they swam to the hand of the captain and took the morsels directly from him. He chased one of the larger sharks and dropped a noose around its body and allowed the shark to pull him through the water with ease. He then stopped and told his thrilled visitors to get their cameras ready. The captain lifted the great shark out of the water with both hands and raised it over his head. The shark never moved or attempted to squirm back into the water. Bob and Erin were amazed at what they had just witnessed. It was thrill enough to be in such proximity of the reef sharks and witness their dorsal fin passing so close to them, but the final act was outrageous.

That day there was a young, scantily clad woman sitting in front of Bob. When she stood up, her *gluteus maximus* was exposed for all to see, while the string remained obscured within the cleavage. Bob had his camera in hand and wasn't about to miss the photo opportunity. The only thing he didn't count on was that Erin noticed him doing it. She became livid with jealousy, and for the next two days, she remained that way. Erin rationalized her own behavior with the notion that she might not be as well-endowed as that woman, but she sure was a hell of a lot richer. Besides, she would soon become a queen. Bob was beginning to have second thoughts about the possibility of marital bliss, and moreover, he noticed she seemed to be preoccupied too often to suit him. Whenever she became upset, she would stare off into space while smiling in a strange fashion.

Another day they were taken to the reef, where they were allowed to walk directly upon it. They had reef shoes, and after the small boat was secured, they were assisted onto the reef's surface. The water was only eight to ten inches above the reef, which was composed of coral and other live ocean creatures. They saw clams with bright-blue lips and many other mollusks colored in pink, yellow, purple, and white. There were beautiful black sea urchins and colored stones interspersed with sand. The reef encircled the island and was open only in a small area. It was this protection that formed the sheltered shallow lagoon.

Each meal was a feast. For breakfast there were set tables with mounds of bananas, melons, papayas, and figs. Other tables revealed many different types of bread rolls and, of course, croissants. Twelve or more different cheeses were always available, as well as homemade jams and French-made marmalades. Cereals, eggs, omelets, and breakfast meats were at the hot table, all cooked to order. Passionfruit, orange, grapefruit, and prune juice adorned the beverage area. The lunches varied daily and presented a variety of fresh fish, meats, and cheeses. The dessert table was overladen with fresh fruit of all types, as well as an assortment of desert pies and cakes. The dinners were always different and elegant. Each evening, wine was available for the asking. Gourmet preparation of fowl, meat dishes, and fish were presented on the menu. The deserts were fabulous and included French pastries, tarts, tortes, pies, cookies, and three flavors of ice cream each evening. Rich, delicious coffee and teas of various types were available also.

At nine-thirty every night, an amateur performance was presented for the guests. Each night there was a different show. They sang, danced, and acted in skits and plays every evening. The participants stemmed from the ranks of the Club's employees. Very talented personnel showcased their proficiencies and, at the end, brought prolonged applause from the audience.

Each evening, Bob and Erin sat at the bar located on the beach. They played the silly games that the host initiated for all the guests at the bar. One evening, the hotel sponsored a dance contest, which began at 10:00 p.m. Bob was selected to be a judge, along with three other guests. The rules of the contest were that contestants danced until they were eliminated by the judges. There would be a selection of at least twenty different dances, and the contest started with about twenty couples. There was one outstanding dance couple that everyone quickly became riveted upon very early in the contest. The judges alongside Bob included two women and a man. One very elderly woman was visiting from France and spoke very little English. The other woman was in her thirties and French. The gentleman was from Greece and in his forties. Bob had a few drinks and thought he would add some humor to the process of elimination on the dance floor. Instead of just tapping the shoulder of the dance team to be eliminated, he placed his large, green, palm leaf hat on the man's head. This, indeed, brought heaps of laughter each time the music stopped. He strolled onto the dance floor, passing the one to be eliminated, and suddenly turned and dropped the hat on the unsuspecting target. The judges were down to the last four couples, when the emcee approached the judges' area and motioned to Bob. He told Bob he had been instructed by his boss that the outstanding couple must be eliminated. When Bob looked aghast, and said they were the best couple, he was told that the couple were not guests of the hotel, and the contest had been meant for guests only. Bob agreed to his request, but when he told the other three judges, they were timid, and each judge refused to personally march onto the floor and eliminate them. Bob said he would do the deed, so the next time the music stopped, he walked on the floor and placed the goofy hat on the head of the man. The crowd had swelled to one hundred or more people, and they screamed their displeasure with his action and even shouted expletives at Bob. They were incensed over the elimination of the best, and they let him know it. Bob took it in stride until Erin ran over to him and shouted in his ear over the noisy crowd. She berated him for the act and called him an idiot. Bob just laughed more then got up on a chair with his goofy hat on his head. He turned to the crowd and bowed to them while removing his hat. The crowd quieted slightly, and Bob announced to them that he was ingratiated with their approval of the judges' decision. Erin was still angry, and until she heard why they were eliminated, she remained so. She told Bob that she had been accosted by a group of newly arrived guests from Chile. They complained that the dance the couple was eliminated from was the La Bomba, and the only ones who were dancing it correctly were the eliminated couple. The Chileans raved on about the insult of it all, and Erin retaliated that she was fed up over the pettiness of the whole thing. She told them that nobody really cares and to get a life! The night ended without further incident.

One night they were witness to a small calamity. A fireworks display was scheduled to begin at 10:00 p.m. at the pier. The fireworks were wonderful and were enjoyed immensely by all the spectators. They were set off at the end of a three-hundred-foot pier that had a thatched roof hut with open sides situated near the pier's end. A rocket accidentally ignited a box of rockets that had been facing toward the beach in the direction of the onlookers. Rockets began to skim over the water toward the beach. Bob and Erin dropped to the ground at the sight of the approaching rockets. They were stunned and recognized immediately that these were not part of the planned show, where most of the other guests thought this was a planned finale. A moment later the roof of the hut went up in roaring flames, which still did not convince all the guests this was not a planned finale. Employees ran in all directions to find hoses. Some were able to find them, but the ends wouldn't attach to each other. They were missing appropriate connectors, so the hoses could not be extended to the end of the pier. "It is a live reenactment of the Keystone cops," Bob remarked to Erin.

The next morning, they walked to the pier to inspect the damaged hut that had been situated at the end. Ashes and a charred deck were all that remained.

The crystal blue, green water was alive with fish of every color. The water appeared as though it were an artist's conception. The canvas was streaked with turquoise, and from it, every shade of blue and green seemed to be birthed. For the effort of a scrap of bread thrown casually into the water they would see the surface burst alive with churning color. Fish, large and small, vibrantly adorned with light blues, purples, reds, and yellows, competed for the feast. Some of the shapes of the fish were outrageous. Their shapes and color looked as if they were created in jest. Bob and Erin walked to the pier after breakfast each morning, armed with bread, and provided their own entertainment.

On another day during one of the game contests, Bob joined the outrigger team. Each day at different times, various games were held for the participating guests. Two people manned the outrigger and followed a racing course. Ten boats were at the ready, and at the whistle, Bob leaped into the front while his partner manned the rear. They were able to get their oars in the water for four strokes when they were struck broadside by another boat, which caused their outrigger (or "canoe," as the Tahitians called them) to capsize. Bob and his partner were in the water, and their craft immediately filled with water and sunk. The entire episode took less than a minute to complete. Everyone was laughing at the chaos, which left them with nothing to do but laugh along with them. During their two weeks at the Club, they played many sports and did much sightseeing. Erin, of course, had discovered the native dress was the Pareo, and she visited every store on the island to find the right colors and designs.

Their assessment of Tahiti was that it had been the best place either one had ever vacationed. Erin was thinking what a wonderful world there was to discover if you had the wealth to do it. She began to daydream traveling to all the exotic places in the world and became overwhelmed with the thought of her inheritance. She mentally calculated she could easily live off the interest of seven million dollars or so. That should provide her with enough after taxes money to satisfy her every desire. She might become too acclimated to a lifestyle of sumptuousness and, who knows, she might have to use up some of the principal. Erin's knowledge of financial matters was so obviously extremely shortsighted.

Bob suggested they should fly to Fiji next. The flight was from Papeete to Nandi, which was on the largest island of Fijis. In Fiji, the letter "n" is always inserted before the letter "d" for purposes of pronunciation. Hence, "Nadi" is pronounced as "Nandi." There are well over four hundred islands in the Fijis, but only three large ones. Viti Levu, Vanua Levu, and Taveuni were all subjected to extreme rainfall, which gave the islands dense tropical vegetation and the intense growth of orchids. They were also mountainous, but their central portions were uninhabited. When they arrived in Fiji, they had crossed the international date line and then found that they had to drive on the other side of the road. Erin complained bitterly about the stupidity of the English until Bob told her the reason for it. He explained that in the days of old when horses were the only mode of transportation, battles were fought on horseback. A weapon was held in the warrior's right hand because most people are right-handed. Riding on the left side of the road gave accessibility and ease for the use of the weapon. Erin never mentioned her anxiety about the driving for one-half hour and then continued to voice other nonstop babble whenever she was in the car.

They drove up the coast on the island of Viti Levu to Suva. After driving for an hour on the dirt road, which was the only type of road in Fiji, they arrived in the Pacific harbor area. The signs pointed to a tourist attraction, and they decided to go. Bob drove the jeep inside the gated parking lot, where a sign indicated the attraction was a replica of an old Fijian village. A native approached Erin and demonstrated his wares. Bob bought a set of wooden dishes and regretted it later when he saw the same item for half the price. He became very angry over the incident and the ability for him to enjoy the rest of the tour was severely hampered. They completed the tour and drove to Suva for a quick visit of the city. Life moved slowly here, and although it had the flavor of a third-world country, it was clean, and there was no evidence of poverty. When they had seen enough, they headed north on the King's Road to Rakiraki. Here at Sunset Point, they viewed the offshore islands. Bob convinced Erin to stay overnight at The Nanunanu Beach Cottages. They were taken to the small island by a motor skiff. The trip took no more than fifteen minutes in calm seas. There was a small, local restaurant that beckoned to them, and inside there were long, wooden tables where the local diners sat. The cuisine was Chinese, with a modified Fijian touch. In the morning, they continued their exploration throughout the large island. They drove on to Lautoka and then to Nadi and now had come full circle.

They found the Fijian people to be very friendly, and everywhere they drove, hands waved and people shouted *Bulla*, which was a greeting like "hello." In the small mountain and inland villages, the people offered to let them remain overnight in their houses. The geography was mountainous, and the lush, green vegetation stood in contrast to the red earth. Modest farms were planted in geometric lines and lay nestled between hilly areas. The carpet of lush green vegetation on the hills and mountains appeared as though it were artificial. Most of the cultivated areas lay next to a lazy river that snaked its way across the region with water that was reddish-brown in color. The distant mountains had no steep inclines or jutting peaks, only a slight foggy mist hovering over them. That evening was spent at the Sheraton Fiji Resort, where they ate dinner on the pier. The dining area was spread over a large portion of the wharf. The water was lit with spotlights, and both saw a poisonous sea snake lurking in the nearby coral while hundreds of brightly colored fish swam by.

Bob had heard that the islands only had two or three helicopters for medical emergencies. Four-hundred-plus islands offered up emergencies that were occasionally difficult to deal with. Diabetes was a rampant problem, and diabetic emergencies were very common. He had heard that a pregnant woman recently died in the throes of labor because the diabetes had not been treated. Prenatal care was a rarity, since the population was spread out over all the many islands. Bob asked questions of various officials regarding medical facilities on the islands. He was encouraged by many to apply formally to the Office of the President for permission to practice medicine in Fiji. It seemed the country recognized medical licensure of the United States, Canada, England and Australia. If you were licensed in one of those countries, you were granted immediate licensure and visa status. The proviso, of course, was that you had to practice somewhere in Fiji for at least fifteen hours a week. Bob thought this might not be a bad place to think about a permanent move. He could dabble, as it were, in medicine, to prevent boredom.

The following morning, they were at the Nadi airport early to catch the flight to Savusavu on the island of Vanua Levu. Erin had become incensed when the ticket agent for Sunflower Airlines asked her to step on the scale. Initially she refused, and only after the agent explained that this was normal procedure so that the weight was calculated correctly for the pilot did she agree. The airlines weighed every item to determine the total number of passengers that the plane could carry safely. After landing they rented the only jeep available on Vanua Levu and drove to Na Koro Resort along the ten-mile-long dirt road. It was situated at the end of the road on the coast. Bob and Erin became friends with the owner of the Resort. He was an Australian who took them all over the island on daily explorations. On one of their trips, they were shown an island that was for sale. Savasi Island was set off on its own and was connected to Vanua Levu by a causeway. The island was fifty-two acres of dense vegetation. It had two homes, which came fully equipped with fishing decks and an excellent sandy bottom beach between them. The asking price was one million two hundred thousand dollars, and Erin tried desperately to get Bob to buy it. He refused to even entertain the possibility, causing Erin to anger, and pout; she didn't speak to Bob for twenty-four hours. She fantasized daily about owning the island and saw herself surrounded by servants living amidst the paradise. When she inherited her money, she would consider buying it for herself to enjoy. After all, she deserved it, didn't she?

After two weeks of exploring Vanua Levu, snorkeling, and sunbathing, they were ready to continue their adventure. During this time, Erin slept less and less each night. She would awaken shortly after one in the morning and conjure up visions of wealth in her mind. One evening she drew a crown on a piece of scrap paper, and the next day Bob found it. When he questioned her about it, she told him she didn't remember drawing it. Bob made a mental note to talk to one of his shrink friends about this odd behavior he was witnessing in Erin.

Next, they flew to Turtle Island to spend another week in paradise. A sea plane carried them to Turtle Island, and as they taxied on the liquid tarmac to the pier, they gazed out the small windows. There were the locals on the pier's end, all adorned in native attire. They exited the plane and were met by song and drink and were taken to the beach and served lunch. Following this, they were oriented to the facility and events. Bob and Erin were led to their burre, a charming, thatched-roof bungalow. There were no windows or screens, only large openings in the wall because there were no insects, and there were no temperature changes. It was always in the eighty to eighty-five range, and if squalls occurred, shutters were easily drawn from the sides of the window opening. Inside there were flowers, and everything was bright and cheerful. Their names had been inscribed on a wood plaque that hung at the door entrance. Each evening before dinner, Fijian troubadours strolled from burre to burre serenading the guests.

The daily routine began with the early dawn sun, the silence broken only by the mild crashing of a wave on the beach. The shores were very white, and when the tide was low, one had to walk out a half a mile to reach water at waist level. Reefs abounded and inched toward the shore, keeping the water shallow, while the climate remained balmy with the temperature of the waters perhaps a bit chillier, at eighty-four degrees. Each morning, Bob would run a designated path around the small island, which was about four miles long. When he returned to the burre, they would breakfast upon the beach near the pier. The simple foods were luscious, and the coffee was aromatic and wonderful. There were included choices of many different tropical fruits to be made daily.

One day they were ferried by boat to the other side of the island, where they spent the day alone on a secluded beach. A picnic basket was provided and delivered by boat shortly before noon. When they were alone, they stripped and lay on the beach, basking in the glorious south pacific sun. Much sunscreen number 40 was used by them both, and after becoming quite warm, they ran into the water. Here they played and frolicked in the calm, beautiful water of

Fiji, where there were no waves to speak of, and the water was only chest high. They had almost concluded a brief interlude of lovemaking on the desolate beach when they both became aware of the sound of an outboard motor. They both scampered for their bathing attire as their lunch was almost upon them. The basket was delivered, and the boat sped away with the promise to return for them at four o'clock. A red tablecloth was spread, and a bottle of chilled, local white wine was removed from the basket. The lunch consisted of crab, fresh fish, fruits, and vegetables and delicious bread with cheese. Their day on the beach had been wonderful, and they were both at peace with the world.

On the next day, Bob complained that he felt as if he was coming down with a viral infection. He had been coughing intermittently all through the night and was feeling quite exhausted. Erin placed her hand upon his head and was startled by the heat of his skin. She told him she was sure he had a fever and suggested that he take some Motrin. Bob did exactly that, but throughout the day his temperature continued to spike. That evening Bob refused dinner because he felt so ill, and his cough continued. The next morning, he complained that he was not any better and was concerned that he was in the middle of nowhere and sick. *Not a very good combination,* he said to himself. He convinced Erin they should cut the vacation short and prepare to return home. Bob thought that perhaps he had contracted a tropical disease, and he wanted to be near medical help. They made all the arrangements with the help of the island manager, whose only source of communication was a ship-to-shore radio. The reservations were finally accomplished, and they were booked to leave the following morning on a Qantas flight. There were only two flights a week from Nadi to Los Angeles on Thursdays and Sundays, which was lucky because the decision to leave early was made on Wednesday.

The flight back was miserable for Bob. His fever was not responding very well to Motrin or aspirin. He dozed off and on and drank a large volume of fluids during the entire trip. Erin had noticed that Bob had lost about six or seven pounds; she was now becoming concerned. Bob had gone through most of his supply of sample medications that he carried with him. He had even taken a course of antibiotics in hopes he might gain the upper hand on his illness, but they had no effect at all. Cough medication with codeine also had no effect on suppressing his cough. At last they arrived at LAX, and they drove home in total silence. When they reached the Antelope Valley, Erin was astounded at how barren it now appeared to her. She had spent the last few months surrounded by lush, green, tropical flora, and now she was surrounded by bleak, ugly, brown desert. She suddenly understood what the words "geographical shock" might really mean. She insisted that Bob call Mark Gaines and see him right away, but he fell asleep.

～39～

DR. LUND FALLS ILL

Erin called Doctor Gaines and explained that Bob was very sick and needed to be seen right away. Gaines told her to bring him right into the office.

"Mark, I think I may have some tropical bug," Bob said.

"Let me get some of your history down, Bob—you know, first things first," said Mark. He then proceeded to take a meticulous medical and travel history from Lund. When he had concluded, Mark examined him thoroughly. He discovered some enlargement of the lymph nodes in the neck and heard rales in the lungs. His temperature was 101.6, and Lund had lost ten pounds.

"I want to admit you to the hospital," said Mark with deep concern.

"I'm not going to fight you on this, Mark," replied Lund.

"Oh, by the way, Bob, since you have been away, your office has been sending lab test results to this office for safekeeping ever since you called your office about a lab mix-up. I guess your staff didn't want to risk the possibility of getting reamed out by you again."

As Bob left the office, he was handed some laboratory reports by Mark's front office girl. He read them as he walked up to the hospital. The reports were those he had ordered on Erin and himself. As he had suspected, she had hepatitis, and his own liver enzymes were abnormal as well. Briefly looking at the lab tests he had ordered on Alex, he froze. He was becoming rapidly confused and thought he would read the reports again later.

Mark wanted desperately to question Bob about Mr. Benson but thought better of approaching the subject now. He would talk with Bob when he was over his illness. There would be plenty of opportunity then.

After Bob was admitted to the hospital, the floor nurse inserted a venous catheter and hung the IV fluids that Dr. Gaines had ordered. The lab was called and responded by drawing four tubes of blood for testing and placed some additional blood into two blood-culture bottles. Two grams of the potent antibiotic Mefoxin were then added to the IV bottle that was to be given every six hours, and a dose of another broad-spectrum antibiotic was given through the IV tubing. Other lab tests and x-rays were then requested, and with oxygen in his nose, Lund felt more comfortable than he had for the last three days. He dozed off peacefully.

The next morning, he awakened to find Mark sitting at his bedside, perusing his chart. Mark looked perplexed and asked Bob some more questions about his recent travels. He told Bob that his chest films revealed an extensive pneumonia, which involved both lungs. He was certain that his initial choice of antibiotics was appropriate, but Mark tried not to show his real feelings about Bob's illness. The truth of the matter was he was very concerned about the pneumonia. Lund's oxygen saturation when breathing room air was only 84 percent, which was far below the normal value of at least 93 percent. This meant that his lungs were not doing very well, and the pneumonia was widespread throughout both lungs. During the next week, Bob's temperature spiked every night, and his appetite waned. He continued to lose weight despite the intensification of calories using total parenteral nutrition. The dietitian calculated his daily requirement of carbohydrates, proteins, and fats as well as trace minerals and vitamins administered through the veins. A large, central venous catheter was inserted under his left collarbone, and the fluid entered the major vein leading to the heart. The central catheter had been a necessary procedure because the high concentrations of glucose would have been too irritating to administer directly into a standard-size vein. IV fat solution, Intra Lipid, was also given through the central line as well. Despite all the nourishment, he still did not stop losing weight; he had dropped another six pounds at the end of the week. Blood cultures were drawn twice a day, and there were still no bacteria cultured. Mark thought he should CAT scan Lund's chest and abdomen to look for hidden abscesses or other hints of the cause of the fever. He ordered the tests to be done right away and asked the radiologist to call him to review the results when the tests were ready. The CAT scans took two hours to complete. Mark met Dr. Stan Richards in the reading room and went over the results with him. The chest scans showed there was a suspicious cavity in the uppermost part of the right-lower lobe of the lung. The rest of the chest findings confirmed there was a diffuse pneumonia present, and the scans of the abdomen were normal. Mark reviewed the chart and became aware of a trend in the platelet count. There was a slight but nevertheless definite drop in the total number of platelets. On admission the count was one hundred eighty thousand, and now, a week later, it was one hundred and ten thousand. Initially the liver function tests were all normal and the white blood count was only slightly elevated at eleven thousand, but now it had risen to twenty-nine thousand. It had now become necessary to deliver higher oxygen concentrations to keep his oxygen saturation level in a normal range.

Mark rubbed his head and yawned. It felt good to stretch and ease the tension in his muscles. He walked into the nurses' room at the end of the hall and poured himself a cup of coffee. After a brief five-minute interlude of relaxation, which was easily achieved by just not thinking about Lund's illness, he felt refreshed. With renewed dedication to solve the diagnostic dilemma, he again reviewed the chart. He listed his findings as progressive pulmonary failure, increasing lung infiltrates, low platelets, and evidence that the liver was not making albumin. Suddenly the thought came to him that Bob might be slipping into acute respiratory distress syndrome. He knew that ARDS was pulmonary failure caused by pneumonia, and that it eventually caused inflammatory changes in the lung, leading the air sacs to then fill with fluid. He just couldn't accept this diagnosis in a sick doctor. This was Mark's first time that he had been called upon to render medical care to an ill colleague. He was losing his objectivity in the matter. When he analyzed his thought processes, Mark saw the problem clearly. Doctors were not supposed to get sick, and certainly they were not to become critically ill. In some unconscious manner, his thinking about Bob's illness had been stopped short from considering all the possibilities. It had been too easy to attribute everything to pneumonia alone because any alternative diagnosis was painfully unacceptable. The need for him to allay his anxiety was accomplished by suppressing the possibility of ARDS into his subconscious.

For the first time ever, Mark now understood why physicians should not ever care for their family or friends. The loss of objectivity could be fatal.

He wrote out a list of orders. All the tests were requested to be done immediately. Mark was now considering the possibility of an early disseminated intravascular coagulation syndrome—commonly called DIC—where the blood begins to clot all over the body.

This he knew was an ominous portend of things to come. The lung failure alone carried a 50 percent mortality rate, but combined with the clotting complication, it was at least 75 percent. *It just isn't fair,* thought Mark. *Bob is only fifty-two years old and had never been sick in his life.* He waited at the nursing station for the lab to call him with answers. In the meantime, Mark walked to Bob's room and observed the digital readout of the pulse oximeter. Despite receiving mask oxygen at fifteen liters a minute, Lund's oxygen saturation had dropped to 72 percent. His respiratory rate was now forty, and Mark knew he had to act quickly. Dr. Lund had now been relegated to the position of a critically ill patient who was totally dependent on the nurses and medical staff. He was transferred into the ICU, where the anesthesiologist was summoned to insert an endotracheal tube for ventilatory support. Dr. Sharpe moved quickly and inserted the tube, which was then connected to the volume ventilator. Mark wrote new orders and increased his oxygen to 90 percent without detecting any change in the pulse oximetry value. He then added six centimeters of positive-end expiratory pressure to the ventilator system. After a few minutes, the oxygen rose to 91 percent, and Mark smiled. At least he had bought some time now that the oxygen level was reasonable.

Lund had slipped into a coma and was still unconscious when Erin walked in to see him. She viewed the scene before her and thought she was having a déjà vu experience. Then she recalled the similar circumstances she had witnessed with Alex months ago. What was even more weird was that Lund was in the same ICU bed that Alex had occupied. She did not appear very upset but expressed just the right degree of concern to be convincing. Dr. Gains sat down with her in the ICU waiting room and brought her up to date about Lund's turn for the worse. She sat quietly and let Mark finish, then she asked him what Lund's chances were for survival. He told her the chances were about 25 percent.

Erin thanked him and left the ICU. Her mind was racing as she drove back to her home. In her confusion, she found herself driving to the condo that she moved from a few months ago. She altered her direction and drove to her new home since becoming Mrs. Lund.

Erin was confused and found herself caught between two opposing emotions. On one hand she felt sad because the possibility of Bob's death loomed so close, but she also felt exhilarated about the prospect of inheriting all his money. This was California and it was a community property state, and she was the only relation to Bob Lund. He had told her he had no close family so she would be the one to inherit his wealth. She felt no guilt about her lack of sorrow for Bob, for she had never loved him. The money was coming to her because she deserved it. After all, hadn't she put up with Alex for years and then Bob? She had been Bob's confidant, lover, and travel companion, and now she would reap her rewards. She poured herself a drink and let her mind wander. *If Lund dies, I'll be worth another seven million dollars or more*, she reasoned. She thought herself quite fortunate and then remembered she hadn't called her attorney for quite a while and reached for the phone. "Hello, Karl Bixby please, Mrs. Lund calling," said Erin in an affected tone of voice.

"Please hold, Erin," replied the secretary.

Erin was fuming. *How dare that bitch call me by my first name. Who does she think she is? Next time I call, I will deal with her!*

"Hello, Mrs. Lund, and congratulations on your marriage to the good doctor. I heard about it only a few days ago at the Rotary Club lunch," said Karl.

"Thank you, Karl, but please call me Erin," she insisted.

"Very well, Erin, what can I do for you?" he asked, as he jotted down the time on his legal pad.

"Have you heard anything from the court about my inheritance?" she asked.

"I have written to the escrow company who handled the closing, and they have referred me to the purchaser. I just received the letter from them last week, and I have called them to arrange a meeting with them, but it hasn't been set yet," answered Karl.

"What do they have to do with it, Karl?" asked Erin with annoyance in her tone.

"I'm really not sure, Erin, because the escrow officer would tell me nothing," responded Karl.

He continued, "I sent them a letter informing them that you have engaged me to represent the estate of your deceased husband, Alex. I also informed them that he was the only living child of a marriage that terminated in a divorce and therefore was the sole heir. Their attorney referred me to the purchaser of the buy-sell agreement, as they have no obligation to disclose anything."

"Well, I don't understand these things; I just want to get it over with," she responded.

"I understand, and I promise to call you as soon as I have a meeting with them," said Karl.

Erin visited the ICU daily and acted out the role of the concerned wife. Lund's clinical condition deteriorated over the next week, during which he regained consciousness for only a few hours. Mark had proven the diagnosis of disseminated intravascular coagulation and had initiated all the known treatment available. Multiple organ failure had ensued, and the end was now in sight. Three days later, Bob Lund died in coma. Erin made the funeral arrangements hastily. She had been through this before and was now well-experienced.

Rick Small and Bill Hendrickson paid an unexpected visit to Erin to pay their condolences.

"We are truly sorry for your loss," said Small.

"Please accept my sympathy as well," said Bill.

"Thank you both for coming. You know, even though I was only his wife for a short time, I feel that we had a unique bond," said Erin. "I will miss him immensely; I loved him so much," cried Erin as she wiped a tear.

"I took the liberty of notifying Bob's attorney in Rhode Island," said Small.

Stunned at this statement, Erin gasped. "You notified his attorney?" she asked with her voice cracking. "Why did you do that?"

"Well, Bob and I were pretty close over the years, and he had no family heir," answered Small.

"But how did you even know that he had an attorney on the east coast?" she asked in a frightened voice.

"Bob had him handle all his personal stuff. He took care of the details for Bob," said Small.

"What details?" asked Erin becoming excited.

"He means that he had him draw up his will," interjected Bill.

"What are you talking about? Bob never told me about any will," said Erin pleadingly.

"Bob had his lawyer draw a will, and it was witnessed by me the day after the closing of the sale," said Small. He hesitated and then continued. "I called the lawyer and told him that Bob had died and asked him to notify his daughter."

The words echoed in Erin's ears. She looked pale and became dizzy. When she recovered, she looked at Small. "He had a daughter. He never told me he had been married," she said.

"Oh," stammered Rick, "He never did marry; he just supported his daughter."

"Do you know any of the details?" she urged.

"Lund told me that he had gotten a nurse pregnant when he was in his late twenties. The mother lived back east and never disclosed the birth of his daughter until she was two years old. He agreed to support her, and the mother agreed to allow visitation. Bob had been close to his daughter over the years. Her name is Shauna, and she is a student at the Rhode Island School of Design in Providence, Rhode Island. She is an artist, and according to Bob she has a lot of talent.

"So, she's been told already of his death?" asked Erin.

"Yes, she called me last night and is flying out for the funeral. I need to call her back and tell her when it will be," he said.

Still in shock over this discovery, Erin said quietly, "The funeral is the day after tomorrow at 1:00 p.m."

"We'll see you then," Bill said and headed for the front door.

～40～
THE ASSETS

On the day of the funeral, Shauna Lund introduced herself to Erin. She was accompanied by a friend of her father's. After the services at the grave side, the mourners were all invited to her home to pay their respects. They were served a variety of lunch items and soft drinks.

"I am very glad to meet you?" said Erin seething with anger. Her intuition told her that there might be more to this story than she was aware of. "To be completely honest with you, Shauna, your dad never told me he had a daughter. Needless to say, I am still in shock about his death and haven't had time enough to sort things out."

"I understand, Erin, and oh, I want you to meet Mr. Dennis Hershel, my father's longtime friend and his attorney," said Shauna very pleasantly.

"Sorry to have to meet you under these circumstances," said Dennis sincerely.

"I am also sorry," Erin replied with pursed lips. She was very anxious and wanted this to be finished. Home sounded awfully inviting. Erin wanted desperately to be alone with her thoughts. There were things she had to think about in solitude.

"If I might have a moment with you in private," said Dennis. He led her away from the crowd that had gathered at the buffet. "Your husband had a will, which I want to inform you about. Can we meet tomorrow?"

Erin felt some assurance now that she had been informed of the will. *The worst-case scenario is that Shaun and I will divide the fortune,* she surmised. Feeling somewhat uplifted, she set the meeting for the next morning at ten at her home. She thought she should call Karl Bixby and ask him to be present in case she had to sign any papers. Maybe Mr. Hershel had brought a certified check for three and one half million dollars with him. She had remembered seeing the reruns of the millionaire television series where the lawyer always did just that.

At ten the next morning, Mr. Bixby, Mr. Hershel, Shauna, and Erin all sat down at the formal dining room table. Shauna had chosen a light-purple blouse and pants that accented her figure. She was a beautiful young woman, very friendly and pleasant. She had no airs about her and was easy to talk to. Even though she offered no threatening demeanor, Erin despised her. This was competition of a different sort, and she couldn't control her jealousy.

"We're all here now, so I guess we can begin," announced Dennis Hershel. He continued as he removed a stack of folders from his briefcase and displayed them on the table in front of him. "Bob Lund's will and last testament is as follows. I will summarize and then give a copy to Mr. Bixby." Erin's heart was beating fast, and she was feeling flushed. Her cheeks felt hot. She was sure that they were all watching her.

Dennis continued his presentation. "I, Robert Lund, being of sound mind do hereby declare this is my last will and testament. I so declare that I am not now, nor have I ever been married. I further declare that I have one living daughter, Shauna Erica Lund of Providence, Rhode Island, and no other living children." Dennis stopped at this point and looked at Erin. She was now pale and appeared very nervous. He went on. "To my daughter Shauna, I leave all my personal belongings and the following: All my stock accounts held in my name and hers. These include treasury notes, stocks, and bonds, and are with the firm of Dean Witter. All certificates of deposit held in my name are at the First National State Bank of R.I." He stopped and looked around the table. Shauna was crying, and it was apparent her sob came from deep within. Erin sat and stared ahead into space, biting her upper lip. The room then became silent.

"Dennis," spoke Karl Bixby, "what is the value of the assets?"

Dennis opened another file and peered over his bifocals. "The certificates of deposit are valued in excess of six million dollars. The Dean Witter stock accounts are worth slightly more than four million."

"You mean he left me nothing?" shouted Erin.

"Take it easy, Erin, said Karl. "What is the status of his local bank accounts and the ownership of this house?" he asked.

"When I spoke to Bob Lund last, he told me he had placed Erin's name on his bank accounts. The house has always been in his name and Shauna's with rights of survivorship."

"What does that mean, Karl?" screamed Erin.

"That means that Shauna owns the house," he answered her softly.

"How can that happen?" she screamed. "I am his wife. I am entitled to half his property."

"Erin, Lund was unmarried when he drew up his will, and he was entitled to leave his money to anyone he wanted. In addition, and I think Mr. Bixby will confirm what I am about to say, the CDs and the stock accounts are all held in rights of survivorship. That means that the survivor owns the assets. The will was drawn to state publicly that he had done this act intentionally. He was not married then, and it was within his right to do so."

"So, she gets ten million dollars, and I get crap. Is that the way it is?" she asked, screaming in a loud voice, pointing her finger at Shauna.

"I'm afraid it is," responded Karl.

The meeting broke up. No one said a word as they all got up from the table and walked to the front door. Erin ran from the room screaming obscenities and slammed the door of her bedroom behind her. The attorneys shook hands, and they all said goodbye.

Erin drank herself into oblivion the rest of the day and night. The next day she awakened with swollen, bloodshot eyes and a splitting headache. She nursed her hangover and put Murine eyedrops into her eyes and then applied ice packs. One hour later, she dressed and took a long shower. Her first visit would be the California Bankers Trust, where Lund had all his accounts.

~41~

A Visit to the Bank

Erin walked briskly into the bank and asked to see the branch manager. "What can I do for you, Mrs. Lund?" asked Mr. Dixon.

"I want to see my husband's bank accounts," she demanded.

"I'll see what I can do for you," said Dixon as he picked up the phone and asked one of his employees to bring him everything they had on Dr. Bob Lund. Sensing her hostility, he tried to be pleasing. "I am sorry for your loss," he said sincerely. She did not respond.

"Here we are now; I have the accounts, Mrs. Lund. The business checking account has a twenty-two-thousand-dollar balance." Erin looked up and, for a moment, held on to the possibility that there was more money. She knew what a cheapskate her husband was and prayed that he had squirreled away more cash right here. He looked through the manila folder and made some notes. Dixon then smiled at Erin and continued, "Oh yes, Dr. Lund had a personal checking account with a twenty-thousand-dollar balance." Erin was now feeling much better than she had before she arrived. *Keep going,* she said under her breath. "There is a two hundred-thousand-dollar certificate of deposit and a savings account with thirty thousand dollars."

"Is that it?" she inquired.

"Yes, Mrs. Lund," answered Mr. Dixon.

"Bob placed my name on all the accounts?"

"Yes, I believe that he took care of all the necessary paperwork except that you will have to sign the signature cards on the accounts before you can withdraw any funds," replied Dixon.

Her spirits now raised, and she said that she would do it now, if he would give her the forms. When she finished, she asked Dixon when the CDs would mature.

"They have another sixty days to run," he answered.

"Well, that's all right, I'll take the penalty now. Mr. Dixon, I want to cash in the two hundred-thousand-dollar certificate of deposit today," she said.

"I'll make arrangements for that right away," he said. "Wait here and I'll be back with the paperwork." Erin was thinking about the real money she was about to get from Alex's estate. Her mind drifted, and she was more at ease with herself than she had been in a long time. With the two hundred thousand dollars, she could leave for a long trip and not return until she was ready. Her trance was abruptly broken by Mr. Dixon who sat down at his desk. He looked concerned.

"Mrs. Lund, I'm afraid you can't withdraw the funds," he said. "There's a small item I overlooked. Dr. Lund pledged the CDs as security for a two hundred-thousand-dollar loan he made a year ago." She couldn't believe what she was hearing. Her hopes were again shattered by her husband. In her mind she reasoned that he had purposely done this to her. "What did he use the money for?" she asked with hostility in her voice.

Mr. Dixon opened the file again and peered at some documents. He then looked up at Erin.

"The money was a line of credit for the medical practice. Doctor never liked to pay interest, so he would use the CD as security. The 6 percent interest we pay on the CD was an offset against the 9.5 percent rate on the loan. Doctor liked the idea that we were only making 3.5 percent. He was kind of eccentric like that, whenever money was the issue."

"Well, how much money is left from the CD now?" asked Erin.

"Let's see," said Dixon as he scribbled down some figures. "Dr. Lund used one hundred sixty thousand dollars, so there would be about thirty-five thousand left over, and I can cash in the CD and issue the balance to you now."

"That would be great," she said. "Oh, by the way, can I use his Visa card?"

Dixon cocked his head slightly and looked askance. "I'd better check the balances on the card," he said. He made a call to the teller, and the computer instantly revealed the information.

"Mrs. Lund, the balance on the card is twenty-four thousand dollars," said Dixon.

"That can't be," shouted Erin. Lund doesn't spend that kind of money. "Well, let's take a look," he said as he entered numbers into the computer on his desk. The screen came alive with words and numbers in a few seconds. "You see here," he said, pointing to the screen. "Airline tickets to Tahiti and Fiji, three thousand dollars; Club Med, seven thousand; Turtle Island, three thousand; and a charge for a jewelry shop in Tahiti for six thousand dollars and other charges for five thousand dollars. It appears you had a great vacation. Now I'm sorry to say the piper must be paid. I will pay the balance off with the thirty-five thousand balance due you from the line of credit loan and will place the eleven thousand balances in your account today. Your other checking and savings accounts amount to another seventy-two thousand dollars."

Erin's mind was spinning. She was angry and depressed, experiencing great difficulty in understanding the six-thousand-dollar jewelry charge in Tahiti. She left the bank very disturbed. By the time she came home, Erin had concluded Bob must have bought her something as a surprise. Even that didn't conjure up any guilt, and it only served to justify her own warped ideas of self-worth. She quickly ran to the bedroom, where Bob's suitcase lay next to the walk-in closet. She threw his clothes on the floor, and then shook the rest of the items out on the floor. A small, brown paper bag was stuck in the elastic side pocket. Erin removed it and removed a small box. A card fell from the bag at the moment she pulled the box from it. She hesitated for an instant and then decided to read it after inspecting the contents of the box. Erin opened the box and was greeted by an exquisite, large, dark, round stone set with diamonds. The ring was exotic, and on the bottom of the box was a small paper. It said "This is a certified black Tahitian opal appraised at ten thousand US dollars." She slipped the ring on her finger, and it fit perfectly. *Leave it to Bob to get a bargain.* Holding the ring to the light, she saw how clear the stone appeared. There were no flaws in it at all. She forgot about her recent disappointment at the bank completely as she admired the beautiful ring. Erin kneeled on the floor and picked up the card that had fallen from the bag and read it. "To Shauna, This is how beautiful you are to me in every way, Love Dad." Erin screamed at the top of her lungs. She ripped the ring from her finger and threw it on the floor then pounded her dresser with her fist. For ten minutes she called Bob Lund every name she could muster. Finally, Erin threw herself on the bed in exhaustion and wept.

When she recovered from the insult, she pulled out her husband's billfold, turned it upside down, and emptied all the contents on the bed. Five hundred dollars in hundreds were put in a pile; she discarded the remaining items. Rage overtook her as she pulled the scissors from her dresser, mumbling the whole time, and picked up one of the Visa cards from the bed. It was different than usual gold cards in that it had the name International Gold Visa on it. Savagely she cut it in half and continued cutting it in tiny pieces, then discarded it with the rest of the items. She picked up another card and turned it over. It too was a Gold Visa and had the name of the Republic Bank on it. She attacked it also with her scissors, speaking vile things to these inanimate objects all the while.

The last things on the bed were a few of Lund's business cards. As Erin was about to drop them in the wastebasket, she saw something written in Lund's handwriting. Curiosity got the best of her, and she looked closely at it. Her name was written clearly, and above her name was a telephone number that she recognized as a San Fernando Valley area code. Under her name were written the digits 17172. *This was interesting,* she thought. *Perhaps tomorrow I will call the number. It could be the number of a secret bank account that I don't know about. That wouldn't surprise me at all. There has been a mountain of secrets I have only recently discovered!*

～42～

SURPRISE, SURPRISE

The telephone awoke Erin from an unrestful sleep. Karl Bixby was on the phone and had asked her to meet him in his office at one that afternoon. He had finally contacted the attorney for US Care and was driving to Palmdale for the meeting. Erin immediately became wide awake and knew that this was her day. She had been dealt too many cards from the bottom of the deck. Now her time had come. She had no doubt that by this afternoon, she would be a millionaire and not the possessor of a paltry seventy-odd thousand dollars. *Boy how times have changed,* she thought. *There was a time not so long ago that seventy thousand sounded like a million. Not now though; I am soon to be crowned queen.* Erin took her time and lounged until eleven, when she decided she ought to look smashing if she were to be exalted into royalty. She spent more time than usual applying her makeup and decided to wear her best outfit. She looked at herself in the full-length mirror and said aloud, "Let the coronation begin."

She drove to Karl Bixby's office in the new office building on Tenth Street and West Avenue M. She entered his office at 12:50 p.m. and announced she was there for a one o'clock meeting. The receptionist said, "Sure Erin, have a seat."

Erin exploded and unleashed all her pent-up emotions on the unsuspecting girl. "I don't know you well enough for you to call me by my first name! Do you have any idea who I am? I am Mrs. Lund to you, and you will always remember that. I insist you treat me in the proper manner, or I will see if I can have you fired for your insolence. I have nothing more to say to you, Bonnie. You are dismissed. Now get out of my sight." Bonnie left her in the waiting room and sobbed softly as she left. Fifteen minutes later, Erin was ushered into the office by another woman.

"Where is Bonnie?" asked Erin in a haughty manner.

"She went home early today. She's sick," replied the secretary. Erin felt good about it. She had dealt with that chronic thorn in the proper way, and now Bonnie was going home to repent.

"Please come in, Mrs. Lund," said Karl. He pulled a chair from the table and assisted in seating her. "This is Mr. Edward Feinstein, who is the counsel for US Care." Ed stood up and extended his hand across the table. He was about forty years old, six feet tall, well-built, and very handsome. Erin put on her best act as she thought about the possibilities of getting together with Ed. She fantasized that once she had the money, he would probably have no difficulty in responding to her request for lunch. After all, she was beautiful and royalty to boot. Erin was finding it very hard to separate reality from fantasy and was now overcome with grandiose ideation.

"Mr. Feinstein, please, the floor is yours."

He smiled at Erin and then began to speak. "As you know, US Care concluded the purchase of The Palmdale Hospital and Medical Group almost three months ago. Our offer and the acceptance of it was made to and by the partnership known as the SLK Partnership. The partners were Drs. Small, Lund, and Kovacs. Approximately three weeks before the partnership closed the sale, Dr. Kovacs met with an unfortunate mishap. He was robbed and murdered right outside the office building. As a result of the loss of that partner, the attorney for the two remaining partners produced the partnership agreement, which provided for a mechanism to disburse the funds." Erin took a big breath and felt better. For a moment, she thought there might have been a problem with the disbursement of the funds from the sale. Now that she heard there was a mechanism that the partnership provided, she could almost see the money.

She closed her eyes and tried to figure out just how much room it would take to store about seven million dollars in hundred-dollar bills. Ed cleared his throat and startled Erin. She had been caught daydreaming and was embarrassed by it. "The partnership," said Ed, "contains a clause on page eleven that spells out the agreement of the partners as to the disposition of a deceased partners interest." He looked at Erin and smiled. "Dr. Lund's instruction was that his interest would go to his daughter. Dr. Small instructed that his interest goes to his wife." Erin was breathing rapidly and finding it hard to concentrate now. "One partner, Dr. Kovacs, agreed to have all his interest divided among the remaining partners. Therefore, when the total sales price of twenty-one and one half million dollars was paid, Drs. Lund and Small each received about ten and one half million dollars each." Erin jumped up and screamed "No, this can't happen to me!" She screamed at the top of her voice, then wept for fifteen minutes while the two lawyers just sat motionless in their chairs looking at each other. Erin finally walked out of the room and mumbled something about a crown on the way out the door.

~43~

TONY THE KNIGHT IN SHINING ARMOR

She was furious. Her money had been stolen by her husband and that idiot bastard, Small. He had to pay; she was dead serious about that. She picked up the phone and placed the call.

"Hello, Tony, this is Erin Lund. Can we meet today? I must speak with you."

"Sure Erin, meet me at the Red Station House on Palmdale Boulevard in half an hour. I'll be in the bar."

She sat down and tried to think clearly. *Tony must have a way to help me. He certainly helped last time I needed him.* She felt confident now and walked out the door.

The Red Station was one of the newer additions to the growing city. What it lacked in fine cuisine, it made up for in the bar.

"She walked into the restaurant and turned to the right, where the bar was located. There were many oversized booths with plush seating and overhead rattan and cane fans. The decor was green and yellow, and the furniture was all cane. From the appearance, Erin easily could imagine she was in the South Pacific again.

She spotted Tony and walked to his table. He stood and greeted her with a hug. He already had a pitcher of beer on the table and poured her a glass.

"I am sorry about your loss, Erin. Is there anything I can do?"

She smiled to herself as she thought of his words. *You don't have the slightest idea what I lost.* She knew he was referring to Bob's death, but that was over now. Her only sorrow was that she didn't inherit all the money she was entitled to receive by her calculation.

"As a matter of fact, you can. I want to pay someone back for screwing me royally." *Boy that is an apropos statement if I ever heard one,* she thought. *After all, am I not a queen.* Her mind wandered and she became glossy-eyed, then she continued. "I want to set Dr. Small up so that he goes to jail for a long time. I want to frame him for a crime." She drew a big breath and went on. "Help me frame him for Kovacs's murder." She stared at Tony while he sipped a beer.

"You're serious, aren't you?" he asked with a smile.

"You bet I am!"

Tony sat back and said nothing for a few minutes. Finally, he looked into her cold, calculating eyes and spoke. "The hit man was a guy named Angie De Toro. He was just recently convicted for the first-degree murder of another person. In California, it's three strikes and you go to jail for life. That's the story, with one more detail. Angie has been asking me to help his wife and kids get by financially, and I said I would do the best I can. Now, just mind you, if he were to agree to my plan, maybe we could pull this off. But I got to tell you, this ain't no twenty-five-hundred-dollar deal. We're talking more like fifty thousand dollars."

Erin said not a word. Rapidly she figured she could afford twenty-five thousand dollars; that would leave her fifty thousand. "Tony, I don't have that kind of money, but I can get you twenty-five thousand dollars."

"Didn't you inherit any dough or get any insurance money?"

"It's a long story, Tony, but if you've got time, I'll tell you all about it." One hour later, when she finished the story and half the beer, Tony had tears in his eyes. He couldn't believe she almost had all that money in her hands, so he accepted her offer and said he would visit Angie in jail that weekend and get back with her on his decision. "Erin, you will have to give the money to me right away if he says he'll do it. I don't think he'll refuse; he has nothing to lose. He's in jail for life now, so what's another conviction? After his wife tells him she has the money, he will confess to having been hired by Small."

Erin thought a moment, but her anger was obvious. "No, Tony, have him confess that both Dr. Lund and Small hired him to do the killing." She thought, *how do you like that Bob, you bastard?* He was just as guilty of cheating her as Small was.

At home she pondered what had just happened to her. Her inheritance had been given to her husband Bob and Dr. Small. Bob had given her money to his daughter, and then he had bought her a beautiful ring as well. She didn't even own the roof over her head. She had a measly seventy-some thousand dollars to her name. That was sure a far cry from the amount that had been usurped from her. Some eight million from Bob Lund and about seven from her father-in-law Kovacs was now only a dream. She decided to go to Lund's office to see if there was anything there that she might gain some benefit from.

When she arrived, she was greeted by the secretary, Anne. Sally, the nurse, had left for another job, but Anne agreed to stay on for a while until things were in order. The patient records had to be transferred to another doctor for continuity of care. Anne told Erin that her husband's mail was piled on his desk. The accumulation in the box on the floor was professional junk mail, but the mail on the desk was personal. She settled into Lund's oversized leather chair and began to sort through the large stack of letters. One hour later, she was about ready to leave, having become exhausted and wounded by paper cuts to her fingers. Begrudgingly, she picked up one more letter. The letter had Cayman Islands stamps on it. This piqued her curiosity, and she opened the letter.

Dear Dr. Lund,

I have accomplished your requests that you outlined for me when you were in the Caymans. The Caymans International Bank Visa Gold Card that was issued to you will be treated as you have requested. The one and one half million dollars that you have placed on deposit will be used to credit your card charges monthly. You will continue to draw 4 percent interest on the funds until they are depleted. The bank has agreed with your instructions that no other cards will be issued until five years from now, unless you request otherwise. If the card is lost or stolen, I, acting in your behalf through your power of attorney, shall be the only one authorized to obtain a replacement. You of course may also do so in person at the bank with proper identification.

The bank has also agreed to honor a transfer of any balance that remains to your daughter Shauna Lund in Providence, Rhode Island, in the event of your death.

Do not hesitate to call me at the above telephone number, if I can be of further service.

Lewis Parsons, Attorney.

Erin cried. If only she hadn't acted so quickly and cut up Lund's International Visa Card, she could have had the use of all that money for five years. She walked around dazed. Her last attempt at the crown was snatched from her by Lund. Never did she think that she might still have the card if she had not exploded in rage over the black opal ring. She was hyperventilating and feeling like she wanted to vomit.

~44~

DR. SMALL GETS HIS SHARE

Rick Small was at home when his doorbell rang. He went to the door, opened it, and was surprised to see two men standing there.

"Good evening, sir," said the taller of the two. "I am Detective Lieutenant Ray Johnson, and this is my partner, Detective Morrison." He opened his wallet and flashed his ID card. "May we come in?"

Dr. Small turned pale and felt his heart begin to race. Beads of sweat appeared on his brow, and suddenly it became difficult to breathe. The room was spinning, and just as he grasped the door for support, Detective Morrison caught his forward motion. In a flash, Ray Johnson had Small's feet, and they carried him to the couch in the living room. Rick was feeling numb all over and realized he was hyperventilating. He tried to slow his breathing by making a conscious effort because he knew the numbness was caused by the hyperventilation. His carbon dioxide levels were falling, thus producing the numbness. With a weak voice, he asked his visitors to elevate his legs to hasten the return of blood to the heart. His guests seated themselves across from the couch and waited. After a few minutes, Small sat up.

"I just got lightheaded. That's the first time that has ever happened," he wiped his brow.

"Have you been ill recently?" asked Morrison.

"No, not at all. I am at a loss to explain it. I came close to losing consciousness, and if you hadn't caught me when I was going down, I probably would have ended up in the emergency room with stitches in my head."

Detective Morrison looked at Ray Johnson and smiled. "We'd like to ask you a few questions about Palmdale Hospital's long-term respiratory care center. Okay?

"Of course, I'll be happy to tell you anything you want to know."

Both Morrison and Johnson removed their notebooks from their pockets. "How long has the care center been in existence?" asked Johnson in a serious demeanor.

"I don't remember exactly, but I think it was started in 1982," replied Rick.

"Who were the owners of the hospital then?" asked Johnson.

"The three of uh . . . us, Kovacs, Lund, and myself," replied Small nodding his head.

"Why was the unit created?" asked Johnson, wrinkling his brow.

"I don't understand your question."

"Well, was there a need for that type of facility in the Antelope Valley?" asked Johnson.

"Uh, I'm not sure. You see, I never was involved in making decisions," replied Small.

"And why was that?"

"The other two were more of the business brains. I just went along with the crowd," replied Small, laughing nervously.

"Was Mr. Carson a patient of yours?" asked detective Morrison.

Hearing the name was enough stimulus to provoke Small to hyperventilate again. He tried to concentrate hard on his breathing in an attempt to slow his rate of breathing. He looked at the floor and tried to shake the floating feeling. Both detectives observed his behavior and nodded to each other. They had been at this business for years and could easily identify the signs of acute anxiety in response to unwanted questions. They were aware they had hit a nerve and were waiting for Small to recover.

Rick's mind focused in on the whole facade they had created almost a year ago. He reasoned that he was in the clear since the only witnesses were his partners, and they were dead. Feeling assured with that, he looked up at the detectives and answered.

"He was Dr. Lund's patient, as were all the respiratory care patients. I made rounds on them a few times a week as did he."

Detective Morrison proceeded to relate the tale of the Benson-Carson switch to Rick. He sat motionless throughout the presentation, and when he had heard the completed story, he just shook his head vigorously. "I just don't know what to say; I had no knowledge whatsoever about any of it." Rick was now feeling more confident than ever. The cops were on a fishing expedition, and he didn't know anything, so he was in the clear. He smiled to himself but was unaware his stupid grin was evident to the detectives.

"Doctor, do you know an Angelo De Toro?" asked Morrison, widening his eyes.

"Who?"

"Angelo De Toro," repeated Morrison.

"No, can't say that I do."

"Tell me Doctor, who received Dr. Kovacs's share of the hospital sale?" asked Detective Johnson.

Small started to feel uneasy. His mouth was dry, and he found it hard to swallow." Uh . . . Lund and I got Kovacs's share according to an agreement we had."

"How much money did you get, Doctor?" asked Johnson.

"About four million dollars," whispered Small. Suddenly he felt ashamed.

"So, you got a windfall because Dr. Kovacs was murdered."

"What do you mean?" asked Small with indignation.

"I mean, Sir, that you had a motive to see your partner dead," said Johnson as he cocked his head to the side and looked askance.

"That is absurd! Kovacs was my friend for more than twenty years," shouted Small in anger.

"Doctor, we have a confession from Angelo De Toro naming you, and Dr. Lund, as the ones who hired him to murder Dr. Kovacs."

Rick Small's face was drained of blood, and he was now in a cold sweat. He couldn't believe what he had heard. He was no murderer. It wasn't his fault he gained half of Kovacs's share after his untimely death. This whole thing was absurd. He felt every heartbeat, and the rapid breathing returned. "I want a lawyer now. I won't answer any more stupid questions without my lawyer."

"Fine, Doctor, please put your hands behind your back." With that, Morrison snapped the handcuffs shut, and they all left the house.

Dr. Small was fingerprinted and held in jail until his lawyer appeared. Mr. Clark Heber, the local criminal attorney, met with the detectives to hear the charges.

"What have you got against Dr. Small?" asked Heber.

He was addressing Lieutenant Johnson, who was quick to answer. "We have a witness who identifies your client and Dr. Lund as the ones who hired and paid him to murder Dr. Kovacs."

"What possible motive would they have?" asked Heber, somewhat confused.

"Small and Lund were to receive Kovacs's share from the hospital sale, which was about eight million dollars total."

"How good is your case, Detective?" asked Heber.

"The DA feels it's a winner. "You know if he gets convicted for murder, he goes up for life or even the chamber!"

"I'll talk to the DA tomorrow about it." Heber then asked to see his client so he might explain the charges against him.

The following morning, Heber called the DA to discuss the case.

"Yes, Clark, hard to believe a prominent physician like Dr. Small would hire a killer, isn't it?" asked Ken Stone, the assistant district attorney.

"What evidence do you have against Small?" inquired Heber.

"I've got the sworn statement of Angelo De Toro identifying Drs. Lund and Small as the ones who paid him five thousand dollars to do the deed."

"Who is this guy, De Toro?" asked Heber.

"Well, he's a felon who we caught a while ago and has admitted to several crimes besides yours. He was tried and convicted for another murder committed in Acton some months ago. He doesn't have a reason in this world to point the finger at Small and Lund unless it's true."

"I'm in shock, I've known Small and Lund for years."

"Look, Clark, since we already have a murder one conviction on De Toro and our calendar is huge, I'll let you plead him as an accomplice. That will probably get him less than fifteen years, but with good behavior, he'll be out in less than ten. That's a lot better than what he's looking at for a first-degree conviction."

"Thanks, Ken, I'll speak to my client about the plea bargain." He hung up the phone and sat back in his chair. There isn't any other way to go; the risk of a possible first-degree conviction was too high. His peers were already hot enough about the medical profession and their greed. He couldn't bear to think what jurors would think about a heinous act committed for the purpose of acquiring an additional four million dollars on top of their own shares of eight million dollars each. His client had no chance of being thought to be innocent but was sure to be proven guilty. As soon as the press published the story about the money, Small was as good as convicted, and a jury was superfluous.

~45~

THE LAST STRAW

She was getting up to leave when Erin recalled the card with her name and a number written below it as well. Now, she thought, *No time like the present. What else can go wrong? Perhaps she got this bank account too!* She dialed the number. "Hello, this is Universal Health Laboratories," said the voice.

"Oh, this is Dr. Lund's office," Erin said.

"May I help you?" replied to the voice.

"Yes, I have what seems like an identification number here, but I don't have the name. This is Mrs. Lund, and I am trying to help Dr. Lund's office today. I'm a bit unfamiliar with everything," answered Erin in a sweet voice.

"Is it a five-digit number?" asked the voice.

"Yes, that's it," Erin responded.

"What are the numbers, please?" the voice asked.

"17172," replied Erin.

"Please hold while I enter the code into the computer," asked the voice.

Erin sat perched on the end of the desk staring at her fingernails. "Hello, are you there?" the voice asked.

"I'm here," answered Erin.

"That test for HIV is positive. It has been confirmed by the Western blot test . . . Hello . . . Hello . . . Mrs. Lund, are you still there??"

~246~

Epilogue

She looked at her surroundings, which seemed unfamiliar. Where was her throne and crown? She was still the queen, wasn't she? Royalty had always been hers. The finances had been a problem for her in the past, but not now. She had wealth beyond imagination, and the queen had rightfully inherited her just rewards. She stared into space speaking words that were unintelligible to all those around her. Her eyes were glassy, and she spoke with pressured speech while her movements were quick and unrelenting. She was pacing back and forth.

The subjects in her royal court were all dressed in white. There were the lords and ladies, princes and princesses, all conversing with her personal advisor who was dressed in an elegant white robe.

He had a gentle understanding face and spent many a day with her deeply immersed in the Queen's problems. Always intent on showing her the greatest of respect and concern, his eyes revealed his compassion for her troubled spirit. He tried in vain to coax her to speak to him about her problems, but she remained aloof, and detached, and spoke only in rhymes and alliteration. The Queen scurried about her garden with broom in hand, announcing that she had found her royal scepter. Her advisor succeeded in convincing her highness to remain on her throne and speak with him. Erin sat and stared blankly into space, but suddenly she seemed transported back into the world of reality. She wasn't certain how long she had been in this state, but she felt deep in her soul it had been for a long time.

Dr. Charles Bailey had been rendering his services since her arrival some two months ago. He became fascinated with her and documented her ability to survive on less than two hours of sleep daily. She spoke with a rapidity of speech and continuous talking, which caused laryngitis. Racing thoughts conjured a flight of ideas, and minor external stimuli distracted her. Occasionally, he noticed that she recognized brief glimpses of reality, only to slip back into the abyss of her fantasy world, where every thought was interpreted as reality. She felt her elevated mood was good, but she was also very irritated. Strong tranquilizers were only now beginning to demonstrate their effect. Now, she remained in the real world for longer periods of time with each passing day. Soon she would be firmly anchored in the present by the medication, and only then might therapy prove successful. Only time would tell.

"They stole my riches," said Erin in a loud voice dripping with disdain.

"Tell me about it, will you?" pleaded Dr. Bailey.

"I had millions of dollars stolen from me," said Erin in tears. "The money was taken by illegal schemes that were formulated to deprive me of my rightful inheritance. I am the Queen, and the wealth belongs to the Royal Treasury. Look, my palace has been reduced to this!"

"Perhaps you can tell me who did this to you?"

"Those who want to see me lose my crown. Those who want to bring me down. Those who want to hear the sound of my scepter tumbling down! Where is my thing, ring king?"

There was a moment of silence, and she blinked her eyes and then shut them tightly.

"I remember I was seated at a long table. Others were present, and then the decree. I was to lose the shoes, but whose?"

"Okay, Mrs. Lund, that was fine for now. I'll be back tomorrow and then we can continue. Will that be all right?"

She sat upright and extended her right arm, pointing her finger at Dr. Bailey and announced, "You make take your leave, I believe, don't deceive, just relieve, no reprieve!"

The End

Author's Note

I wrote this book in 1996 about thirty years after Medicare insurance became law. Medicare coverage had grown in leaps and bounds, extending patient coverage, and new medical treatments came to the forefront, as did the creation of large medical groups.

This began the cheating by doctors, hospitals, medical groups, and health insurance companies. Health insurance companies began to deny needs for patient services, and the others billed false charges or charges for services never rendered. They were all complicit in motivation by the almighty dollar. Medicare became a prime target.

This became the stimulus for me to write the medical thriller, *Prognosis Guarded*. All the patient episodes and their diagnoses were true as I encountered in fifty years of medical practice in the hospital. My specialty is internal medicine, pulmonary disease, and hospitalist.

I took my literary license to create a scenario devised to cheat Medicare; other cheaters were real.

Marvin Ginsburg, MD, FACP, FCCP